OECD Development Pathways

Multi-dimensional Review of Panama

VOLUME 2. IN-DEPTH ANALYSIS AND RECOMMENDATIONS

OECD
dev
DEVELOPMENT CENTRE

This work is published under the responsibility of the Secretary-General of the OECD. The opinions expressed and arguments employed herein do not necessarily reflect the official views of the member countries of the OECD or its Development Centre.

This document, as well as any data and any map included herein, are without prejudice to the status of or sovereignty over any territory, to the delimitation of international frontiers and boundaries and to the name of any territory, city or area.

Please cite this publication as:
OECD (2018), *Multi-dimensional Review of Panama: Volume 2. In-depth Analysis and Recommendations*, OECD Development Pathways, OECD Publishing, Paris.
https://doi.org/10.1787/9789264302549-en

ISBN 978-92-64-30253-2 (print)
ISBN 978-92-64-30254-9 (PDF)

Series: OECD Development Pathways
ISSN 2308-734X (print)
ISSN 2308-7358 (online)

The statistical data for Israel are supplied by and under the responsibility of the relevant Israeli authorities. The use of such data by the OECD is without prejudice to the status of the Golan Heights, East Jerusalem and Israeli settlements in the West Bank under the terms of international law.

Photo credits: Cover design by the OECD Development Centre.

Corrigenda to OECD publications may be found on line at: *www.oecd.org/about/publishing/corrigenda.htm*.

Foreword

Economic growth matters, but it is just one facet of development. Policy makers should focus their attention on ensuring that their country's development path is sustainable and that the lives of their citizens improve. This requires reconciling economic, social and environmental objectives.

OECD Development Pathways is a series that looks at multiple development objectives beyond an exclusive focus on growth. It recognises well-being as part and parcel of development and helps governments identify the main constraints to more equitable and sustainable growth by undertaking a multi-dimensional country review (MDCR). Governments trying to achieve economic, social and environmental objectives need to understand the constraints they face and develop comprehensive and well sequenced strategies for reform that take into account the complementarities and trade-offs across policies. The MDCR methodology is based on quantitative economic analysis, as well as qualitative approaches including foresight and participatory workshops that involve actors from the private and public sectors, civil society, and academia.

The MDCRs are composed of three distinct phases: initial assessment, in-depth analysis and recommendations, and implementation of reforms in the identified key areas. This approach allows for a progressive learning process about the country's specific challenges and opportunities that culminates in a final synthesis report to inform reforms in the country.

The MDCR of Panama is the third review, following that of Peru and Uruguay, to be undertaken by the OECD in Latin America. The MDCR of Panama – Volume 1, Initial Assessment was launched in October 2017. This second volume, In-depth Analysis and Recommendations, focuses on three key constraints for inclusive development in Panama, namely skills and formal jobs, regional development and financing for development.

This MDCR is designed to help Panama formulate development strategies, and identify and support the policy reforms needed to achieve further sustainable and inclusive development. This review comes at a time when Panama is achieving high economic growth but further policy action is needed to expand socio-economic benefits across all economic sectors, regions and households. A forthcoming volume, based on the recommendations presented in this second volume, will present the necessary conditions and actions for making reform happen. These analyses support Panama's own development agenda towards achieving a brighter future for its citizens.

Acknowledgements

Multi-dimensional Country Reviews are the result of a collaborative effort of the OECD and the country under review. Work on this second phase of the Multi-dimensional Review of Panama was carried out by the OECD Development Centre in collaboration with the OECD Centre for Entrepreneurship (CEF) and the OECD Centre for Tax Policy and Administration (CTP), together with support from the Ministry of Economy and Finance of Panama.

Mario Pezzini, Director of the OECD Development Centre, guided and oversaw the review. The Multi-dimensional Country Review process is led by Jan Rielaender, Head of the MDCR Unit and Angel Melguizo, Head of Latin America and the Caribbean Unit, both at the OECD Development Centre.

The review was co-ordinated by Sebastián Nieto Parra, Deputy-Head of Latin America and the Caribbean Unit at the OECD Development Centre, and drafted by Juan Carlos Benítez, Paula Cerutti, Juan de Laiglesia, Rene Orozco and Sebastián Nieto Parra (OECD Development Centre); Maria Varinia Michalun and Isabelle Chatry (OECD Centre for Entrepreneurship); and Agustin Redonda (Council on Economic Policies). The tax and benefit incidence analysis was done by Sandra Martinez under the guidance of Nora Lustig (Commitment to Equity (CEQ) Institute Tulane University). Additional inputs were provided by Lyse Marques and Nathalia Montoya Gonzalez (OECD Development Centre). The team is grateful for the insightful discussions, data provided and comments made by Federico Bonaglia, Juan Vázquez Zamora, Carine Viac and Agustina Vierheller (OECD Development Centre); Monica Bhatia, Bert Brys, Céline Colin and Jeremiah Coder (OECD Centre for Tax Policy); Dorothée Allain-Dupré and Oscar Huerta-Melchor (OECD Centre for Entrepreneurship); Patrick Lenain (Economics Department); Catalina Covacevich (OECD Directorate for Education and Skills); and Paolo Falco (OECD Directorate for Employment, Labour and Social Affairs).

Various ministries and public agencies provided useful support during the authors' visit to Panama in October 2017 as well as throughout the production of the report. The role of the Ministry of Economy and Finance, the main counterpart for this report, was particularly valuable, both technically and analytically. Special thanks go to Vice Minister Gustavo Valderrama Rodríguez, Director of Public Policies Marissa Echevers, and Rubilu Rodriguez from the same Directorate for all their support. The Panamanian Embassy in Paris, member of the OECD Development Centre's Governing Board provided crucial support in the realisation and production process of this report.

Other ministries and public agencies also contributed largely, namely: the National Institute of Statistics at the Office of the Comptroller General of the Republic of Panama, the Panama Canal Authority, the Ministry of Development and Social Inclusion, the Ministry of Education, the Ministry of Energy, the Ministry of Health, the Ministry of Labour, the National Secretariat of Energy, AMUPA (Association of Municipalities of Panama), the Vice Ministry of Indigenous Affairs, Kuna Yala Comarca, the National Decentralization Secretariat, the Panama City Town Hall and the Ministry of Government. Finally, the team is grateful to the participants of two workshops hosted by the Ministry of Economy and Finance in Panama in November 2016 and October 2017 that brought together stakeholders from a broad set of backgrounds to identify global trends that could affect Panama's future development.

Other international organisations have been very supportive for this MDCR through discussions and comments during the production of the report: the Development Bank of Latin America (CAF), the Economic Commission for Latin America and the Caribbean (ECLAC), the Inter-American Development Bank (IDB), the International Labour Organization (ILO), the International Monetary Fund (IMF), and the World Bank.

The team is grateful to Kristine Douaud for editing the manuscript and to the OECD Development Centre's Communications and Publications Unit, especially Delphine Grandrieux, Aida Buendia and Elizabeth Nash and to Agustina Vierheller from the OECD Development Centre's Latin America and the Caribbean Unit for their excellent support in editing, laying out and producing the report.

Table of contents

Tables

Figures

Boxes

Follow OECD Publications on:

http://twitter.com/OECD_Pubs

http://www.facebook.com/OECDPublications

http://www.linkedin.com/groups/OECD-Publications-4645871

http://www.youtube.com/oecdilibrary

OECD Alerts http://www.oecd.org/oecddirect/

This book has...

StatLinks

A service that delivers Excel® files from the printed page!

Look for the *StatLinks* at the bottom of the tables or graphs in this book. To download the matching Excel® spreadsheet, just type the link into your Internet browser, starting with the *http://dx.doi.org* prefix, or click on the link from the e-book edition.

Acronyms and abbreviations

AEOI	Automatic Exchange of Information
ALMP	Active Labour Market Policy
AMPYME	Autoridad de la Micro, Pequeña y Mediana Empresa (Micro, Small and Medium-sized Enterprise Authority)
AMUPA	Asociación de Municipios de Panamá
ARP	Argentinian peso
BEPS	Base Erosion and Profit Shifting
BRL	Brazilian Real
CAF	Development Bank of Latin America
CCS	Social Security Agency
CEDLAS	Center for Distributional, Labor and Social Studies of the University of La Plata
CEQ	Commitment to Equity
CFC	Controlled foreign company
CFZ	Colón Free Trade Zone
CGET	French General Commission for the Equality of Territories (Commissariat Général à l'Egalité des Territoires)
CIAT	Inter-American Center of Tax Administrations
CIT	Corporate income tax
CNC	Centro Nacional de Competitividad
CoG	Centre of Government
CRS	Common Reporting Standard
CSS	Caja de Seguridad Social
DIPRENA	Dirección de Presupuesto de la Nación
ECLAC	Economic Commission for Latin America and the Caribbean
EIU	Economist Intelligence Unit
EOIR	Exchange of Information on Request
FAP	Fondo de Ahorro de Panamá (Sovereign Wealth Fund)
FCM	Federation of Canadian Municipalities

FDI	Foreign Direct Investment
GDP	Gross Domestic Product
GRP	Government of the Republic of Panama
IBFD	International Bureau of Fiscal Documentation
IDB	Inter-American Development Bank
IDV	Instituto para Desenvolvimiento do Varejo
IMC	Intermunicipal co-operation
IFARHU	Instituto para la Formación y Aprovechamiento de Recursos Humanos
ILO	International Labour Organization
IMF	International Monetary Fund
INADEH	Instituto Nacional de Formación Profesional y Capacitación para el Desarrollo Humano (National Training Institute)
INEC	Instituto Nacional de Estadísticas y Censo (National Institute of Statistics and Census)
INFOTEP	Instituto Nacional de Formación Técnico Profesional
ITSE	Instituto Técnico Superior del Este (Higher Technical Institute of the East)
LAC	Latin America and the Caribbean
LABLAC	Labor Database for Latin America and the Caribbean
MDCR	Multi-Dimensional Country Review
MEF	Ministerio de Economía y Finanzas (Ministry of Economy and Finance)
MEDUCA	Ministerio de Educación
MGI	McKinsey Global Institute
MICI	Mecanismo Independiente de Consulta e Investigación
MIDES	Ministerio de Desarrollo Social
MIT	Middle Income Trap
MITRADEL	Ministerio de Trabajo y Desarrollo Laboral
MPMP	Municipal Performance Measurement Program
MSMEs	Micro, Small, and Medium-sized Enterprises
NFPS	Non-financial public sector
OECD	Organisation for Economic Co-operation and Development
PAB	Panamanian Balboa
PED	Planes Estratégicos Distritales
PEG	Plan Estrategico de Gobierno
PIAAC	Survey of Adult Skills

PISA	Programme for International Student Assessment
PIT	Personal Income Tax
PPP	Purchasing Power Parity
SEDLAC	Socio-Economic Database for Latin America and the Caribbean
SEZs	Special Economic Zones
SIMEI	Sistema de Recolhimento em Valores Fixos Mensais do Tributos do Simples Nacional
SIMS	Labour Markets and Social Security Information System
SME	Small and Medium-sized Enterprises
SSC	Social Security Contributions
SUBDERE	Subsecretaria de Desarrollo Regional y Administrativo
SUNAT	Peruvian tax administration
TADAT	Tax administration diagnostic assessment tool
TERCE	Third Regional Comparative and Explanatory Study
TVET	Technical and Vocational Education and Training
UN	United Nations
UNDP	United Nations Development Programme
UNESCO	United Nations Educational, Scientific and Cultural Organization
USD	United States Dollar
VAT	Value Added Tax
VRR	VAT Revenue Ratio
WTO	World Trade Organization

Executive Summary

This second volume of the Multi-dimensional Country Review (MDCR) of Panama builds on the results of the first one, which identified the main constraints to advancing citizens' well-being and achieving more sustainable and inclusive development. It provides recommendations in three key areas to address these constraints: skills and jobs, territorial development, and financing for development. A third volume will propose a way of prioritising policy interventions and a framework for measuring policy implementation.

Panama has experienced considerable socio-economic progress and improved well-being in recent decades. However, not all sectors, regions and people benefitted at the same level, resulting in a dual economy. Progress stemmed mostly from economic growth and improvements in labour productivity in the modern tradeable service sector – mainly financial intermediation and trade, logistics and communications activities. The Canal and the Special Economic Zones have played a considerable role in the country's economic performance. Although the country has a formal sector with high wages in specific activities linked to global trade, export capacity and productivity remain low in the rest of the economy. The industrial and agricultural sectors only offer subsistence and informal jobs to most workers, thereby enhancing income inequality among Panamanians. This explains why Panama is considered as a dual economy.

Panama's inclusive and sustainable development will largely depend on the ability to achieve three main objectives: building better skills and formal jobs; promoting the catching-up of lagging regions and reducing territorial disparities; improving the taxation system and enhancing the contribution of the private sector in financing for development.

Building better skills and creating formal jobs for all Panamanians

In Panama, workers' skills remain poor and informality is high, challenging both social inclusion and productivity. Three quarters of the Panamanian workforce is low to medium-skilled and informality affects 40% of total workers. Informality poses a double threat: large losses for workers in the form of low savings and inadequate social protection, as well as a lack of upskilling opportunities; and low productivity and loss of revenues for firms and the wider economy.

To promote better skills and more formal jobs, Panama should implement an integrated package of socio-economic policies. First, Panama needs to create better conditions for productive development by increasing export diversification in agro-industry and upgrading existing services. Second, investment is required to increase access to and the quality of secondary and technical education. These measures should be accompanied by stronger active labour market policies, with the effective participation of the private sector. Third, an integrated pension system should be designed to increase the incentives to be formally employed and mitigate the pervasive impact of informality. Fourth, the skills and formalisation package should generate greater incentives for employees to formalise workers, for example by partially subsidising the social contributions of low-income workers and establishing a simpler scheme to determine minimum wages. Fifth, the formalisation of small and medium-sized enterprises (SMEs) and independent workers will require greater efforts to reduce red tape and administrative costs associated with formal status. Finally, more resources should be devoted to enhance supervision and enforcement of labour laws, including through greater inspection efforts to supervise informal workers in formal firms.

Strengthening regional development policy to boost inclusive growth

Regional development policy is an underutilised lever that would help Panama continue on its growth trajectory and achieve more inclusive socio-economic outcomes. Regional disparities across provinces and *comarcas* in terms of productivity, social cohesion and well-being outcomes are persistent in the country. Better strategic planning and implementation frameworks across different levels of government are necessary to support regional development and boost well-being and prosperity. The state should design policies and create conditions to catalyse greater investment across all regions, especially in the lower-performing ones, and invest more and more effectively at sub-national level.

To design and implement a regional development agenda, policy action in several domains is necessary. First, such an agenda must strengthen multilevel governance practices. This requires adjusting normative and institutional frameworks for regional development and building greater capacity and resources at sub-national and especially municipal levels. Second, it should support a new paradigm approach to regional development that introduces regional development plans, creates regional development funding mechanisms and builds performance measurement systems. Finally, it must enhance horizontal and vertical co-ordination capacity by creating a high-level inter-ministerial body and a dedicated unit for regional development policy. This presupposes the need to build vertical dialogue mechanisms and promote inter-municipal co-operation.

Improving the taxation system and promoting private sector involvement

Panama's total tax revenues have remained stagnant during the last two decades at close to 16.6% of GDP (vs. 22.7% in Latin America and the Caribbean and 34.3% in OECD economies in 2016). Revenues from the Canal – at 4% of GDP – and other state-owned enterprises have partially compensated for low levels of public revenues. Improving the prospects of tax revenue collection would provide a stable long-term source of income to finance key social and productive policies. Revenues should be increased by improving the tax collection system rather than by raising rates. Likewise, mobilising private sector investment through a sound regulatory and institutional public-private partnerships system is an additional source of effective financing for development.

Policy actions are needed to improve the taxation system and encourage private sector investment to support financing for development. First, promote further compliance, transparency and accountability within the fiscal framework by establishing an independent fiscal council. Second, enhance the tax system's efficiency by adopting a methodology to measure and report tax expenditures on an annual basis; by revising benefits provided to economic sectors, as the tax system might be subsidising otherwise unprofitable businesses or firms within these sectors; and by broadening the tax base by scaling back tax benefits provided to well-established and consolidated industries within Special Economic Zones. Third, increase the redistributive power of the tax system for instance by including the currently exempted "13th wage" and turning personal income tax allowances into tax credits. Fourth, modernise the tax administration by integrating critical processes to improve efficiency and reduce administrative costs, as well as by continuing the development of electronic invoicing to fight fraud and tax evasion. Finally, adopt and implement norms for public-private partnerships with sound regulatory and institutional frameworks.

Chapter 1. Overview: Towards a sustainable and inclusive high-income country

After nearly three decades of strong macroeconomic performance and some social improvements, Panama should now embark on a new reform agenda to become a sustainable and inclusive high-income country. This chapter highlights the socio-economic improvements Panama has achieved in recent decades thanks to strong economic growth and consequent poverty reduction. Its growth model is characterised by a dual economy in which a small number of activities, including those related to the Canal and Special Economic Zones (SEZs), have exhibited high productivity growth but limited job creation. This chapter therefore urges greater productivity in sectors that contribute to job formalisation to reduce disparities in income and among regions. As developing these policies requires further resources, taxation system improvements and greater mobilisation of private sector investment through public-private partnerships are needed. This chapter presents the main results of implementing policy actions in the three areas studied in this report: skills and jobs, regional development, and development financing.

Panama has experienced considerable socio-economic progress and improved well-being in recent decades. Gross domestic product (GDP) per capita grew significantly between 2006 and 2016, at an average of 5.5% annually – faster than the average of 1.5% in Latin America and the Caribbean, and 0.7% in Organisation for Economic Co-operation and Development (OECD) countries–, narrowing the gap in GDP per capita with developed countries. Moreover, Panama is on the verge of becoming a high-income economy. In addition, the level of poverty (defined as the share of people living on less than USD 3.20 at purchasing power parity [PPP] per day) dropped by more than half between 2005 and 2016, to 7%. Similarly, extreme poverty, or those living on less than USD 1.90 PPP per day, is only one-fifth what it was in 2005, affecting 2.2% of the population in 2016. Furthermore, Panama performs relatively well in most OECD well-being dimensions compared with countries at the same level of development (OECD, 2017).

Panama's impressive economic performance and social improvements in the past decade have not been achieved without challenges. Most of the economic growth and improvements in labour productivity are due mainly to investment and commerce, both retail and wholesale. Furthermore, the Canal and, to a lesser extent, the SEZs have played a considerable role in the country's economic performance, which explains why Panama is often characterised as a dual economy.[1] Although the country has a formal sector featuring high wages in specific activities linked to global trade (Bussolo et al., 2012), export capacity and productivity remain low in the rest of the economy, particularly in the industrial and agriculture sectors. In addition, similar to other Latin American economies, the shadow economy has contributed to Panama's economic performance but its total contribution, which is difficult to assess, has not benefited most of the population or the state. In terms of social welfare, although poverty rates have fallen considerably in the past decade, income inequality has improved very little. The share of income held by the top 10% of the population has been high (close to 40%) since 2005, and many of the people who escaped poverty in recent years remain vulnerable to slipping back into poverty if there is an economic slowdown.

To address these challenges, Panama should embark on a new model of development to promote continuous, sustainable and inclusive growth, and well-being for all citizens. Although Panama is set to become a high-income economy soon, challenges to sustainable and inclusive growth imply that reforms are needed in the process of moving from middle- to high-income status. These include policies to enhance skills and productivity, as well as labour market reforms to promote the creation of formalised jobs. Further, inclusiveness and extending economic benefits to other sectors and across all provinces and *comarcas* requires improvements in the institutional framework as well as capacity building for a regional development policy. Finally, policies to adjust the tax structure, strengthen tax administration and promote greater private sector involvement through public-private partnerships must be implemented to finance development.

This chapter summarises how Panama should upgrade its drivers of economic growth and improve its social policies to support an inclusive and sustainable high-income country. First, the chapter provides an historical overview of socio-economic development in Panama and the main characteristics of current macroeconomic performance. Second, it presents the main challenges to promote further development. Finally, it highlights from a multidimensional perspective the constraints to boosting inclusiveness and sustainable growth, namely skills and labour market policies, regional development policy and financing for development. This final section summarises the main policy implications and actions to be adopted, and they are analysed in greater depth in subsequent chapters of this review.

Three decades of socio-economic progress in Panama

Following the economic and political crisis at the end of the 1980s, macroeconomic performance considerably improved in the 1990s. Political unrest, with citizens demanding an end to 21 years of dictatorship and corruption, coupled with an economic crisis (GDP per capita decreased by 1.7% between 1985 and 1990, and by more than 15% in 1988 alone), led to the removal of Manuel Antonio Noriega from power in 1989 (Chaikin, 2013; OECD, 2017). In the 1990s a stable macroeconomic framework, based upon improved debt sustainability, saw average annual economic growth reach 5.5%. This contributed to a reduction of extreme poverty (defined as living on less than USD 1.90 per day, 2011 PPP) by close to 8 percentage points during the 1990s, to less than 15% at the end of the decade.

The socio-economic gains exhibited in the 1990s have accelerated since the beginning of the 21st century. As a result of the Torrijos-Carter treaties, signed in 1977 and progressively implemented until 1999, revenues from the Canal have become a key source of income to Panama. Panama's adhesion to the World Trade Organisation (WTO) at the end of 1997 has seen the country benefit from increased global trade. Over the last ten years, levels of investment in Panama have been higher than OECD and Latin American averages. In the period 2006-16, GDP per capita grew an average of 5.5% annually (vs. 3.3% in the 1990s), thereby helping to reduce the GDP per capita gap with high-income countries. Similarly, extreme poverty continued to decline dramatically and is only one-fifth that observed in 2005, encompassing 2.2% of the population in 2016. Finally, the OECD well-being framework shows that Panama is doing relatively well compared to countries with similar levels of development, particularly in areas such as social connections, life evaluations, life expectancy and, more generally, material conditions. For instance, more than three out of four Panamanians report being satisfied with their living standards (OECD, 2017).

Current challenges reveal that new engines for sustainable and inclusive growth are needed

The favourable macroeconomic performance of the past decade, which has been a key driver of the recent social progress, has lost impetus in the past few years. The Dominican Republic and Panama are leading Latin American economies in terms of annual economic growth. According to both the Economic Commission for Latin America and the Caribbean (ECLAC) (2018) and the International Monetary Fund (IMF) (2018), GDP is expected to grow at 5.6% in Panama for 2018, well above the projections for the region (2.2% and 2.0% according to both institutions, respectively). However, annual GDP per capita growth has declined since 2012, from 9.9% in 2011 to 3.2% in 2016, and labour productivity remains well below OECD countries (Figure 1.1). Less promising economic conditions have impacts beyond GDP. Indeed, the effect of growth, rather than reducing inequalities, was responsible for most of the reduction in poverty of recent decades.

Figure 1.1. GDP per capita and labour productivity in Panama

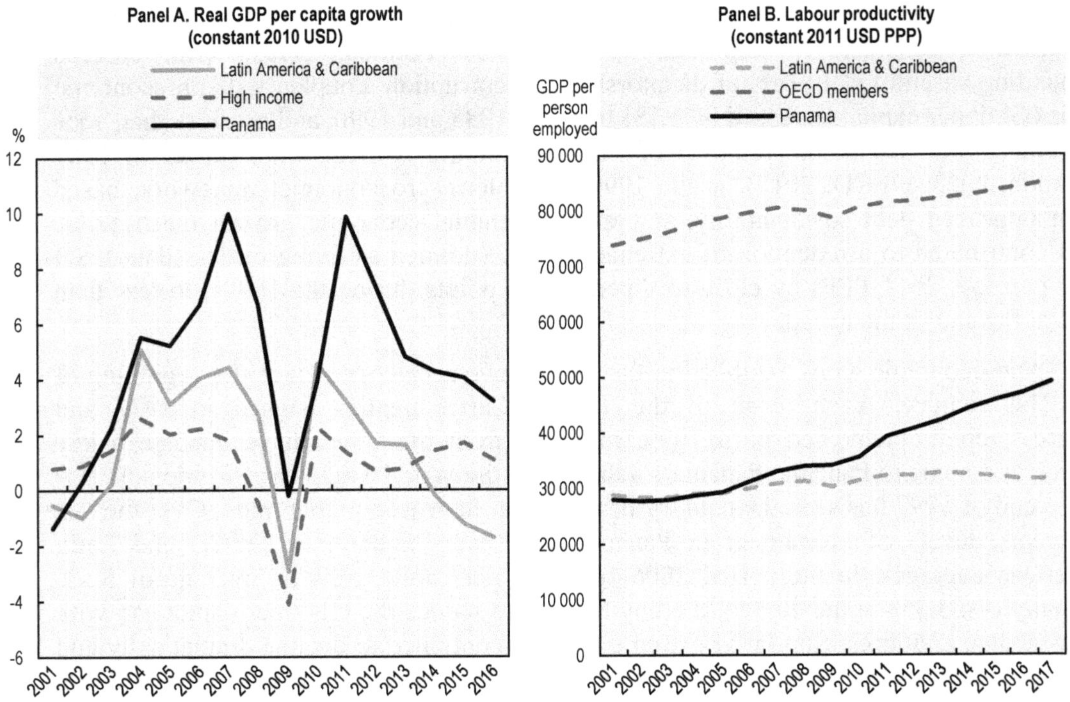

Note: Panel B: Labour productivity refers to GDP per person employed at constant 2011 USD PPP.
Source: Based on World Bank (2018), *World Development Indicators* (database).

StatLink http://dx.doi.org/10.1787/888933776654

Furthermore, dynamic growth in recent decades has been concentrated in only a few activities and regions, benefitting only a small proportion of the population. Gains in GDP growth and labour productivity growth in recent decades were in part the result of a dual economy. The Canal and to a lesser extent the SEZs have played a considerable role in Panama's economic performance. In contrast, other regions and sectors, in particular the industrial and agricultural sectors, exhibited low levels of export capacity and productivity. In that context, the lack of co-ordination among public institutions to deliver an effective national strategy for development remains a concern in Panama (OECD, 2017). In addition, estimates show that the shadow economy has been important in Panama, as in other Latin American economies. This includes the production of goods and services that are deliberately concealed from public authorities to avoid payment of taxes, social security contributions or certain administrative procedures (Schneider, Buehn and Montenegro, 2010). While shadow economy activities are reflected in the state of the official economy, such as the GDP per capita, they are not considered in state revenues thereby affecting the quality and quantity of publicly provided goods and services for all citizens.

Figure 1.2. Activity status by single year of age and socio-economic status (2016)

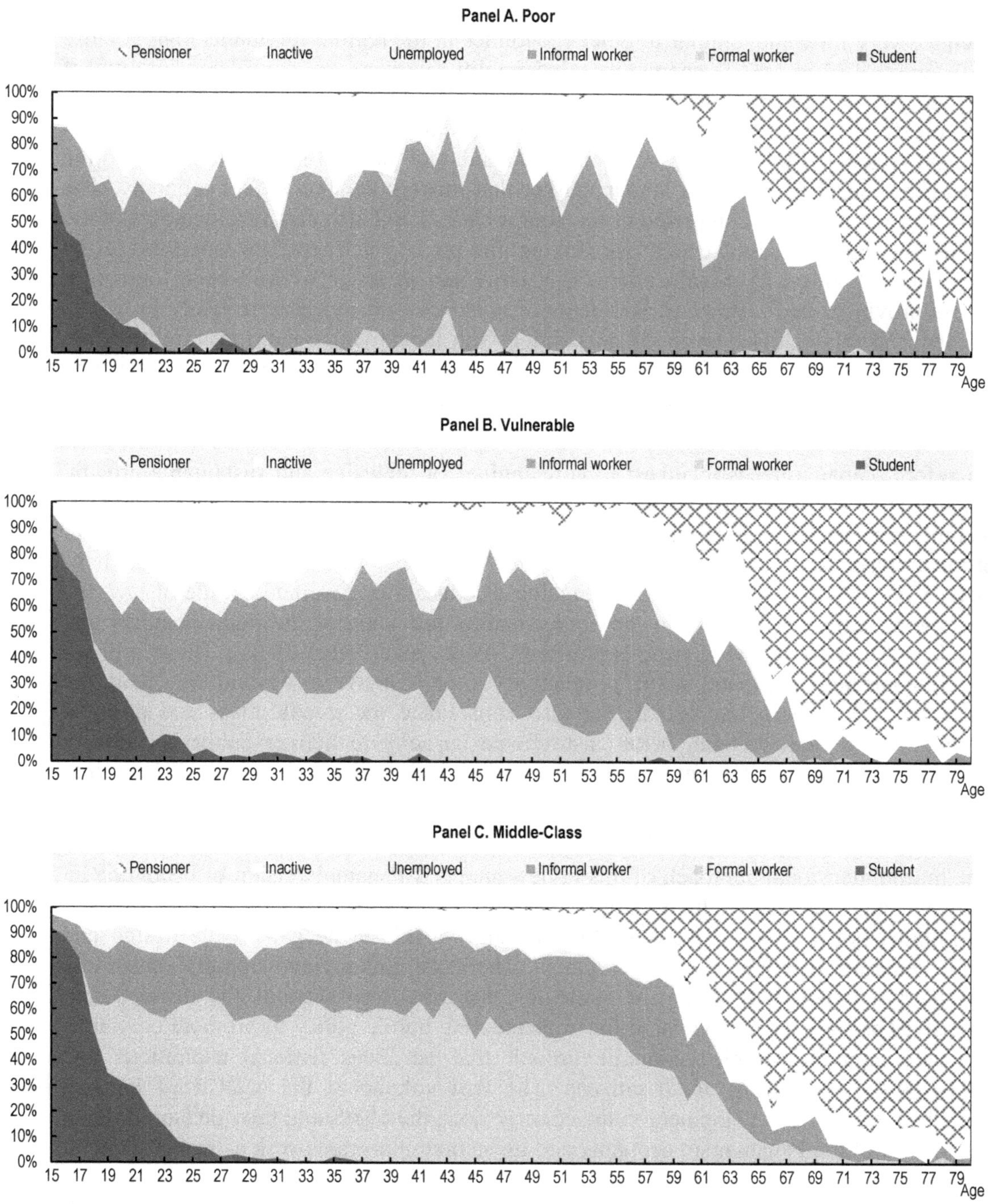

Notes: Socio-economic classes are defined using the following classification: "Poor" = individuals with a daily per capita income of USD 4 or lower. "Population at risk of falling into poverty" = individuals with a daily per capita income of USD 4-10. "Middle class" = individuals with a daily per capita income of USD 10-50. Poverty lines and incomes are expressed in 2005 USD purchasing power parity (PPP) per day. Legal definition of informality: workers are considered informal if they do not have the right to a pension when retired.

Source: OECD calculations based on data provided by INEC.

StatLink http://dx.doi.org/10.1787/888933776673

Consequently, despite the reduction of poverty in the past decades, spatial and income disparities remain in Panama. While the share of the population living in poverty has declined considerably, significant inequalities continue to exist. The Gini coefficient declined very little and, similar to other economies in the region, it remains high at close to 0.48 (vs. 0.32 in OECD economies). Informality (workers are considered informal if they do not have the right to a pension when retired) also persists, accounting for more than one-third of non-agricultural employment. The large proportion of unprotected own-account or low-skill informal jobs on the one hand, and the high-skill formal jobs on the other, have resulted in a dual labour market that mirrors Panama's dual economy. The former group is largely comprised of the poorer classes, but also contains members of the vulnerable middle classes, which risk sinking into poverty and represent one-third of the population (Figure 1.2). Finally, there is a large gap in terms of well-being outcomes across provinces and *comarcas*. Residents of *comarcas* are much more likely to live in poverty and report lower levels of satisfaction with their living conditions, and they are also at greater risk of having informal jobs. However, low outcomes in material and living conditions are also evident in some provinces as well, generally those that are rural, and regardless of whether they have a high percentage of indigenous inhabitants.

Therefore, Panama needs to invest in new engines of inclusive and sustainable growth. Panama is on the verge of becoming a high-income country, but overcoming the middle-income trap (MIT) will require a set of public policies designed to improve labour productivity across all sectors. Following the experiences of other countries that have tackled the MIT, improvements in the quality of education, governance, rule of law, the taxation system and liquidity in the equity market are some of the main domains that should be prioritised (Melguizo, Nieto-Parra, Perea and Perez, 2017). These policies should contribute to expand labour productivity to other activities beyond the Canal, the SEZs and the construction sector, but also consolidate the middle class and promote formal jobs. In that context, better institutional capacity to deliver public services to citizens is fundamental to move towards further inclusive development. Taking into consideration the regional disparities, a national strategy, in partnership with sub-national actors, should be delivered to enhance regional development.

The multidimensional approach of this review supports Panama's vision of becoming an inclusive and sustainable high-income economy. The entire process of the OECD's Multidimensional Country Review (MDCR) aims to close the gap in the design and implementation of policies for development. Therefore, this review supports Panama by formulating national development strategies that take into account the development objectives and the means available for implementing public policy to promote equitable, inclusive, and sustainable economic growth that advances national aspirations and improves the well-being of all citizens. The first volume of the MDCR of Panama described economic development in the country since the 1980s and provided an in-depth assessment of the Panamanian economy and its institutional framework as well as state of well-being today. It also identified the main constraints to sustainable and inclusive development, and proposed topics for further analysis in the second phase of the MDCR. A participatory workshop held in October 2017 with policy makers, civil society representatives and participants from the private sector discussed topics identified as fundamental to boost inclusive development (Box 1.1). The results of the workshop were considered when recommendations and the analysis presented in this review were drawn up.

Box 1.1. The three phases of the MDCR of Panama and the participatory workshops

This review is composed of three distinct phases:

- The first phase aimed to identify the main constraints to achieving sustainable and equitable improvements in well-being and economic growth. That report, entitled "Initial Assessment", was the first volume and was launched in October 2017.
- This second phase further analyses the key constraints identified in the first report to the formulation of policy recommendations that can be integrated into the development strategy of Panama. This second volume is entitled "In-depth Analysis and Recommendations".
- The final phase of the MDCR will provide support for the implementation of these recommendations. As for other Latin American economies, this final phase is particularly relevant in Panama given the complexity of both the political economy and the policy-making process to make reform happen (Dayton-Johnson, Londono and Nieto-Parra, 2011). The third volume is entitled "From Analysis to Action".

For each phase, in addition to the publication of a report, a series of workshops was organised. The policy recommendations in this volume are informed by the participatory work stream of the MDCR of Panama. A workshop entitled "Opportunities for the future in Panama: Territorial inclusion, formal jobs, financing" was held in Panama City on 12 October 2017. The workshop brought together thirty-five participants from the administration, the private sector and civil society to discuss policy options to respond to the three main challenges identified in the first phase of the MDCR of Panama (OECD, 2017).

Based on the governmental learning methodology, workshop participants selected key topics to concentrate on in a prioritisation exercise and formed thematic groups to discuss (i) territorial development, (ii) sustainability, (iii) capacities and human capital, (iv) financing development, (v) co-operation and social dialogue, (vi) formal jobs and (vii) state capacity. Each of these groups then identified policy solutions to Panama's most pressing development problems. On the basis of policy proposals from the OECD team and from participants, the workshop participants discussed, and suggested additions and amendments to, the policy recommendations that are included in each chapter of this review.

Volume 2 of the MDCR presents in-depth analysis of, and outlines recommendations for, the three topics identified in Volume 1 as key constraints to inclusive development in Panama:

- building better skills and creating formal jobs for all Panamanians (Chapter 2)
- strengthening regional development policy to boost inclusive growth (Chapter 3)
- improving the taxation system and promoting the private sector's involvement to support financing for development (Chapter 4).

The overview of the main findings and policy actions for these three topics follows. In-depth policy recommendations are covered specifically in each of the following chapters of the report.

Building better skills and creating formal jobs for all Panamanians

Informality remains high in Panama and is a challenge for social inclusion and productivity. Although Panama's economic growth has served to create more than half a million jobs since 2003, informality remains higher than in other countries with similar levels of GDP per capita such as Argentina, Turkey and Uruguay. In 2016, informality still affected around 40% of non-agriculture workers and almost 50% of workers overall. Informality poses a double threat: large losses for workers in the form of low savings and inadequate social protection, as well as a lack of upskilling; and low productivity and loss of fiscal revenues for firms and the wider economy.

Inequalities in the labour market start early, highlighting the need for better access for all Panamanians to quality education and skills. Young workers from poor or vulnerable families are more likely to have informal jobs than those from the middle class. Youth from these households leave school earlier than their peers in better-off households, and when employed they work mainly in informal jobs. At age 15, six out of ten youths living in poor households are in school; at age 30, however, nine out of ten are informal workers or inactive. In vulnerable households, six out of ten young people aged 30 are working in the informal sector or inactive. This shows that informality especially affects those in the lowest quintiles of the income distribution and thus a certain degree of labour market segmentation exists in Panama, making the transition from school to work a particularly relevant stage in young people's careers and futures.

Furthermore, the dual economy has translated into a dual employment market, which in turn largely explains income inequality in the country. On one hand, Panama has a strong and productive modern tradeable service sector – mainly financial intermediation and trade, logistics and communications activities surrounding the Canal and the SEZs – which steered the country's recent economic growth. These sectors are skills intensive but create relatively little employment. On the other hand, the less productive services sector, the agricultural sector and in some measure the manufacturing sector, in which own-account workers and micro-productive units have proliferated, offer subsistence and informal jobs to most workers.

To promote better skills and better jobs for all Panamanians, certain policy actions should be taken into account (the policy recommendations are developed in depth in Chapter 2):

- Create better conditions for productive development by including formalisation as a key item in a national development strategy and a well-co-ordinated approach to increasing economic diversification in agro-industry and upgrading existing services.
- Develop better and relevant skills by increasing the access to and quality of secondary and technical education, as well as strengthening active labour market policies such as training programmes with effective participation of the private sector, in particular for young people.
- Increase the incentives to be formally employed and mitigate the pervasive impact of informality by developing an integrated pension system, by providing alternative schemes to incorporate independent workers, domestic workers and temporary agricultural workers in the social security system and also by communicating the benefits of formality and the risks of informality.
- Generate incentives for employers to formalise workers by partially subsidising the social contributions of vulnerable workers, or by establishing a simpler scheme to determine minimum wages.

- Supervise and enforce labour laws by increasing efforts to supervise informal workers in formal firms.
- Boost the formalisation of small and medium enterprises (SMEs) and independent workers by reducing red tape and administrative costs associated with formal status.

Strengthening regional development policy to boost inclusive growth

Regional development is a lever to help Panama continue on its growth trajectory and achieve more inclusive socio-economic outcomes. Regional disparities across provinces and *comarcas* in terms of productivity, social cohesion and well-being outcomes are persistent in the country. In improving strategic planning and implementation frameworks, well-being and economic prosperity can be better promoted in the key multisector policy area of regional development. The state should therefore invest effectively in regions, including the lower-performing ones, to encourage sustainable growth in Panama.

There is a pressing need to define and implement a strategic approach to regional development in order to help mitigate the risk of *ad hoc* growth in some areas of Panama. Projections indicate that the greatest population growth is expected in some of the least advantaged territories, where quality of life and well-being outcomes are already low, particularly in the *comarcas,* Bocas del Toro, and Los Santos. In addition, Panama City is also expected to grow significantly and the challenge will be to ensure adequate infrastructure, housing, amenities, and public service delivery capacity to keep up with growing demand, while also maintaining or improving quality of life. While appropriate spatial and land-use planning are fundamental to meeting the challenges represented by such growth, they complement and contribute to a regional development policy; they do not replace it.

Consideration should be given to strengthening the normative and institutional frameworks supporting regional development. Currently, there is no overarching strategy to guide regional development in the long term, nor is there an explicit regional development policy to serve as a road map in the medium term. The implementation of regional development initiatives is spread across line ministries, with each territory introducing and executing its sectoral objectives and plans. At the national level, regional development is consequently fragmented and sector-driven, with limited effectiveness and a lack of concrete results. At the sub-national level, newly introduced District Strategic Plans (*Planes Estratégicos Distritales*) combine development and land-use planning, and are designed with the Strategic Government Plan 2015-2019 (*Plan Estratégico de Gobierno*) and the National Strategic Plan 2030 (*Plan Estratégico Nacional con Visión de Estado-Panamá: 2030*) in mind.

To design and implement a regional development agenda for all provinces, *comarcas* and municipalities, certain policy actions should be taken into account (the policy recommendations are developed in depth in Chapter 3):

- Strengthen multilevel governance practices to better support regional development by adjusting normative and institutional frameworks for regional development and building sub-national, especially municipal, capacity and resources. Inspiration could be drawn from practices in Finland and Slovenia (legal frameworks), the United Kingdom (White Papers), Sweden (state strategies), France (state-region planning contracts) and New Zealand (regional growth programmes).

- Support a "new paradigm" approach to regional development. Several actions are required: (i) develop a national regional development policy that clearly articulates national territorial development objectives and priorities; (ii) introduce provincial and *comarca* regional development plans; (iii) create regional development funding mechanisms; (iv) build performance measurement systems; and (v) consider stronger partnerships between the public and private sectors when launching future regional development agencies. Countries such as Colombia, France, Ireland, Mexico and Sweden are good examples of these practices since they have taken diverse approaches to formalising their regional development strategies.
- Enhance horizontal and vertical co-ordination capacity by creating a high-level interministerial body and a dedicated unit for regional development policy. This presupposes the need to build vertical dialogue mechanisms and promote intermunicipal co-operation. Sweden's Forum for Sustainable Regional Growth and Attractiveness offers a successful example of vertical co-ordination, and countries such as Chile, Greece, Iceland, the Netherlands, New Zealand and Ukraine have mechanisms to support intermunicipal co-operation.

Improving the taxation system and mobilising private sector investment to support financing for development

Panama's total tax revenues have remained stagnant during the last two decades. At 16.6% of GDP in 2015, total taxes and social security contributions in Panama remain well below those of the OECD (34.3% of GDP) and Latin American and Caribbean countries (22.7% of GDP) (OECD/ECLAC/CIAT/IDB, 2018). However, revenues from the Canal and other public enterprises have partially compensated for low levels of revenue intake.

Improving the prospects of tax revenue collection would provide a stable long-term source of income to finance inclusive growth. To ensure financing for development in Panama, citizens' willingness to pay taxes – known as "tax morale" – is fundamental (OECD/CAF/ECLAC, 2018). Revenues can be increased by improving tax collection instead of raising rates. This is particularly evident for indirect taxes. Furthermore, Panama provides a wide array of tax benefits that affect the system's efficiency by potentially providing incentives to firms within sectors that would not be profitable in the absence of tax expenditures. Moreover, exemptions, deductions and other special treatments affect both the vertical and horizontal equity of the tax system. Finally, evasion and fraud linked to the weak institutional capacity of the tax administration office affect tax collection in Panama.

Better private sector involvement, through public-private partnerships, is an additional source of effective financing for development; Panama therefore needs to update its current legislation on public-private partnerships. In 2011, a law proposal was withdrawn at the Congress, and the 1988 law regulating concession projects, including roads and airports, is outdated. The establishment of sound regulatory and institutional frameworks for public-private partnerships should promote sustainable investment projects for development in Panama.

To implement a policy framework that effectively increases financing for development in Panama, certain policy actions should be taken into account (the policy recommendations are developed in depth in Chapter 4):

- Ensure macroeconomic stability and bolster international creditworthiness by establishing an independent fiscal council to promote compliance, transparency and accountability within the fiscal framework.
- Enhance the tax system's efficiency by adopting a methodology to measure and report tax expenditures on an annual basis; by ending subsidisation of otherwise unprofitable businesses or firms; and by expanding the tax base by scaling back tax benefits provided to consolidated industries within SEZs.
- Promote higher equity and the redistributive power of the tax system by for instance expanding currently exempted services in the value-added tax base or by expanding the personal income tax base to include the currently exempted "13th wage" (a bonus paid at the end of the year), since those that earn more benefit the most.
- Modernise the tax administration by integrating critical processes to improve efficiency and reduce administrative costs, or by continuing the development of electronic invoicing to encourage compliance by fighting fraud and tax evasion.
- Adopt and implement new norms for public-private partnerships with sound regulatory and institutional frameworks. These include the creation of a public-private partnerships unit, transparent and competitive auction processes, effective and efficient participation of citizens in the grant process for environmental and social licences, the execution of land permits, and fiscal accounting for public-private partnerships to avoid using concessions as an option for fiscal space.

Notes

[1] There are three major SEZs, each one serving a distinct purpose. The Colon Free Trade Zone (CFZ), the pioneering SEZ, specialises in re-exporting and manufacturing for exports. The more recent Panamá Pacífico is a residential and industrial zone that seeks to attract multinational headquarters, service companies and high-value-added manufacturing firms, among others. Finally, the City of Knowledge is orientated towards knowledge-intensive enterprises, privileging innovative enterprises, research institutions and international organisations.

References

Bussolo, M. et al. (2012), "Distributional effects of the Panama Canal expansion", *Economia*, Vol. 13/1, Brookings Institution Press, Washington, DC, pp. 79-129, www.jstor.org/stable/41756783.

Chaikin, D. (2013), "Controlling corruption by heads of government and political elites", in Larmour, P. and N. Wolanin (eds.), *Corruption and Anti-Corruption*, ANU Press, pp. 97-118, http://www.jstor.org/stable/j.ctt2tt19f.9.

Dayton-Johnson, J., J. Londono and S. Nieto-Parra (2011), "The process of reform in Latin America: A review essay", *OECD Development Centre Working Papers*, No. 304, OECD Publishing, Paris, http://dx.doi.org/10.1787/5kg3mkvfcjxv-en.

ECLAC (2018), "Actualización de proyecciones de crecimiento de América Latina y el Caribe en 2018", April 2018, Economic Commission for Latin America and the Caribbean, https://www.ce Panamanian Balboa.org/sites/default/files/pr/files/tabla-proyecciones_crecimiento_abril-2018_esp.pdf.

IMF (2018), *World Economic Outlook* (database), International Monetary Fund, https://www.imf.org/external/pubs/ft/weo/2018/01/weodata/index.aspx (accessed April 2018).

Melguizo A., S. Nieto-Parra, J. R. Perea and J. Perez (2017), "No sympathy for the devil! Policy priorities to overcome the middle-income trap in Latin America", *OECD Development Centre Working Papers*, No. 340, OECD Publishing, Paris, http://dx.doi.org/10.1787/26b78724-en.

OECD/CAF/ECLAC (2018), *Latin American Economic Outlook 2018: Rethinking Institutions for Development*, OECD Publishing, Paris, http://dx.doi.org/10.1787/leo-2018-en.

OECD/ECLAC/CIAT/IDB (2018), *Revenue Statistics in Latin America and the Caribbean 2018*, OECD Publishing, Paris, http://dx.doi.org/10.1787/rev_lat_car-2018-en-fr.

OECD (2017), *Multi-dimensional Review of Panama: Volume 1. Initial Assessment*, OECD Development Pathways, OECD Publishing, Paris, http://dx.doi.org/10.1787/9789264278547-en.

Schneider, F., A. Buehn and C.E. Montenegro (2010), "New estimates for the shadow economies all over the world", *International Economic Journal*, Vol. 24/4, Taylor & Francis, pp. 443-461.

World Bank (2018), *World Development Indicators* (database), https://data.worldbank.org/products/wdi (accessed February 2018).

Chapter 2. Building better skills and creating formal jobs for all Panamanians

This chapter explores how labour markets can be a lever to help Panama increase equity and find a path towards inclusive growth. It argues that Panama's dual labour market has been both the cause and a consequence of Panama's large inequalities. Panama's successful economic growth in the past decade has been based on a growth model that encompasses labour market inequality. While the productive tradeable service sector offers formal jobs for a few skilled workers; many low-skilled Panamanians are self-employed or informally employed in small, low-productive, non-tradeable service sector or agriculture firms. This chapter discusses a comprehensive policy package that would rebuild the social contract in Panama from a quality employment perspective. This chapter covers policies to strengthen education quality, endow workers with better skills, mitigate the perverse effects of labour informality and provide labour incentives to promote better quality jobs.

Quality employment is a key element in a country's growth and development process. At the same time, it is central to a strong social contract, understood as a tacit pact between the state and citizens (OECD/CAF/ECLAC, 2018). Although Panama has a relatively small, young population, employment is a crucial element since it acts as a link between quality economic growth, poverty reduction and income equality.

Panama's dual labour market is both a source and a reflection of Panama's large inequalities. The scarcity of good employment opportunities has been one of Panama's long-lasting obstacles to making the labour market more inclusive, displaying significant variations across levels of education, income and regions. Panama's successful economic growth model of the past decade has reinforced labour market duality. The productive tradeable service sector – mainly financial intermediation and trade, logistics and communications activities surrounding the Canal and the Special Economic Zones (SEZs) – that led Panama's strong growth offers formal jobs for a few skilled workers in Panama City and Colón. In contrast, many working-age Panamanians encounter severe labour-market difficulties. Most of them are self-employed or informally employed in small, low-productive non-tradeable service sector or agriculture firms in the outskirts of Panama City and the provinces.

Strong economic growth has provided new, quality employment for some low-skilled workers, mainly in construction and transport, making the labour market more inclusive. The expansion led by the productive and competitive tradeable services sector spiked the demand for both public and private infrastructure. To fulfil this demand, the non-residential construction sector grew for more than a decade at a rate that is equivalent to doubling its stock of structures every four years. Large infrastructure projects, such the expansion of the Canal, the renovation of Tocumen airport, office buildings, warehouses and telecom infrastructure, generated a demand for low-skilled workers. Between 2003 and 2017 the construction sector created one out of every five new jobs and more than doubled its labour force. As such, construction absorbed some of the labour released by agriculture and fishing and provided low-skilled workers with more productive and better paying jobs. This employment shift can probably explain some of the improvement observed in informality and inequality reduction within these years.

Yet, the demand for non-residential construction cannot grow indefinitely at a higher rate than the rest of the economy – and in fact it has already started to slow down –, presenting a risk of losing some of the progress achieved in employment, poverty and inequality (Hausmann, Espinoza and Santos, 2016).

Creating formal quality productive jobs for future generations is Panama's main challenge in terms of poverty and inequality reduction. While the tradeable services sector has led Panama's growth and employment story for some decades, its poor direct employment creation capacity and the economic deceleration of the past five years has raised concerns. Though Panama is still growing at a strong pace – average annual rate of 5.6% between 2013 and 2017 –, the number of people out of work in Panama rose for the first time since the 1990s, reaching 6.1%, as a result of weakening labour demand and the subsequent drop in the number of new, salaried jobs created. Likewise, informality has gone back to its pre-boom growth path. Going forward, if the economy does not change its ability to generate employment, Panama will need to grow at an annual average of almost 6% of gross domestic product (GDP) for the next ten years to create enough jobs for future generations and fulfil its demographic dividend.[1]

To continue on the path towards a more inclusive labour market and avoid the dual market trap, Panama has to work on a policy package that includes economic diversification and better education. Employability barriers in Panama are mainly related to scarce formal job opportunities and insufficient work-related capabilities, but also poor market regulation, lack of law enforcement and poor financial incentives to look for a job (such as low potential pay, low-quality jobs and no unemployment insurance).

The remainder of this chapter is structured as follows: it begins with an overview of employment and informality in Panama before going on to examine the main drivers of Panama's labour market duality. These are: i) sectoral labour intensity and productivity differences; ii) firm size and self-employment; iii) pension coverage; iv) education and skills; and v) enforcement of labour laws. Assessing these drivers is key to making the Panamanian labour market strong, sustainable and inclusive, to reduce inequalities and to improve the lives of all Panamanians.

High labour market duality, informality and inequality

The high incidence of informality is one of the most salient features of Panama's labour market. Informality is a key obstacle to making Panama more inclusive and labour productive. Although Panama's economic growth has created more than half a million jobs since 2003, almost one-third of those jobs are poor-quality, informal jobs. Moreover, since 2012 two-thirds of all new jobs were informal (INEC, 2017). Informal workers are defined here as those workers (salaried and self-employed) who are not affiliated to social security systems (do not pay pension contributions) and therefore will not have the right to a pension when retired. Informality represents large losses for workers (in the form of social protection, low savings or upskilling), for firms and the wider economy (reducing productivity and tax revenues, for instance). Its interaction with contributory social-protection systems creates a vicious cycle: the majority of informal workers contribute irregularly, if at all, thereby weakening the systems which then provide insufficient support to workers when they need it. At the same time, insufficient savings accentuate old-age poverty.

Informality is high and affects the most vulnerable workers

The informal sector in Panama is smaller than in most Latin America countries, but large by Organisation for Economic Co-operation and Development (OECD) standards. Despite recent progress, labour informality remains higher than in other countries with similar levels of development such as Argentina, Turkey and Uruguay. In fact, in 2016, labour informality still affected around four out of ten non-agricultural workers and almost half of all Panamanian workers, especially affecting those in the lowest quintiles of the income distribution and thus contributing to inequality (Figure 2.1).

Figure 2.1. Informality rates in Panama and selected Latin American countries (LAC)

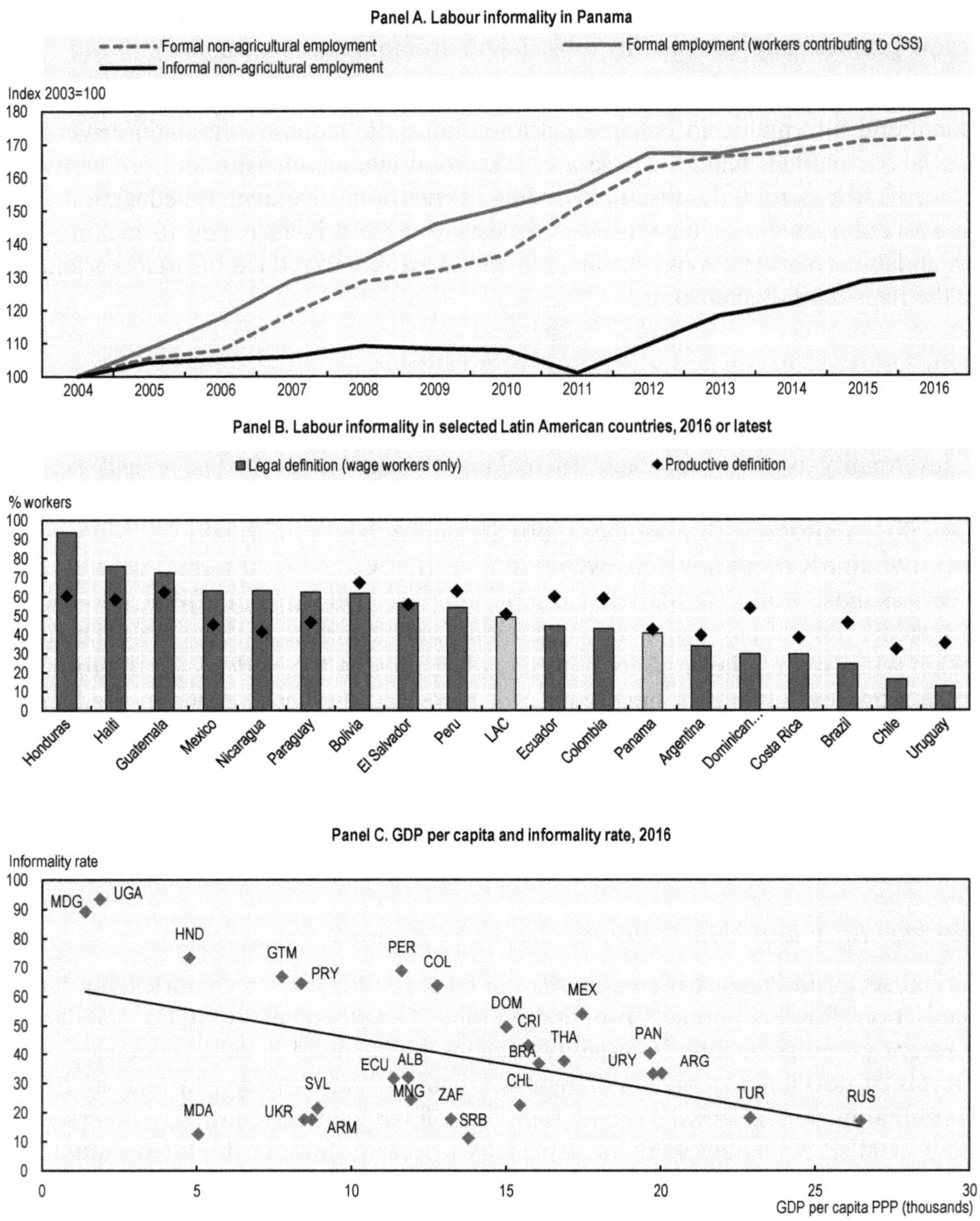

Notes: Legal definition of informality used unless specified: workers are considered informal if they do not have the right to a pension when retired; for cross-country comparability rates are calculated for wage and salary workers only. Productive definition of informality: workers are considered informal if they are salaried workers in a small firm, non-professional self-employed, or zero-income workers. For Panel B, LAC average of 17 countries: Argentina, Bolivia, Brazil, Chile, Costa Rica, Colombia, Dominican Republic, Ecuador, El Salvador, Guatemala, Haiti, Honduras, Mexico, Nicaragua, Paraguay, Peru, Uruguay. Data for Argentina are only representative of urban areas and wage workers.

Source: OECD calculations based on data provided by INEC (National Institute of Statistics and Census of Panama), OECD and World Bank tabulations of SEDLAC (CEDLAS and World Bank, 2016), ILO, ILOSTAT (2017) and IMF (2017), *World Economic Outlook* (database).

StatLink http://dx.doi.org/10.1787/888933776692

Box 2.1. Job quality in Panama

Overall job quality, a multi-dimensional concept capturing several job characteristics that contribute to the well-being of workers, is relatively low in Panama. The *OECD Job Quality Framework* is structured around three dimensions that are closely related to people's employment situation: earnings quality (a combination of average earnings and inequality); labour market security (capturing the risk of unemployment and extreme low pay); and the quality of the working environment (measured as the incidence of job strain or very long working hours). These three dimensions jointly define job quality and should be considered simultaneously, together with job quantity, when assessing labour market performance. The OECD (2015a) has adapted the job quality framework to emerging economies by taking into account their labour market specificities, such as the weakness of social protection (inadequacy of benefits and low coverage of social insurance schemes), the relative high rates of working poverty, and the more limited data available for these countries.

Similar to other Latin American countries, Panama's job quality is much lower than the OECD average in two out of the three dimensions. The results show special concern on the quality of earnings and risk of entering extreme low-pay status. Earnings inequality is particularly large in Panama. The levels of earnings inequality are more than three times higher than that in OECD countries as in most emerging economies (Figure 2.2) (OECD, 2015a).

Figure 2.2. Earnings are lower and more unequal than in OECD economies

PPP-adjusted international dollars, 2010 (High inequality aversion, α= - 3)

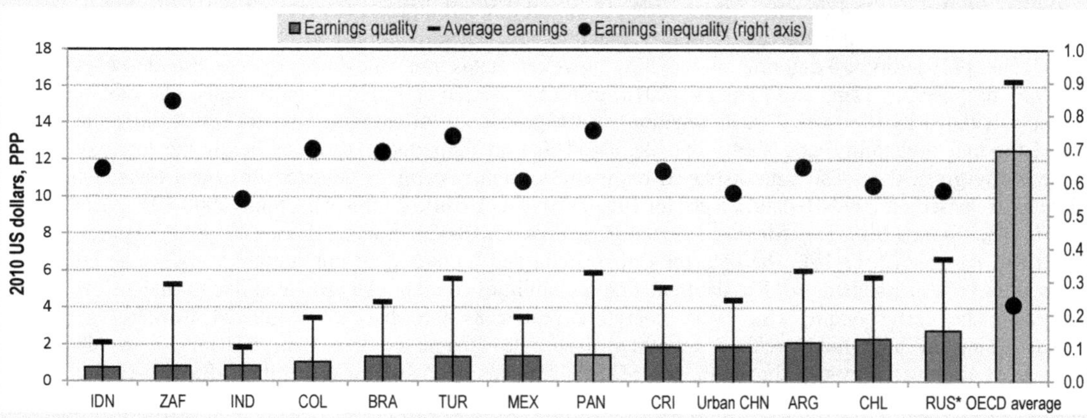

Note: Calculations are based on net hourly earnings and concern 2013 values, except for Brazil (2009), Chile (2009), China (2009), Argentina (2010), India (2011) and Panama (2016). The OECD average is a simple cross-country average of earnings quality. Data for Argentina are representative of urban centres of more than 100 000 inhabitants. The figures for Russia are based on imputed data on households' disposable income from information on income brackets, and therefore include the effect of net transfers. Individual hourly income for two-earner households was calculated using available information on partners' employment status and working hours.
Source: OECD calculations based on national household -Encuesta Continua de Hogares- (INEC, 2016) and OECD (2015b).

StatLink http://dx.doi.org/10.1787/888933776711

The risk of workers falling into extreme low pay in Panama is high. Although workers in other emerging economies such as India, Mexico and Colombia face higher risk of workers falling into extreme low pay; Panama's risk of falling into extreme low pay more than triple that of Argentina, Brazil and Costa Rica. Moreover, social transfers are not fully able to reduce this risk which translates into higher levels of overall labour market insecurity than in most OECD countries (2015a).

Figure 2.3. Labour market insecurity due to extreme low pay is higher than in OECD economies

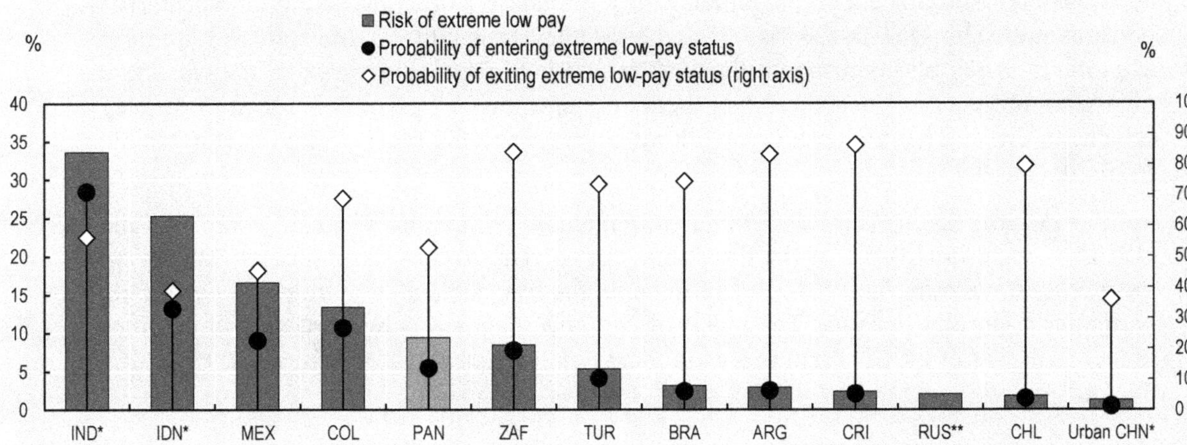

Notes: The low-pay threshold is set at USD PPP 1 in terms of net hourly earnings and corresponds to a disposable income per capita of USD PPP 2 per day in a typical household of five members with a single earner working full-time. The choice of the household size follows Bongaarts (2001) and is based on data from Demographic and Health Surveys. Country rankings are generally robust to changing the low-pay threshold. The probability of entering and exiting low-pay status are calculated by the pseudo-panel methodology proposed by Dang and Lanjouw (2013) using the sample of employed individuals. The risk of low pay is calculated by (the scaled transformation) of the probability of entering low-pay status times the inverse of the exit probability, and shows the likelihood that an individuals' earnings below the low-pay threshold at any given time. The data displayed represent net hourly earnings adjusted for social transfers. Calculations are based on 2009-10 data, except for Brazil (2009-11), Chile (2009-11), China (2008-09), Costa Rica (2010-12), India (2011-12), Mexico (2010-12), Russia (2010-12), South Africa (2010-12), Turkey (2011-12) and Panama (2013-16). The data for China, India and Indonesia do not contain transfers, so an insurance rate of 0% is assumed. For Russia, transition probabilities could not be estimated due to categorical income data. The corresponding risk figure therefore represents the share of employed working-age individuals living in households with a monthly disposable income of less than RUB 6000, which corresponds to an hourly low-pay threshold of USD PPP 1.14 (as of 2010) for a member of a two-earner family working full-time.

Source: OECD calculations based on national household -Encuesta Continua de Hogares- (INEC, 2016) and OECD (2015b).

StatLink http://dx.doi.org/10.1787/888933776730

Figure 2.4. Job quality is worst for informal than formal workers

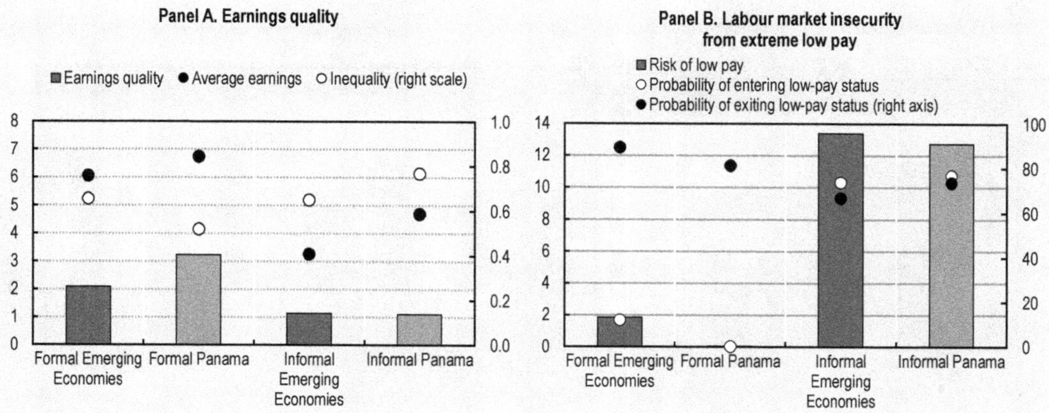

Note: Figures represent unweighted country averages across all sampled emerging economies except Indonesia. Due to missing information, China was excluded from the calculation of labour market security in Panel B. Classification between formal and informal status is based on social security payments (employees) and business registration (self-employed), except for Colombia and Russia where information on work contract (written or not) was used, and Panama where information pension contributions was used for all workers.

Source: OECD calculations based on national household -Encuesta Continua de Hogares- (INEC, 2016) and OECD (2015b).

StatLink http://dx.doi.org/10.1787/888933776749

Informal jobs in Panama have poorer earnings quality and larger insecurity from the risk of low pay than formal jobs, similar to other emerging economies. Figure 2.4 uses the job quality framework to measure the quality gap between formal and informal jobs in Panama along two dimensions of the OECD Job Quality Framework. Although earnings inequality is similar among formal and informal workers; on average, formal workers earn more than informal workers. Thus the earnings quality of formal workers is substantially higher. Lower average earnings for informal workers are consistent with the perception that informal jobs are less productive. In addition, the analysis of upward and downward earnings mobility reveals that downward mobility is generally higher in informal jobs, whereas upward mobility is significantly larger in formal jobs. This means that workers holding informal jobs face a higher risk of wage loss as well as fewer opportunities for wage improvements.

Source: OECD Employment Outlook 2015.

The incidence of informality is much higher for workers from poor and vulnerable households, youth, and the less educated, perpetuating the vicious cycle of inequality and low productivity (Figure 2.5). In fact, labour informality and low skills are strongly connected, decreasing as workers attain higher levels of education. Almost 70% of the working population with only primary education are employed in unregistered jobs, compared with only 33% of those who attained a tertiary degree. Likewise, youth are more likely than their adult counterparts to end up in informal employment (INEC, 2017).

Figure 2.5. Informality enhances inequality

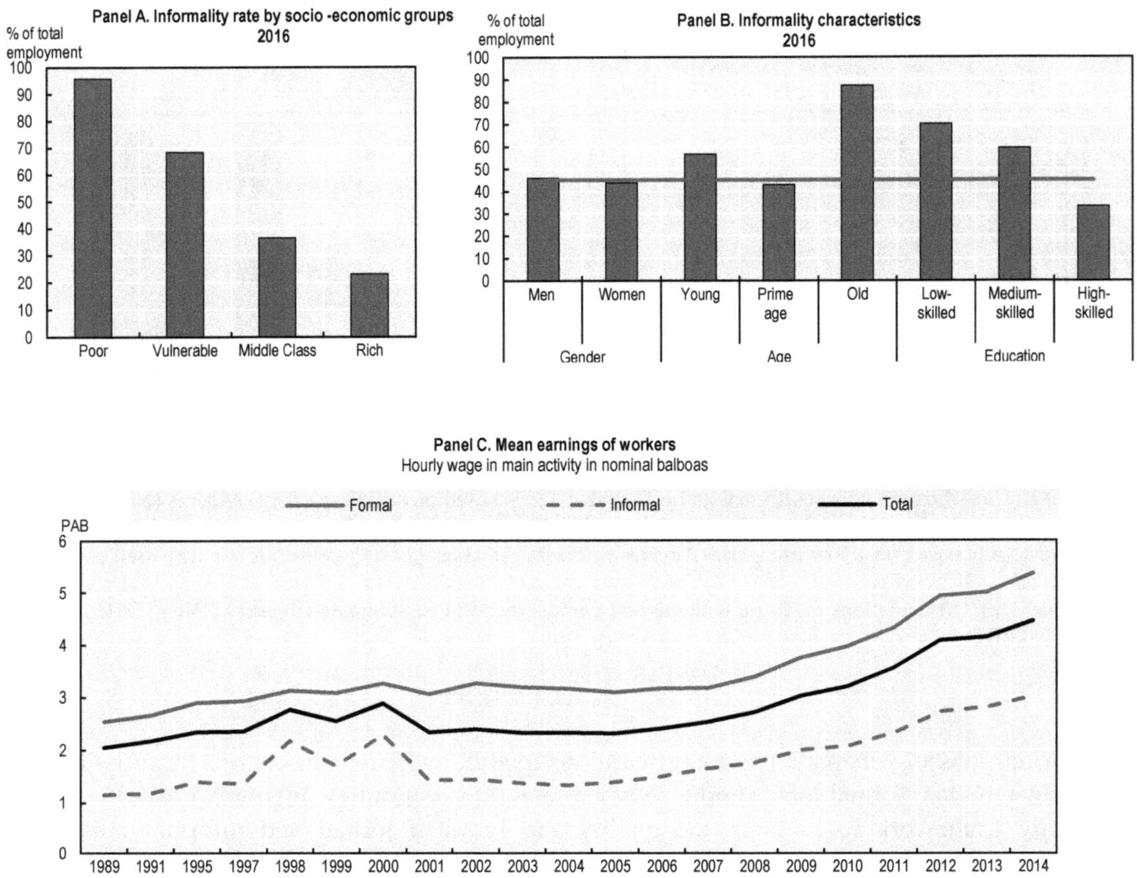

Notes: PAB = Panamanian Balboa.[i] Panels A and B: Legal definition of informality: workers are considered informal if they do not have the right to a pension when retired; for cross-country comparability rates are calculated for wage and salary workers only. Panel C: Productive definition of informality: workers are considered informal if they are salaried workers in a small firm, non-professional self-employed, or zero-income workers. A firm is considered small if it employs fewer than five workers. The three skills level groups are formed according to years of formal education: low=0 to 8 years, medium=9 to 13 years, and high=more than 13 years.

Source: INEC (2017), CEDLAS and World Bank (2016), SEDLAC (Socio-economic Database for Latin America and the Caribbean), http://www.cedlas.econo.unlp.edu.ar/wp/en/estadisticas/sedlac/.

StatLink http://dx.doi.org/10.1787/888933776768

Inequalities in the labour market start early. Young workers from poor or vulnerable families are more likely to hold informal jobs than those from the middle class. Likewise, youth from these households leave school earlier than their peers in better-off households (Figure 2.6). At age 15, six out of ten young people living in poor households are in school; at age 30, however, eight out of ten are informal workers or inactive. In vulnerable households, six out of ten young people aged 30 are working informally or inactive. In contrast, remarkable differences are observed among consolidated middle-class households: nine out of ten of youth are in school at age 15, while six out of ten have a formal job at age 30.This suggests that a certain degree of labour market segmentation exists in Panama, making the transition from school to work a particularly relevant stage in young people's careers and futures (OECD/CAF/ECLAC, 2016).

Figure 2.6. Activity status by single year of age and socio-economic status (2016)

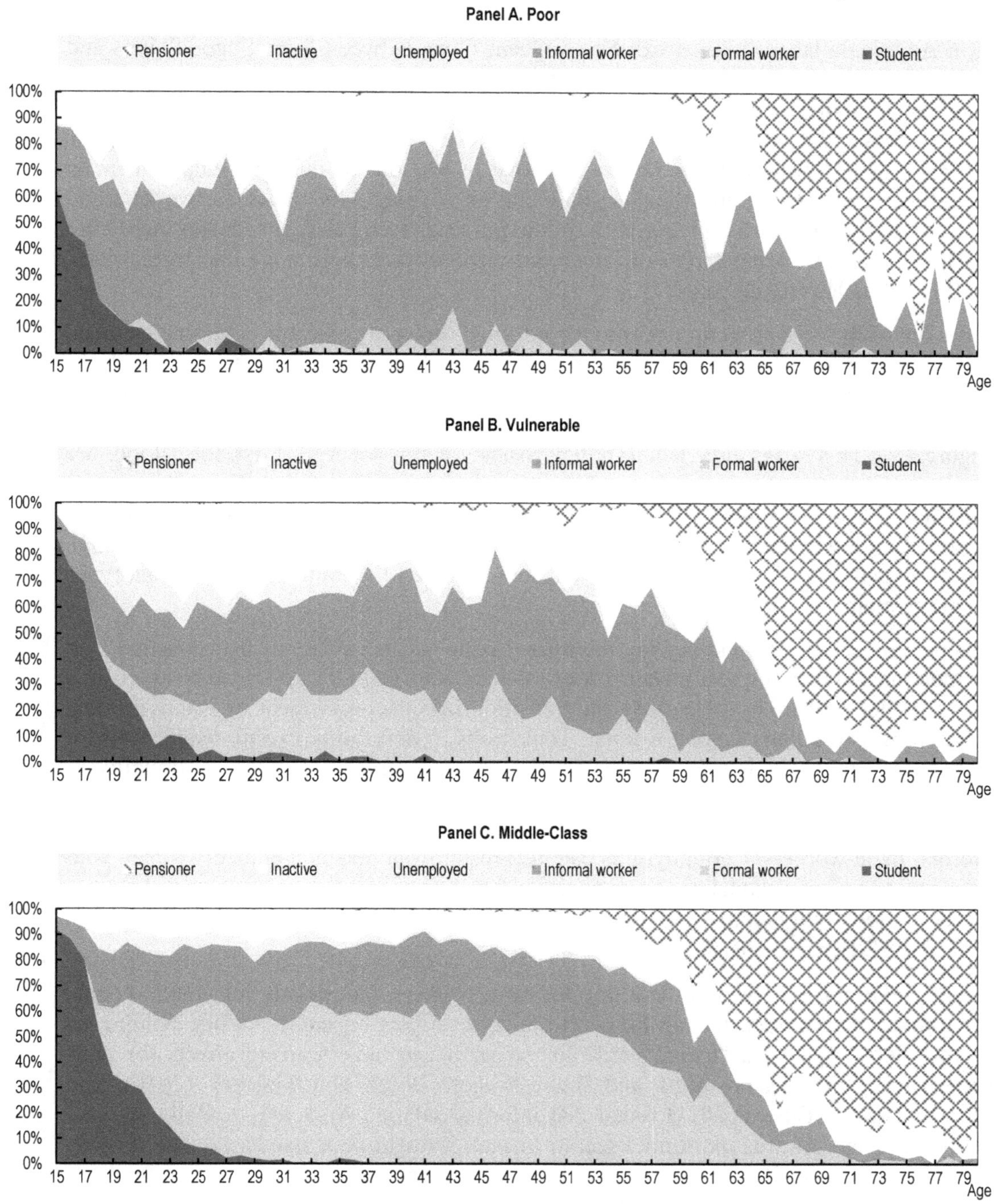

Notes: Socio-economic classes are defined using the following classification: "Poor" = individuals with a daily per capita income of USD 4 or lower. "Population at risk of falling into poverty" = individuals with a daily per capita income of USD 4-10. "Middle class" = individuals with a daily per capita income of USD 10-50. Poverty lines and incomes are expressed in 2005 USD purchasing power parity (PPP) per day). Legal definition of informality: workers are considered informal if they do not have the right to a pension when retired.

Source: OECD calculations based on data provided by INEC.

StatLink http://dx.doi.org/10.1787/888933776673

Box 2.2. The informality trap

Latin America's labour market exhibits frequent flows between formal "good" jobs and informal "bad" jobs (Bosch, Melguizo and Pages, 2013). Flows out of informal jobs are more common than those out of formal jobs, as a considerable number of informal workers make the transition into formal jobs every year. Panel data capturing the dynamics of how workers aged 30 to 55 move in and out of informal employment in Argentina, Brazil, Chile and Mexico show that on average 34% of female workers and 29% of male workers who are currently in the informal sector will not remain there after a year (Figure 2.7). Almost 10% of female informal workers will move into formal jobs, and 22% of males will do so.

Flows out of the formal sector and into the informal sector are sizeable, stressing the need to place better incentives to stay in, or move towards formality. On average, 15% of workers who are currently in the formal sector will not be so within a year. Almost 10% will be informal workers a year later, compared with 3% who will be unemployed (Figure 2.7). This raises three labour policy issues in Latin America. First, formal jobs are scarce, and more quality jobs are needed. Second, unemployment benefits might not be generous enough to support the unemployed while they look for quality jobs, forcing them to take lower-quality jobs instead. And third, in some countries, the relatively high cost of formalisation for workers might encourage some of them to prefer informal types of employment.

This pattern of entering and leaving the formal sector is also evidence that informal jobs are more unstable owing to a higher risk of job loss. Informal jobs appear to be associated with a higher probability of making the transition into unemployment or inactivity than formal jobs, particularly among women. Transitions from informality into unemployment do not seem much higher for women than men, while transitions from informality to inactivity are quite high for women. Almost two out of three informal female workers who transition out of informality every year become inactive, compared with only 14% of informal male workers. Certainly, this can also result from personal choice. Women who are planning to leave the labour force soon for family reasons, for example, may be more likely to look for more flexible work, and thus self-select into informal work (OECD/CAF/ECLAC, 2016).

Overall, informal jobs seem to be a trap for most workers, particularly for youth, women and low-skilled workers, having long-term adverse effects on equity. While holding an informal job might be a "springboard" for some, it can have scarring effects for most workers' employment prospects and future wages. Bosch and Maloney (2010), and Cunningham and Bustos (2011) found that informal salaried work may actually act as a preliminary step towards the formal sector. In fact, it might be a standard queue towards formal work, especially for younger workers, which can serve as training time and not necessarily harm an individual's career path. However, Cruces, Ham and Viollaz (2012) found strong and significant scarring effects in Argentina: people exposed to higher levels of unemployment and informality in their youth fare systematically worse in the labour market as adults (OECD/CAF/ECLAC, 2016). Additionally, informal firms generally provide workers with fewer opportunities for human capital accumulation and are less productive (La Porta and Schleifer, 2014). All of this might thus pose an additional burden in earnings and career advancement to the most vulnerable (OECD/CAF/ECLAC, 2016).

Figure 2.7. Flows in Latin America's labour market

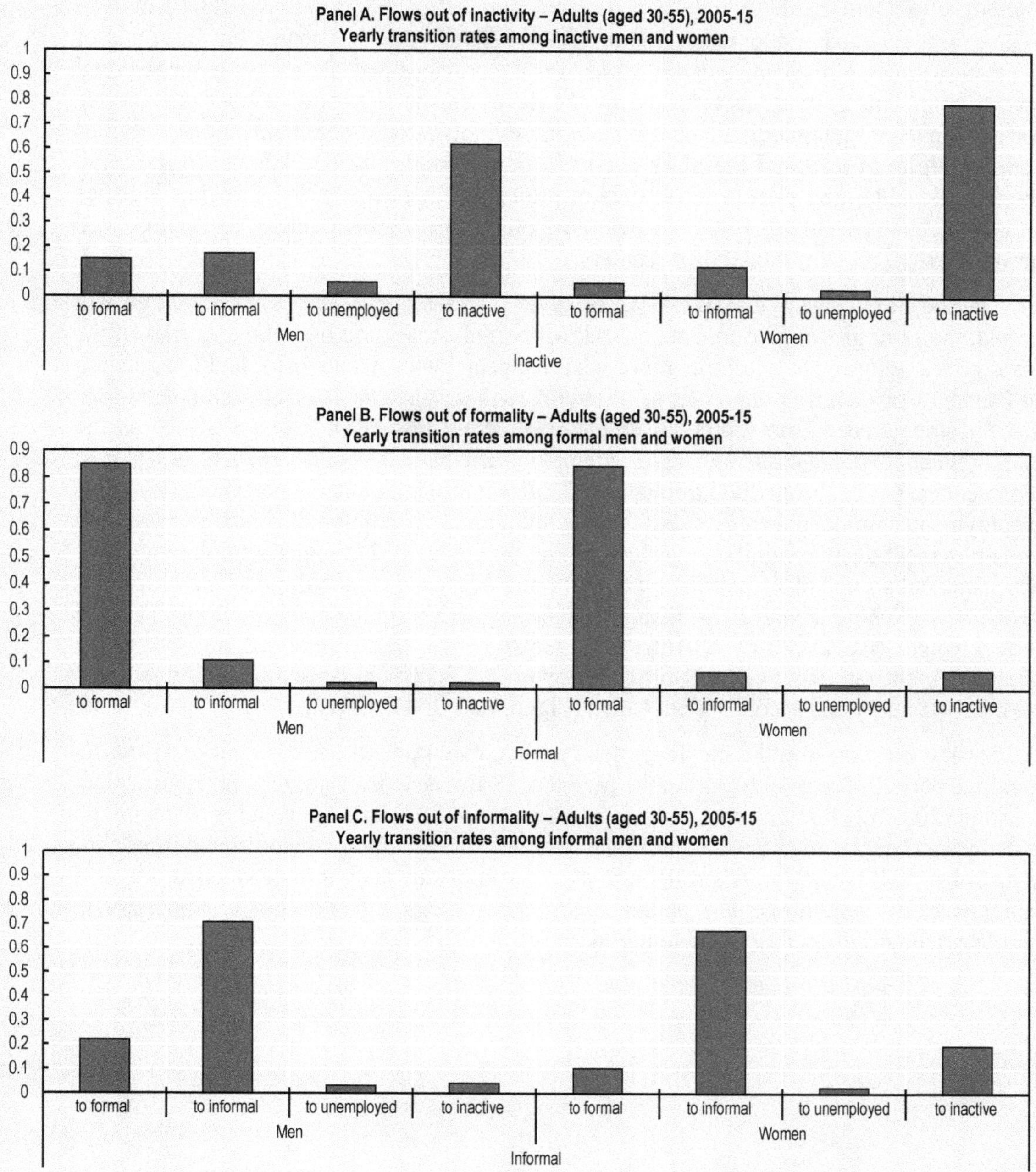

Notes: Results show yearly transition rates into and out of informality. This analysis is limited to urban populations in four countries (Argentina, Brazil, Mexico and Chile) owing to data limitations. Data for Argentina are representative of urban centres of more than 100 000 inhabitants. Legal definition of informality: workers are considered informal if they do not have the right to a pension when retired.
Source: OECD and World Bank tabulations of LABLAC (CEDLAS and World Bank, 2016).

StatLink http://dx.doi.org/10.1787/888933776787

Informality goes hand in hand with the Panama's dual economy and dual labour market

Overall, strong and steady growth has led to job creation in Panama between 2001 and 2017 at an average annual employment growth of 3.4% (INEC, 2017). Panama has been one of the fastest-growing economies in the world over the previous decade, at double the regional growth rate. This growth has been led by the development of a modern tradeable service sector – financial intermediation and mainly trade, logistics and communications activities surrounding the Canal and the SEZs –, which mostly employ skilled labour. At the same time, both public and private infrastructure projects demanded by this growing logistics service sector have fuelled further growth through non-residential construction and created new – formal – jobs for non-skilled workers.

This period of expansion (2001-17) can be divided in three sub-periods: an initial growth period, the peak growth period, and slow-down period. Analysing only the extremes of the period does not provide a full picture of what happened with employment and job creation in Panama. As such it is important to differentiate these three stages. As overall economic growth strengthened from 2003-07, employment grew fast at an average of 4% as the employment to population ratio rose, unemployment halved and informality fell almost 3 percentage points. From 2007 through 2012, informality fell almost 7 percentage points as employment continued to grow, but both employment to population ratio progress and unemployment decline significantly slowed. Finally, since 2012 Panama's employment rate has stagnated around 60% (population aged 15 and over) and informality has increased as a result of weakening labour demand and the subsequent drop in the number of new, salaried jobs created (ECLAC/ILO, 2016). This slowdown is also reflected in the rising unemployment rate (6.1% in the third quarter of 2017), which especially affects workers with only primary and secondary education (Figure 2.8) (INEC, 2017).

Formal job creation is still a challenge for Panama, even though employment grew during the three periods. It was only during the period of fastest economic growth and employment creation (2007-12) that informality significantly decreased. While the benefits of economic growth can trickle down to the informal, without formal employment-oriented policies, growth by itself cannot be relied upon to translate spontaneously into productive jobs and better working conditions. The pattern and sources of growth are equally important in reducing labour informality in the long run.

Figure 2.8. The improvement of labour market conditions is slowing

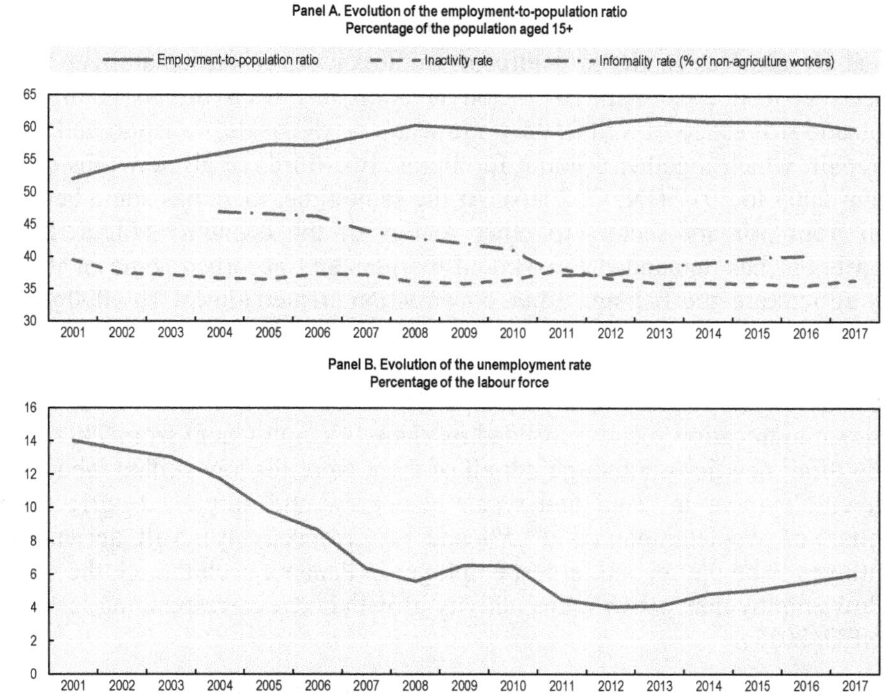

Note: Legal definition of informality: a worker is considered informal if (s)he does not have the right to a pension when retired.
Source: OECD calculations based on data provided by INEC.

StatLink http://dx.doi.org/10.1787/888933776806

Figure 2.9. The employment structure is changing for low-skilled workers

Percentage of workers employed by sector

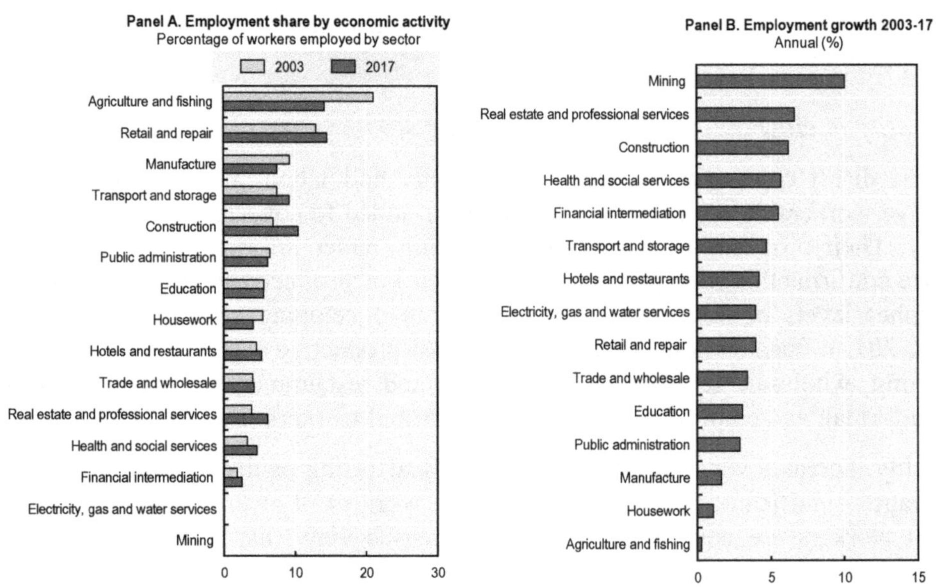

Source: OECD calculations based on data provided by INEC.

StatLink http://dx.doi.org/10.1787/888933776825

Growth resulted in some changes in the employment composition of Panama during the last decade, especially for low-skilled workers. The high demand for non-residential construction, and goods and services created changes in GDP composition that have been accompanied by changes in the structure of employment, in particular over the high-growth spell between 2003 and 2012. Job creation has been driven mainly by the construction and real estate as well as the trade sector – wholesale, transport and storage – retail and repair, which together account for almost two-thirds of all new jobs created in Panama from 2003 to 2017 (INEC, 2016). At the same time, there has some been labour reallocation from primary sectors to other sectors of the economy (Figure 2.9). The construction boom has demanded low-skilled workers and absorbed some of the labour released by agriculture and fishing. While construction created almost 100 000 jobs since 2003 (16% of all new jobs) and expanded its share of employment from 7% to 10%, agriculture created only 27 000 new jobs from 2003 to 2016 (5% of all new jobs) reducing its employment share from 21% to 15%. To a lesser extent, the transport, storage and communication sector expanded its share of employment from 7% to 9% and created 12% of all new jobs, although not all of them were for low-skilled labour. At the same time, employment in retail and repair also grew and surpassed agriculture and fishing in share of people employed (14.5% and 14% respectively). Still, agriculture and fishing continues to be the second largest employer in Panama even though the sector has registered low employment growth, low activity growth and a corresponding loss of share of GDP (INEC, 2017).

This employment shift can probably explain some of the improvement observed in inequality since the early 2000s. As low-skilled workers moved from agriculture to construction and transport jobs their salaries increased and informality fell. Yet, now that the construction boom is expected to decelerate and the modern service sector demanding high skills is expected to continue leading growth, there is a risk of losing some of the progress achieved in terms of poverty and inequality (Hausmann, Espinoza and Santos, 2016).

Creating formal high-quality productive jobs for future generations stands out as one of Panama's main challenges in the next decade. While the dual economy has led Panama's growth and employment story for some time now, it is time for other sectors to play a more important role in creating jobs.

Informality is closely linked to productivity

The most direct connection between productivity and labour informality is that low-productive workers do not produce enough value-added to cover the costs of being hired formally. Their production remains profitable only under informal working conditions. Evidence confirms this strong correlation between low productivity and high informality, with higher levels of informality concentrated in developing countries (La Porta and Shleifer, 2014). Panama is no exception; the least productive sectors such as agriculture and fishing, wholesale retail and repair, hotels and restaurants, and manufacturing are highly informal, and employ two-thirds of all informal workers (Figure 2.10).

Informality increases wage dispersion, negatively affecting equity. Formal workers earn, on average, significantly more than informal workers. Lower average earnings for informal workers are consistent with the consensus view that informal jobs are less productive.

Figure 2.10. Relative productivity and labour informality in Panama, 2016

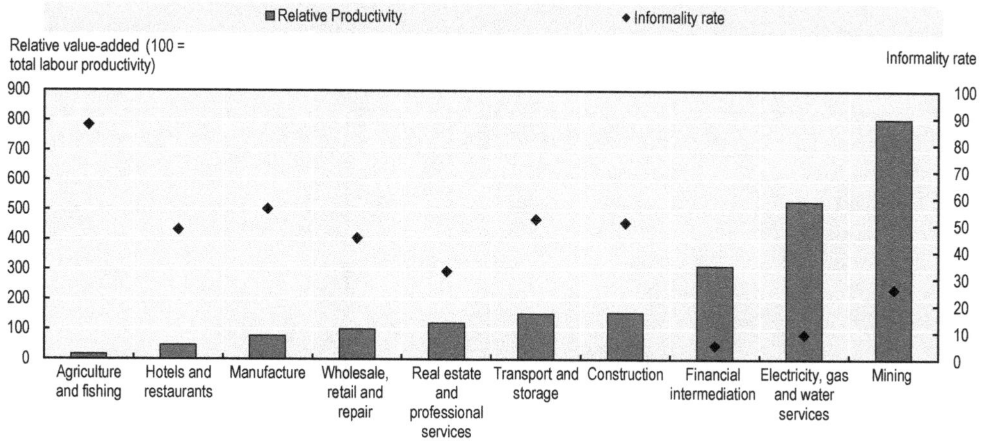

Note: Legal definition of informality: workers are considered informal if they do not have the right to a pension when retired. Labour productivity is measured as the annual value added (the value of output less the value of intermediate consumption) per employee.
Source: OECD calculations based on data provided by INEC.

StatLink http://dx.doi.org/10.1787/888933776844

The productivity level of a large share of informal workers leads to an output per worker that does not cover the minimum costs of formal hiring (i.e. the minimum wage). If labour income is used as a proxy for labour productivity, then the productivity of almost two-thirds of workers in Panama is below the minimum wage they would need to be paid if they were hired formally (plus the social security contribution costs). Low productivity, then, is a functional barrier to formality for these workers, as employers will not readily bear the costs of the formalisation of workers who do not produce enough to cover the costs. In fact, labour income of more than half of informal wage workers – around 65% – remains below the average minimum wage of PAB 423, while 47% of them remain below the least generous minimum wage in Panama of PAB 253 and 85% of them remain below the highest minimum wage in Panama of PAB 725. The income distribution of own account workers is very similar to that of informal wage workers with two out of three own account workers earning less than average minimum wage (Figure 2.11).

On the other hand, the productivity of formal workers appears sufficient to bear these costs. Only 8% of formal wage workers earn monthly salaries close to or below the average minimum wage of PAB 423 (and less than 2% of formal wage workers less than the lowest minimum wage of PAB 253). Although it appears that the minimum wage is too low to be binding for most formal jobs, it may affect the formalisation decision of a significant share of workers. The minimum wage plays a benchmark role, which can be seen by the density of informal workers earning between the highest and lowest minimum wages (Figure 2.11).

Figure 2.11. Informality and earning, 2016

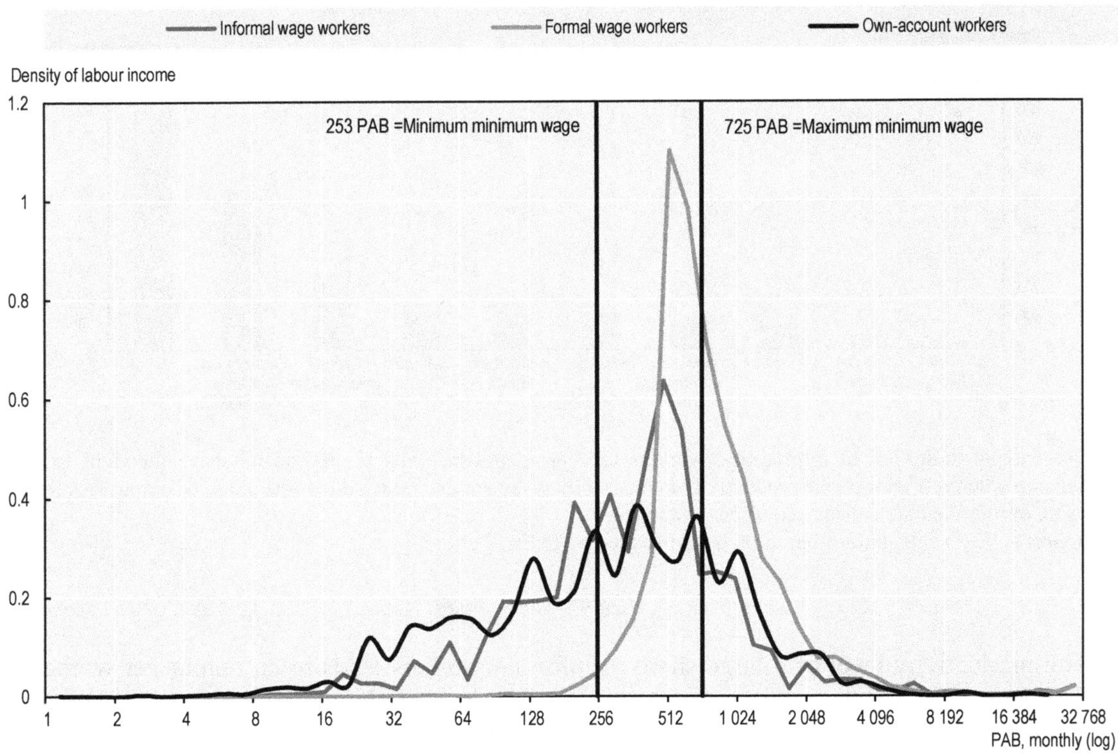

Notes: Legal definition of informality: workers are considered informal if they do not have the right to a pension when retired. Kernel estimates of monthly-equivalent labour market incomes for dependent workers based on their classification as formal or informal. The horizontal bars represent the lowest and highest minimum wage of the minimum wage matrix (PAB 253 and PAB 725 respectively in 2017).
Source: OECD estimates based on microdata from Encuesta de Propsitos Multilpes of 2016 (INEC, 2016).

StatLink http://dx.doi.org/10.1787/888933776863

Differences in informality rates across regions are closely linked to differences in productivity levels as well as to the proportion of social security over total labour costs. There are significant differences in total labour costs (partly related to the complex minimum wage matrix) and the wedges on workers' wages (implied formalisation costs – that is, the portion of the total labour costs that goes towards paying taxes and social security contributions) between departments, urban and rural settings, and geographic areas (Figure 2.12). In general, urban settings have higher labour costs, more so in Panama where the minimum wage matrix differentiates among urban and rural areas establishing a lower minimum wage for workers in rural areas. Moreover, although formalisation costs are proportional among all departments, there is greater variance with respect to total labour costs. Informality tends to be lower in geographic locations where the total labour cost is further from the minimum labour cost (i.e. Coclé, Boca del Toro, Darién and the *comarcas*). In this regard, the presence of competitive and productive industries such as the financial sector or the Canal and the SZEs compared to low-productive agriculture and fishing, retail and repair, and hotels and restaurants are better indicators of higher levels of income and, thus, of higher labour costs and lower levels of informality (Céspedes, Lovado and Ramirez, 2016; OECD, 2015a).

Figure 2.12. Informality, wages and productivity by province

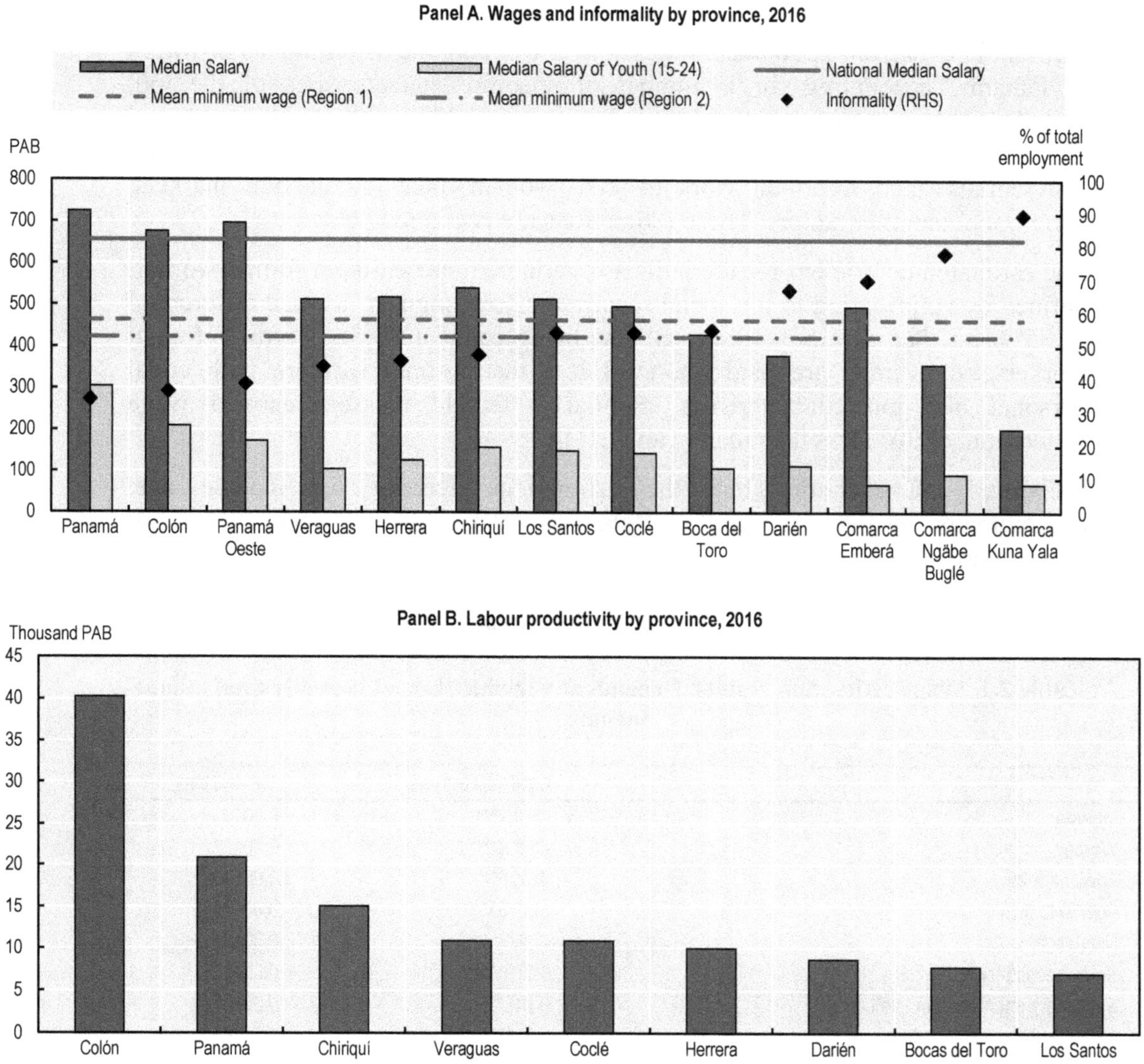

Notes: Legal definition of informality: workers are considered informal if they do not have the right to a pension when retired. Labour productivity measured as the value added (the value of output less the value of intermediate consumption) over the annual average personnel employed per month.
Source: OECD calculations based on data provided by INEC.

StatLink http://dx.doi.org/10.1787/888933776882

Box 2.3. Estimating wage differentials for informal and female workers

Household data from 2016 make it possible to estimate the determinants of wages in Panama, accounting for a number of specific characteristics of the job, including characteristics of the worker, the employer and also regional differences. Such wage estimations also allow an approximation of the wage differentials that informal workers and women face on labour markets, conditional on other factors. These estimations are presented below.

The estimated coefficient for the indicator variable representing a formal worker, defined by contributing to the social security system, suggests a wage differential of 35% less than formal workers, all else being equal. In other words, informal workers on average are paid one-third less than formal workers with equal personal and job characteristics. Similarly, female workers earn a wage differential of 30% less than men (Table 2.1).

Individual characteristics that the estimations account for include age, approximated by three age groups. Relative to those aged between 29 and 64, youths earn less while older workers earn more. Educational attainments of the individual are accounted for in the estimations through five different categories. Predictably, wages are rising with higher educational attainments.

Table 2.1. Wage estimation results. Dependent variable: Log of monthly total labour income

	Coefficient estimate	Standard error
Informal	-0.347***	0.00149
Women	-0.308***	0.00137
Age under 25	-0.156***	0.00196
Age 50 to 60	-0.0135***	0.00148
Illiterate	-0.227***	0.00464
Some secondary education	0.179***	0.00196
Secondary education completed	0.345***	0.00198
Some post-secondary education	0.511***	0.00241
Tertiary education completed	0.903***	0.00219
More than 5 years with current employer	0.164***	0.00129
Public sector employee	0.313***	0.00287
Domestic employee	0.185***	0.00396
Hours worked	0.0230***	0.00005
Constant	4.616***	0.00461
Fixed effects for 12 major regions	included	
Fixed effects for 21 industries	included	
Observations	14 412	
R-squared	0.547	

Notes: *, ** and *** denote significance at 10%, 5% and 1%, respectively.
Source: OECD estimates based on microdata from *Encuesta de Propsitos Multilpes* of 2016 (INEC, 2017).

A productive transformation is needed to create more and better jobs

Informality is directly linked to Panama's dual economic structure. On one hand, a small share of the working population – less than 20% – is employed in the high-productivity industries such as the financial intermediation sector and the modern tradeable service sector – logistics, communications, transport, trade services, and information – which mostly consist of formal jobs but create little employment. On the other hand, almost half of the population works in low-productivity, informal services and agriculture. This contributes to labour market segmentation: informal and formal sectors are largely separated, with a large informal sector consisting mainly of many poorly educated agricultural, retail or construction own account or microenterprise workers running firms that add little value, and a formal sector of educated workers who run bigger, more productive firms in the tradeable services sector.

The most productive sectors create little employment

Panama's employment it is still concentrated in low-productivity, informal sectors. Although the construction boom created new formal jobs, two out of three workers in Panama are employed in a sector with below average labour productivity such as agriculture and fishing, retail and repair, and hotels and restaurants, a fact that might be at the core of the large income inequality in Panama (Figure 2.13). Moreover, half of the Panamanian construction workers are still employed informally, while the activity is expected to slow down. This demonstrates both the inverse relationship between productivity and informality and that Panama's economy is not currently conducive to increased formal job creation.

Relative productivity across sectors shows some particularities of the Panamanian economy: a highly productive modern tradeable service sector, a fast-growing construction sector and a low-productivity non-tradeable service sector. The labour productivity of Panama's financial sector and logistic sector activities – trade, repackaging services, and transportation, storage and communications – are between 2.5 and 3 times the total labour productivity (Figure 2.13). These are the internationally competitive activities that have driven Panama's economic growth in the last two decades. Additionally, the construction and real-estate sectors have made significant gains in productivity, driven by expansion of the Canal and the renovation of Tocumen airport, office buildings, warehouses, telecom infrastructure, shopping malls and other infrastructure demanded by the modern service sector. At the same time, the non-tradeable service sector – mainly retail and repair, hotels and restaurants, education, health and social services – halves the total labour productivity of Panama but employs half of the working population. The analysis on the basis of sector-level data is limited by the level of detail available in labour statistics. For example, Figure 2.13 bundles private and public education and health services as well as all sectors in manufacturing, whose productivity levels are very different. More notably, it aggregates all trade and wholesale activities, while there are large productivity gaps between Panama Canal-related activities, the SEZs, and other types of wholesale. Likewise it considers the agricultural, livestock, hunting, forestry and fishing sectors as a whole as well as aggregate all restaurants and hotels whose productivity levels are very heterogeneous across the country under the same category.

Figure 2.13. Productivity and the distribution of labour in Panama, 2016

Relative value-added as a percentage of workers and employment by economic sectors

(y axis: 100 = total labour productivity and x-axis: % of employment)

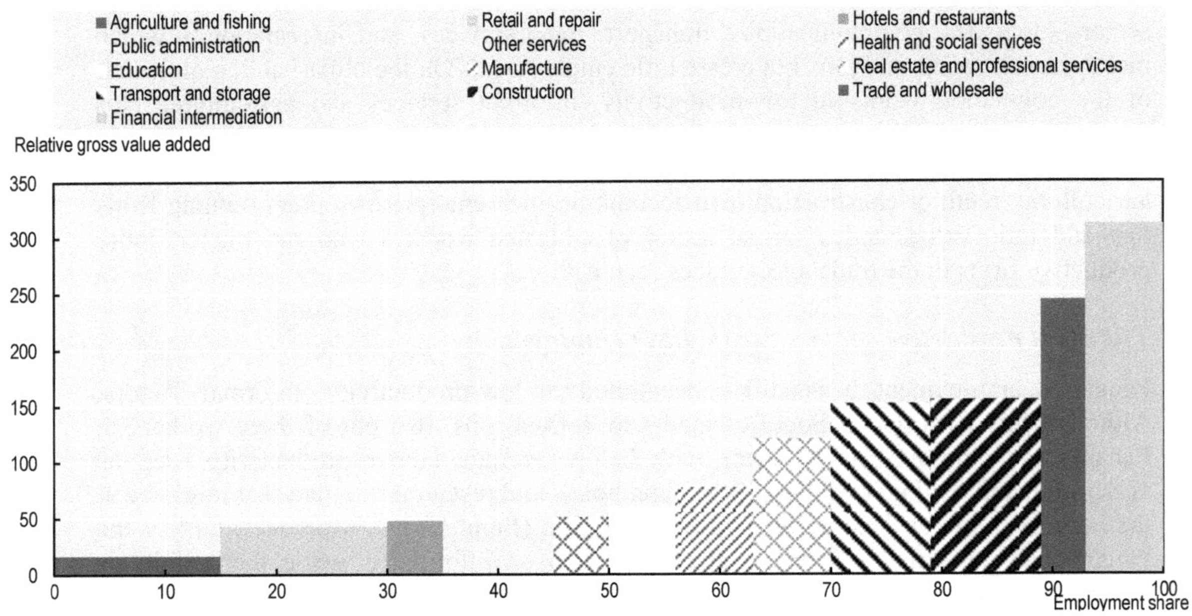

Note: Labour productivity is measured as the annual value added (the value of output less the value of intermediate consumption) per employee.
Source: OECD calculations based on data provided by INEC.

StatLink http://dx.doi.org/10.1787/888933776901

There are significant productivity gains to be realised through labour reallocations from less to more productive sectors as well as through endowing workers with better skills (Figure 2.14). Three of the five sectors that employ the largest shares of the population (retail and repair, agriculture and fishing, and manufacturing) are among the sectors with the lowest productivity. Although labour productivity in retail and repair –the largest employment sector in Panama– has increased, it still very low (43%) compared to overall labour productivity. Similarly, labour productivity in agriculture, livestock, hunting, forestry and fishing – which has dropped in the past decade – is only 16% of the average productivity, while the sector employed 14% of the workforce in 2016 – the second largest employment sector. In addition, labour productivity in hotels and restaurants is less than half the average productivity and has great potential in a country that has natural resources to serve as a worldwide vacation destination.

Figure 2.14. Productivity increases are led by within-sector growth with a few exceptions

Percentage

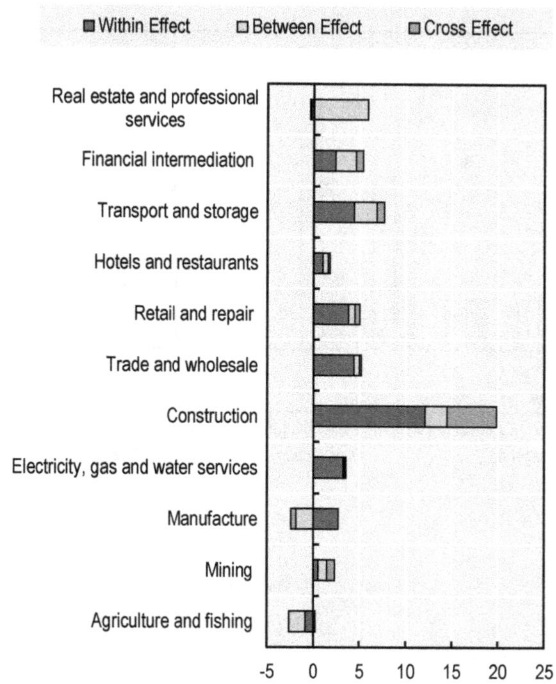

Notes: The total change in productivity can be broken down into a within-industry effect, measuring the average yearly growth of output per employed person driven by technical change and capital accumulation; a between-industry effect measuring compositional shifts in sectoral shares of employment and relative price changes driven by reallocation of labour resources between sectors; and cross effect measuring the productivity gains which are driven by increases in the employment/market shares of firms whose productivity is increasing quickly, driven by the interaction between productivity changes and employment shares. In particular, the cross-sector effect represents the joint effect of changes in employment shares and sectoral productivity. This term is positive if, on the average, labour goes to sectors whose productivity is growing.

Source: OECD calculations based on data provided by INEC.

StatLink http://dx.doi.org/10.1787/888933776920

Productivity gains in most major sectors in the past 13 years have been achieved with overall falling elasticity of job creation to economic growth. Figure 2.15 shows the growth in real gross value added, employment, and employment elasticity of growth across the sectors with the largest employment shares in the economy. The employment elasticity is a measure of the percentage change in employment associated with a 1-percentage-point change in economic growth. It represents a convenient way of summarising the employment intensity of growth or sensitivity of employment to output growth. As such, it can indicate the ability of an economy to generate employment opportunities for its population – as a percentage of its growth process – as well as used to track sectoral potential for generating employment (Islam and Nazara, 2000). A positive employment elasticity of growth indicates that increased output is associated with increased employment. An elasticity lower than 1 indicates that output is growing more quickly than employment, signifying both increases in productivity and in employment.

Figure 2.15. Employment elasticity across selected sectors in Panama, 2003-16

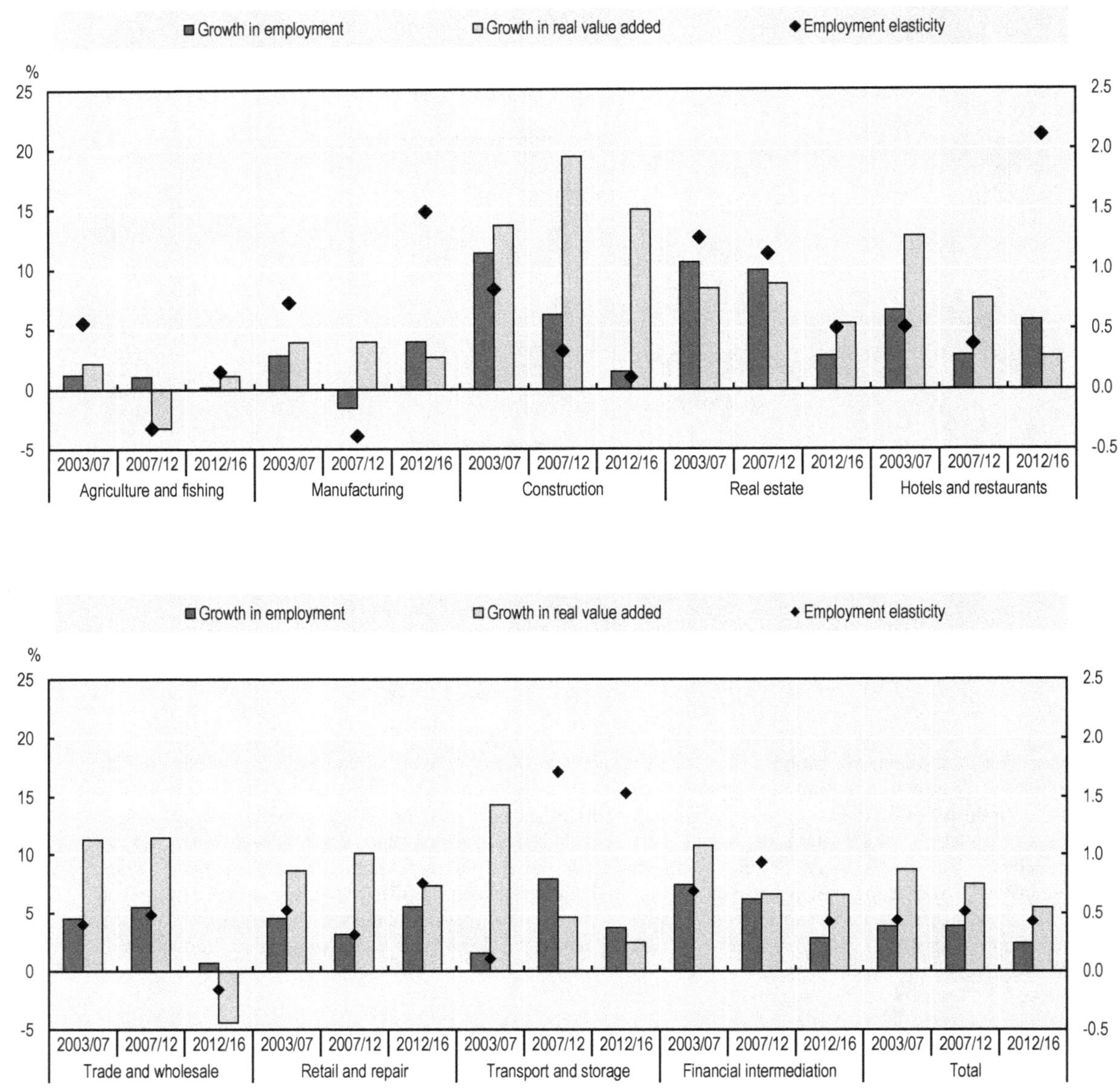

Source: OECD calculations based on data provided by INEC.

StatLink http://dx.doi.org/10.1787/888933776939

Elasticity varies considerably across sectors ranging from transport and storage, which experienced the most job-friendly growth, to agriculture, which has seen a reduction of its workforce. Most of the big actors in the services sector, including construction, real estate, trade and wholesale, transport, storage and communications, have generally been employment intensive during the past decade. They have also experience falling elasticity since fast employment growth was accompanied by steady productivity growth. As a result, their job creation capacity is slowing down. These sectors have created considerably fewer new jobs since 2012 compared to what happened at the beginning of the 2000s. Greater employment generation in these sectors is crucial to benefit from the demographic dividend as well as to reduce informality.

Additionally, the trend in the manufacturing, restaurant and hotel sector, and transport and storage where elasticity is above 1 and growing, is a call to attention. Manufacturing, restaurants and hotels are among the sectors with the lowest productivity in the economy – below the aggregate average – and their employment shares are growing; a further fall in productivity could be a cause for concern. Fostering labour reallocation towards more productive services is therefore an avenue to increase overall productivity in the economy.

Overall, the aggregate employment elasticity estimates for Panama have increased during the period of fastest economic growth. It varied from 0.44 during 2003-07 to 0.51 during 2007-12 and back to 0.43 from 2012-17. This implies that for every 10% change in real GDP, there is about 4.3% change in employment. Going forward, although stepping up the employment intensity of growth would be hard since elasticity is close to 0.5, it is the relative cost of capital vis-à-vis labour and the nature of investment demand that will determine to what extent growth would be job-creating. On a rough basis, about 400 000 new workers will need a job in the next 10 years. If Panama's employment intensity of growth stays constant the economy will need to grow at almost 6% GDP annually for the next decade to meet the demographic dividend.

Promoting value-added economic activities to generate sustainable growth and employment

The noted link between employment, informality and productivity levels, along with Panama's economic structure, indicate productive transformation as a key policy area to promote more formal jobs in the medium to long term (OECD, 2017). Policies that favour formal job creation should be combined into longer-term planning, with a strong link to the broader national development strategy. Creating formal jobs requires the promotion of an economy which, from the supply side, has workers with higher levels of productivity and skills and, from the demand side, can create good-quality formal jobs to absorb those workers.

Panama needs to spur economic activities so that they overtake construction and allow the country to continue growing at a sustainable pace. The country should promote more complex economic activities in the provinces to help decentralise growth and make it more inclusive (Hausmann, Espinoza and Santos, 2016; Agosin et al., 2014).

On one hand, Panama could further upgrade and expand the service sector to new activities. There is a need to increase value-added in exports, and in particular the export of services, which remains the most important component in the export profile. While exports on services represent close to 95% of total exports, the services' value-added generated for these exports remains low compared to benchmark economies. Transitioning from infrastructure-driven growth (i.e. investments in the housing market in Panama City, the Canal and Tocumen airport) to more diversified and knowledge-driven growth requires better and higher investments in innovation. Panama began to promote innovation and to invest in science, technology and research in 2004. Promoting innovation in a small, service-oriented economy such as Panama's is challenging. The country has managed to increase domestic research capabilities and to introduce incentives to invest in innovation. Panama is still far from achieving the critical stage to improve its innovation capacities and to score well in traditional innovation indicators consistent with its level of development (see OECD, 2017).

On the other hand, Panama could invest in value-added regional manufacturing such as agro-industry products. Panama's exported goods have "low complexity" and share few connections with more sophisticated products. Panama's current export basket of goods is mainly composed of low-complexity products, which comprise close to 76% of goods. High complexity products amounted only to 5% (Hausmann, Morales and Santos, 2016). Moreover, the proximity of Panama's current export basket of goods to more sophisticated goods is low. The basket of goods remains rather isolated, clustered around raw materials and far from capital-intensive activities, where the largest potential to develop new high-value-added products lies (Hausmann, 2012). An export basket of goods that relies on merchandise that is labour-intensive to produce, and uses low levels of technology and processing, creates few linkages with the rest of the economy. In turn, the lack of linkages limits the possibilities for incorporating further value-added into the exports (OECD, 2017).

The development of international tourism is another opportunity for Panama to consolidate a diversification strategy. Foreign tourism flows have increased at an average annual rate of 9%. The core of international tourism in Panama comes from the United States and neighbours Colombia and Venezuela, with 307 458, 307 076 and 235 023 registered visitors in 2015 from a total of 1 946 290 visitors, which represents almost half of tourism. Still, Panama lags behind benchmark countries such as Costa Rica, the Dominican Republic and Uruguay which had between three to six million tourists in 2016. The emergence of tourism as a promising sector should be developed hand in hand with both the strengthening of the modern tradeable service sector and positioning of the country as a logistics hub, which will provide the perfect air and water connectivity to foster broader international tourism and territorial development. The decentralisation of tourism-related activities remains an essential objective for the government in coming years. To this end an ambitious capacity-building programme is being implemented with local municipalities.

Additionally future benefits of the Canal and the tradeable service sector should expand to other sectors and regions to increase competitiveness and equity in Panama. The sectoral shifts and rising wages in the Canal cluster underscore a larger concern about loss of competitiveness and concentration of economic activities. In addition to rising labour costs, the rising prices of intermediate goods and labour will make the agricultural, manufacturing and certain service sectors less competitive. While the Canal is a fundamental source of high-quality jobs and high salaries, there is a risk of increasing the concentration of production and exports around it unless the Canal's direct benefits and spillovers are further expanded in Panama.

The *Plan Estratégico de Gobierno 2015-2019* (Government Strategic Plan 2015-2019) anticipates the Canal will diversify activities towards energy including generating electricity, exploiting the trade of liquefied natural gas and liquefied petroleum gas, and bunkering (GRP, 2014). The expansion may allow the development of hub-spoke economies (i.e. moving cargo from smaller to larger vessels for the longer hauls). Construction of shipyards in the Atlantic entrance of the Canal for post-Panamax ships is also foreseen, as well as carrying out top-off operations for ships that do not satisfy the draught restrictions.

Furthermore, investment in infrastructure beyond Panama City is particularly necessary given the country's geography, increasing competitiveness and fostering of local tourism. At the same time new infrastructure projects in the provinces could open up profitable opportunities, generate employment and promote local economic development.

Boosting formalisation in independent workers and firms

Informality can take place either by election or by exclusion. Workers and firms may make a rational choice to operate informally based on a cost-benefit analysis. However, they may also be pushed into informality if the conditions and costs imposed by formality preclude it as an alternative, e.g. make the job unsustainable or the firm unprofitable (Perry et al., 2007). Three scenarios emerge based on cost-benefit rationales: 1) informality by choice, when both firms and workers perceive the costs of formality to outweigh the benefits; 2) informality for evasion, when firms remain informal, even if the benefits of formality outweigh the costs; and 3) informality by exclusion, when workers work informally, even if the benefits of formality outweigh the costs and they would be willing to assume those costs, because there are no formal jobs available (OECD, 2016a).

Labour informality is largely explained by self-employment and small informal firms

A significant share of informal employment in Panama is not voluntary and rather a necessity for most workers involved. One traditional explanation in the literature is that a large share of informal employment is the result of low levels of formal job creation and as a result many workers lack occupational alternatives. The self-employed represent by far the largest group of informal workers in Panama at 54% of total informal workers, followed by 15% of informal wage workers who work for informal firms, 14% of informal wage workers who work for formal firms and 9% domestic workers (Figure 2.16).

Figure 2.16. Composition of informal workers in Panama, 2016

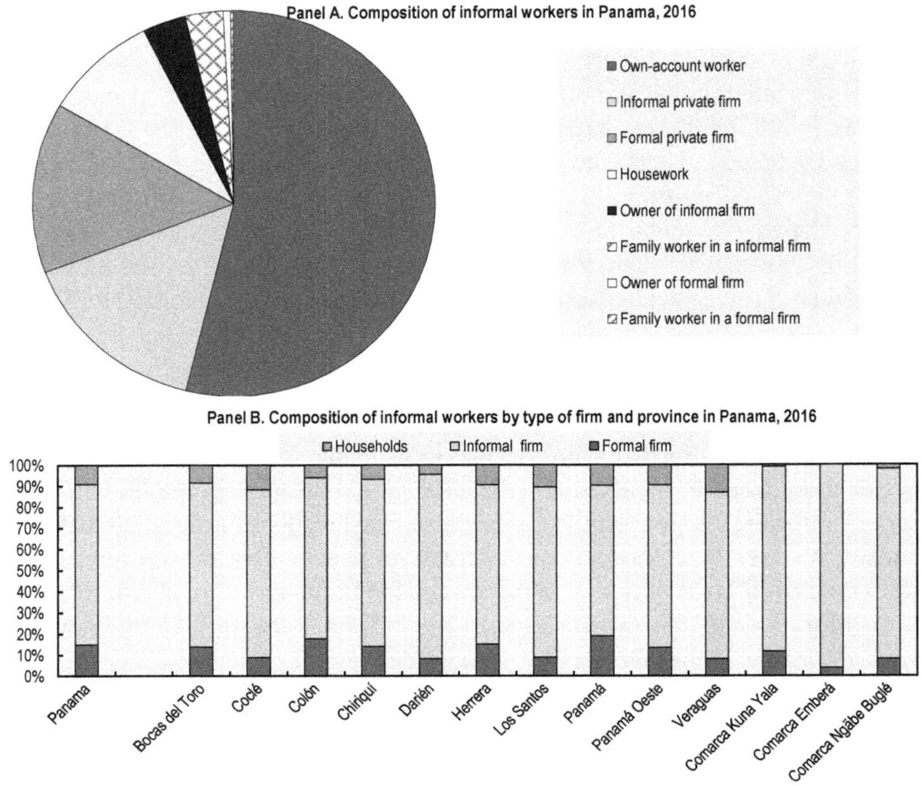

Note: Legal definition of informality: workers are considered informal if they do not have the right to a pension when retired.
Source: OECD calculations based on data provided by INEC.

StatLink http://dx.doi.org/10.1787/888933776958

The labour market in Panama is also dual in terms of employment by firm size. Almost half of total employment in Panama is composed by informal workers in micro, small, and medium-sized enterprises (MSMEs), especially dedicated to agriculture but also manufacturing, construction, commerce and transport, while most of the other half of the working population is employed in formal large firms: 43% of workers are employed in firms of less than 5 workers where informal rates are as high as almost 90%, while another 40% is employed in firms with more than 50 workers where most of the employment is formal (INEC, 2017) (Figure 2.17). In 2010, the first MSMEs survey done under the initiative for the Economic Inclusion of the Informal Sector in Panama (PASI for its acronym in Spanish) found that Panama has nearly 200 000 MSMEs that employ almost 430 000 workers, which means an average of 2.2 workers per MSME (CNC, 2010).

Figure 2.17. Employment composition and informality by firm size in Panama, 2016

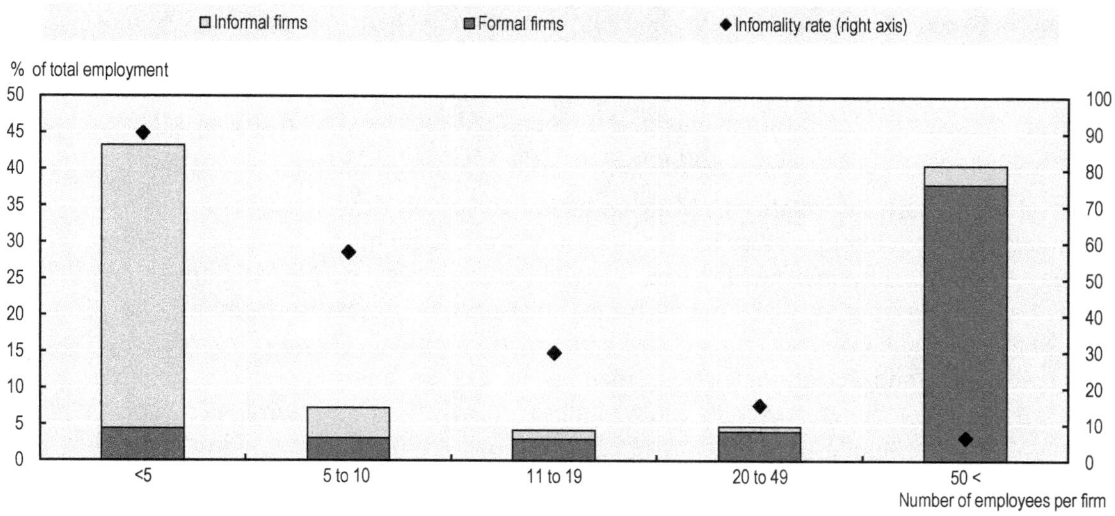

Note: Legal definition of informality: workers are considered informal if they do not have the right to a pension when retired.
Source: OECD calculations based on data provided by INEC.

StatLink http://dx.doi.org/10.1787/888933776977

Almost half of the MSMEs have only one worker and constitute a quarter of the employment generated by the sector. Two–worker companies constitute 21% of MSMEs and generate 19% of employment; companies with 3 to 5 workers represent a quarter of the MSMEs and generate almost a third of the sector's employment. MSMEs with 6 to 20 workers account for 6% of the total number of companies and 24% of employment (CNC, 2010).

Labour informality is extremely high among MSMEs and firms show different levels of compliance. Only 11% of all MSMEs pay the social security quota for all its workers and 9% pay for only some workers; while 59% of companies do not pay social security for any workers. Yet, 21% of the MSMEs employees have social security for other circumstances, for example, they are covered by the social security of their families or are pensioners (CNC, 2010).

Labour informality among MSMEs goes hand in hand with firm informality. PASI identified bottlenecks that MSMEs face to register and operate formally. As such, they classified companies by five main types of informality: (i) those that do not register workers at the *Caja de Seguridad Social* (CSS – Social Security Agency) Social Security Agency (68%); (ii) those that do not pay for workers' social security (79%); (iii) those that do not have a single taxpayer registry (67%); (iv) those that lack an operation permit (66%); and (v) those that lack the local government/municipality permit (60%). Only 6% of all MSMEs[2] comply with all requisites (CNC, 2010).

A large number of informal MSMEs serve as subsistence employment for poor and vulnerable women. The majority of most informal business owners have had poor access to education – 27% did not complete secondary, 20% only finished primary school, and 15% had no education. Additionally, there is a strong gender bias in the sector: 57% of informal businesses are owned by women and 32% are owned by men, while only 10%

are owned jointly. It is important to highlight that most business owners felt they made more money under the informal sector, which is particularly important as their enterprises represent between 75-100% of their household income. Their vulnerability is most evident through the fact that 40% of PASI-surveyed enterprises were unable to gain financing due to lack of collateral and are highly indebted to informal forms of finance. Moreover, almost 40% of informal business owners had previously owned an informal business, demonstrating a systemic and long-term trend (CNC, 2010).

Recent efforts to curb informality in MSMEs have focused on firm registration and have had limited results. Although there has been a lot of work done by Autoridad de la Micro Pequeña y Mediana Empresa (AMPYME – MSME Authority), few MSMEs are formal. In fact, Panama has put in place a number of measures to foster the formalisation of firms. These include a portal to ease the creation of a firm – *Panamá Emprende* –, training services, and fiscal incentives, such as access to financing and a two-year exemption from income tax for new micro firms with a turnover cap of PAB 150 000 (Law No. 33 of 2000) which covers over 100 000 firms. Firms in this scheme are included in a special registry that also grants them access to a number of other support services provided by AMPYME. Still, some firms, especially small and medium firms, have benefited from little reduction of overall formalisation costs.

The incorporation of productive units under Law No. 33 of 2000 is too broad. The main objective of this law is to establish a regulatory regime to promote the creation, development and strengthening of MSMEs, which it clearly defines. Medium-sized firms are defined as firms with turnover of between PAB 1 million and PAB 2.5 million. The inclusion of such firms under the small and medium-sized enterprises (SME) umbrella is debatable and can cause difficulties in the implementation of SME policy since firms with a turnover of around PAB 2 million have very different registration and operating constraints than firms with a turnover of PAB 150 000.

Moreover, innovative legislation passed in 2013 that would enable the incorporation of microenterprises and facilitate tax requirements has not been implemented. Law No. 132 of 2013, which regulates the creation of limited liability microenterprises, could also serve as a productivity-enhancing tool since it forces microenterprises to separate firm bookkeeping from household accounts.

A reason why MSME legislation has not been more effective in reducing labour informality among MSME workers is that the efforts to facilitate the inclusion of MSME workers in the social protection system has not been implemented. There have been no developments between the CSS and the institutions supporting MSMEs to foster labour formalisation. Although Law No. 33 states that the CSS and AMPYME should seek the massive incorporation of own account workers and MSME employees in the social security system, little has been done to create the appropriate mechanisms to promote labour formalisation that is financially sustainable for MSMEs and especially for independent workers. Neither *Panamá Emprende* nor the SME registry are explicitly linked to social security, nor to any of the special regulations for SMEs, including the payment of social security contributions, which are handled by the CSS. Moreover, the limited liability microenterprise law does not incorporate any stipulations to facilitate pension savings for owners and employees.

Simplify the tax burden for MSMEs and independent workers

MSME taxpayers of low fiscal significance in Panama undoubtedly constitute the most difficult sector to control and formalise. For the purposes of their identification and the design of a tax regime that recognises their taxpaying capacity and needs, they should be distinguished by i) their economic magnitude and ii) their economic activity. In terms of economic magnitude it is important to differentiate owners, independent workers and employees since the formalisation constraints they face are different and so is the proper policy response.

Panama could implement a simplified tax regime open to individuals, single-owner firms and micro units. This regime could encourage micro producers and retailers to become formal through the payment of a small monthly fee contingent on the level of annual sales being less than PAB 150 000 – which represents 96% of micro and small enterprises and accounts for 82% of the employment of the sector (CNC, 2010). At the same time the CSS should adapt its contribution quotes for independent workers both in terms of frequency and payment method and enforce the mandatory contribution of independents to the CSS in order to reduce labour informality and ensure that all workers have pension savings.

A simplified tax and pension scheme could serve as an attractive and efficient way to formalise independent workers – also called single-person microenterprises. Simplified regimes reduce the administrative burden and make it easier for low-income, informal taxpayers to comply with both the tax and social security regime by paying several taxes – such as the sales tax, pension and health insurance – in a single payment. The primary objective of its implementation is not to increase the collection of taxes but to reduce the regressive effect of compliance costs for small firms, avoiding overburdening the tax administration with a large number of small taxpayers whose revenue collection is very limited. At the same time, by including pension contributions it reduces the fragmentation derived from the contributory schemes of the formal/informal labour market, and promotes universal coverage of the population in the health and pension dimensions of social protection.

Earlier experience in Latin American countries shows that simplified regimes for small taxpayers should favour simplicity over equity of the system. As such, the fixed-fee system by category appears as the more advisable system since it does not require firms to fill out a complex and detailed income tax form. Categories should be defined by gross revenue or turnover in conjunction with a secondary parameter such as physical magnitude, number of employees or electricity used, as well as to distinguish between economy activities. Special regimes that are exclusively based on revenues or turnover encounter several operational problems since revenues and billing are difficult to control at such small scales. At the same time, relying solely on income can perpetrate the so-called "fiscal dwarfism" effect, forcing companies to stay small so as not to have to pay higher taxes. Finally, it is very important that simplified regimes be updated regularly (González, 2006).

Box 2.4. The simplified tax regime in South America: A labour formalisation tool

In the face of persistent informality among small taxpayers, Argentina and Brazil together with most South American countries developed simplified tax regimes to incorporated self-employed workers and microenterprises into their tax registries. Although these schemes are different among countries, they facilitate the payment of one or more taxes and ensure a minimum level of social protection (pensions for old age and/or health) to a large number of small taxpayers.

The Argentine *Monotributo* is a simplified tax regime that ensures independent workers and microenterprises comply with their tax obligations. In a single monthly payment it concentrates workers' obligatory payments for social security contributions (health insurance and pension savings), income tax and value-added tax of the goods and services sold. Payments fees are fixed according to 11 presumptive categories defined on each individual worker or microenterprise's turnover, number of employees, square metres of land used, electrical energy consumed and rent. Moreover, payments are differentiated among workers and firms that provide services from those that sell goods.

The eligibility requirements of the Argentine *Monotributo* are simple. Any independent microenterprise or co-operative worker with a maximum of 3 members can register under this scheme if their annual gross income is lower than ARP 1 050 000 (around USD 52 000) for those selling goods or ARP 700 000 (around USD 35 000) for those providing services. Additionally, independent worker, microfirm or co-operative cannot register under this scheme if they sell imported goods, or goods have a per unit price higher than ARP 2 500 (around USD 125).

Similarly, the *Simples* and the *Sistema de Recolhimento em Valores Fixos Mensais do Tributos do Simples Nacional* (SIMEI) schemes replace multiple tax obligations with a single payment in Brazil. The former is especially designed for MSMEs and the latter for independent workers up to an annual turnover cap of BRL 60 000 (around USD 16 500). Under the Brazilian corporate legislation, microenterprises are defined as those that have an annual gross income equal to or lower than BRL 120 000 (around USD 33 000) and small enterprises as those that register an annual gross income higher than BRL 120 000, but equal to or lower than BRL 1 200 000 (around USD 330 000).

Simples is a progressive tax based on firms' monthly gross revenue, firms' activity and tax on industrialised products (IPI) contribution, which offers lower rates compared to the payment of all them separately. This regime allows the unified collection of municipal, state and federal taxes replacing the payment of the corporate income tax, social contributions on net profits, social contributions paid by companies, contributions for social security financing, IPI, tax on the circulation of goods and interstate transportation services (ICMS), tax on services (ISS), and employer's social security contribution. In addition, MSMEs under the *Simples* regime are exempt from paying several taxes including the contributions to social services such as Sesc, Sesi, Senai, Senac, Sebrae and the employer's syndicate contribution.

Likewise, SIMEI replaces the federal income tax from *Simples* for a fixed monthly fee. SIMEI payments are composed by the social security contribution (5% average minimum wage), a flat fee of BRL 5 for the state tax ICMS and a flat fee of BRL 1 for the municipal tax ISS. *Simples* and SIMEI also provide access to benefits such as support for maternity, illness and retirement, among others.

All three schemes promote registration and financial inclusion. While *Simples* and SIMEI allow registration in the National Registry of Legal Entities, which makes it easier for enterprises to open bank accounts, make loan applications and issue bills; the *Monotributo* offers a one-month payment refund to independent workers and microenterprises that comply with all monthly payments during a calendar year using debit or credit cards.

Facilitate the operation of formal businesses

Panama should extend the use of methods to incorporate SMEs as well as contribute to reduce firms' operating costs related to formalisation. Although the creation of *Panamá Emprende* encourages the registration of firms in Panama by introducing a computer system that automates, facilitates and reduces the time and costs of opening a new business, it does not simplify or reduce administrative and operational costs for SMEs. Efforts should be made to make AMPYME's' unique registry a useful tool for MSMEs. Registration in *Panamá Emprende* does not result in the automatic granting of benefits. Regularly updating the registry's information as well as linking it to all the benefits enumerated in Law No. 33 of 2000 is essential to prevent the registry from becoming an extra administrative burden for MSMEs. Additionally, AMPYMEs could work on alternative ways to reduce the compliance costs of operating formally by analysing the costs and procedures MSMEs face while operating among different economic activities and regions, as well as working on ways to reduce barriers to MSMEs' access to international goods and capital markets.

Panamá Emprende should serve as a tool to facilitate municipal licensing. Panamanian MSMEs need several municipal licensing levels and administrative procedures in order to operate. Some of these are costly, but mostly they are another level of bureaucracy for MSMEs. To relieve MSMEs from such burdens, the existing *Panamá Emprende* one-stop shops and online portal could be used for licensing procedures at both local and national levels. This would result in better co-ordination among national and local administrations in terms of business regulation, and also help to reduce red tape and recurrent costs associated with formal status.

Establish a clearer and simpler system to determine minimum wages

Panama has a complex minimum salary matrix. Every other year the government of Panama institutes a new minimum salary matrix though executive decree. The matrix is fixed by the national government following the advice of the Minimum Wage Commission and details the salary adjustment according to region, economic activity and size of the firm. The 2017 matrix lists 81 different hourly minimum wages that range from 1.53 to 3.47 PAB per hour. The agricultural sector has the lowest minimum wage and SEZs and airport workers the highest one.

Most of the minimum wages have increased at similar rates since the late nineties. This indicates that aggregate considerations dominate over sectoral or firm-level productivity considerations, generating a general increase of salaries. In practice, the evolution of minimum wages sets a floor to the evolution of sectoral minimum wages, which may erode competitiveness in certain industries. The reliance on national negotiations to set sectoral minimum wages is a symptom of the weakness of collective bargaining in the country.

Over the past decade, aggregate labour productivity growth in Panama has been coupled with the growth in salaries. Figure 2.18 compares growth in aggregate labour productivity (real value added per worker) with two measures of real labour compensation: national real median wage and the median of all minimum wages for urban regions. From 2004 to 2012, the minimum wage growth followed closely the growth in productivity. Yet, since 2012 it has fallen slightly below productivity. Conversely, median wage growth fell below productivity growth from 2004 to 2007 and corresponded closely to productivity from 2008 through 2016. This comparison suggests that increasing productivity appears to raise real wages for the typical worker in Panama. However, this is not the case for all workers in all sectors.

Figure 2.18. Evolution of productivity and wages in Panama

Index 2004=100

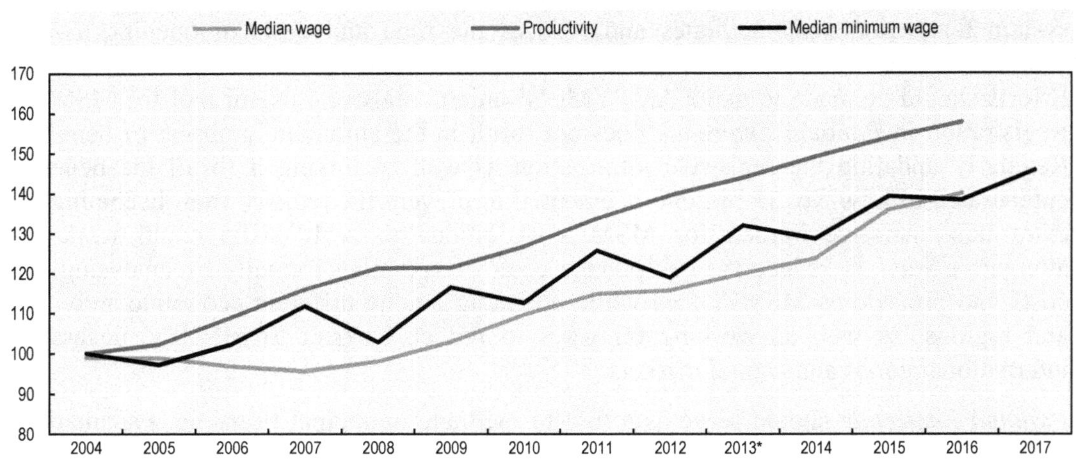

Note: Labour productivity is measured as the annual value added (the value of output less the value of intermediate consumption) per employee. The median minimum wage represents the median of all minimum wages for region 1.
Source: OECD calculations based on data provided by INEC and Ministry of Economy and Finance.

StatLink http://dx.doi.org/10.1787/888933776996

At the sector level, labour productivity growth in most sectors has decoupled from real median compensation growth. In the tradeable service sector, productivity and wages follow very different paths (Figure 2.19). In fact, in trade and wholesale, and transport and communication, for example, productivity fell after an initial spike, while wages continued to increase. This suggests that firms were not able to adjust wages to respond to the fall in productivity. Instead, they adjusted the quantity of employment as explained earlier in this chapter. On the contrary, in the non-tradeable service sector, where informality is more pervasive, wage growth remained significantly below productivity growth, implying that raising productivity is not sufficient to raise real wages for the typical worker in these industries. Both patterns suggest that there is a role for public policies to ensure that productivity gains are better shared in some industries, while not eroding competitiveness in other industries.

Figure 2.19. Evolution of productivity and wages in Panama by sectors

Index 2004=100

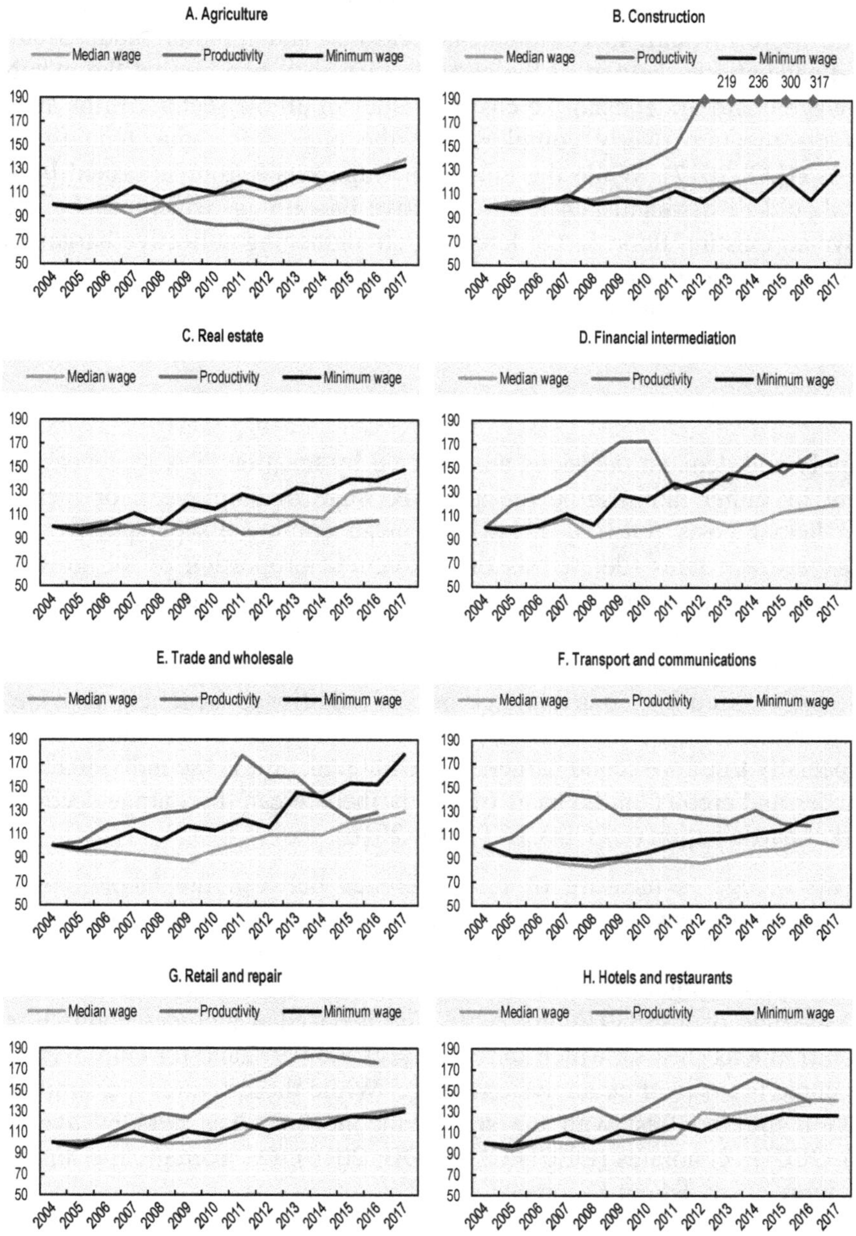

Notes: The minimum wage for primary activities was calculated as the simple average of all minimum wages for workers in agriculture, livestock, hunting, forestry, aquaculture and fisheries; the minimum wage for transport and communications is the average of the minimum wage for workers in transport within SEZs, waterways, aerial and complementary activities, ports, international airports, storage, deposit and mail, as well as workers in telecommunications and network maintenance; the minimum wage for retail and repair is the average of the minimum wages of workers in both small and large retail and repair firms; the minimum wage for hotels and restaurants is the average of the minimum wages of workers in small and large hotels and restaurants. The minimum wage for real estate is the average of the minimum wages of workers in real estate, rental and business activities. Labour productivity is measured as the annual value added (the value of output less the value of intermediate consumption) per employee by sector.
Source: OECD calculations based on data provided by INEC and Ministry of Economy and Finance.

StatLink http://dx.doi.org/10.1787/888933777015

A clear and simple scheme to determine minimum wages is easier to implement and monitor. Complex minimum wage systems offer flexibility to tailor the evolution of the minimum wage to the conditions in each sector. However, more complex minimum wage matrices are more difficult to communicate, enforce and monitor, and require higher institutional capacity on the part of the state. In fact, they require that the members of a minimum wage board understand the characteristics of all the sectors, firms and regions. Thus, systems that are overly complex, like the one in Panama, tend to lose their effectiveness (ILO, 2017). While the minimum wage sets a floor informed by technical criteria, it should be distinguished from collective bargaining, which can be used to set wages above an existing floor. In the long run, strengthening collective bargaining at the firm or sector level would make the current complex matrix unnecessary. As working conditions would be negotiated between workers and firms and/or sectors, salaries would better reflect productivity changes guaranteeing both workers and firms profit from them.

Reduce the cost of formally hiring low-income workers

Labour supply and demand decisions are affected by taxation. Tax systems might deter employment by either diminishing the after-tax wage of employees, or increasing the employer's labour costs (OECD, 2011a). From an employee's perspective, larger net personal tax average rates (defined as the tax/benefit proportion of the gross wage an employee pays/receives after taking into account all mandatory income taxes and social security liabilities and cash transfer benefits) and net personal marginal tax rates (defined as the proportion of an additional unit of wage-earning income that is paid in respect of taxes and social security contributions net of additional benefits) provide greater incentives to reduce the worker's labour supply and/or entry to the labour market. The latter is especially true for second earners. When the tax unit is the individual, the loss of tax allowances and credits on the basis of family income can discourage second earners' labour market participation (OECD/CIAT/IDB, 2016).

Panama's tax wedge, a measure of the difference between the labour costs and an employee's take-home pay, is similar to that of other Latin American economies. The tax wedge on average wage earnings in Panama is 22.9% of total labour costs. This is 1.2 percentage points higher than the average in LAC countries (21.7%) but lower than the OECD average of 35.9% (Figure 2.20). The tax wedge includes compulsory social security contributions (SSCs), which for employees are 9.9% and for employers 13%. No personal income tax is paid on an average wage. While these figures are similar to those for the region they contrast with the significant income taxes paid by average wage workers in OECD economies (OECD/CIAT/IDB, 2016). On average, the higher the tax wedge, the more costly labour becomes.

Figure 2.20. Income tax plus employee and employer social security contributions, 2013

Percentage of labour costs

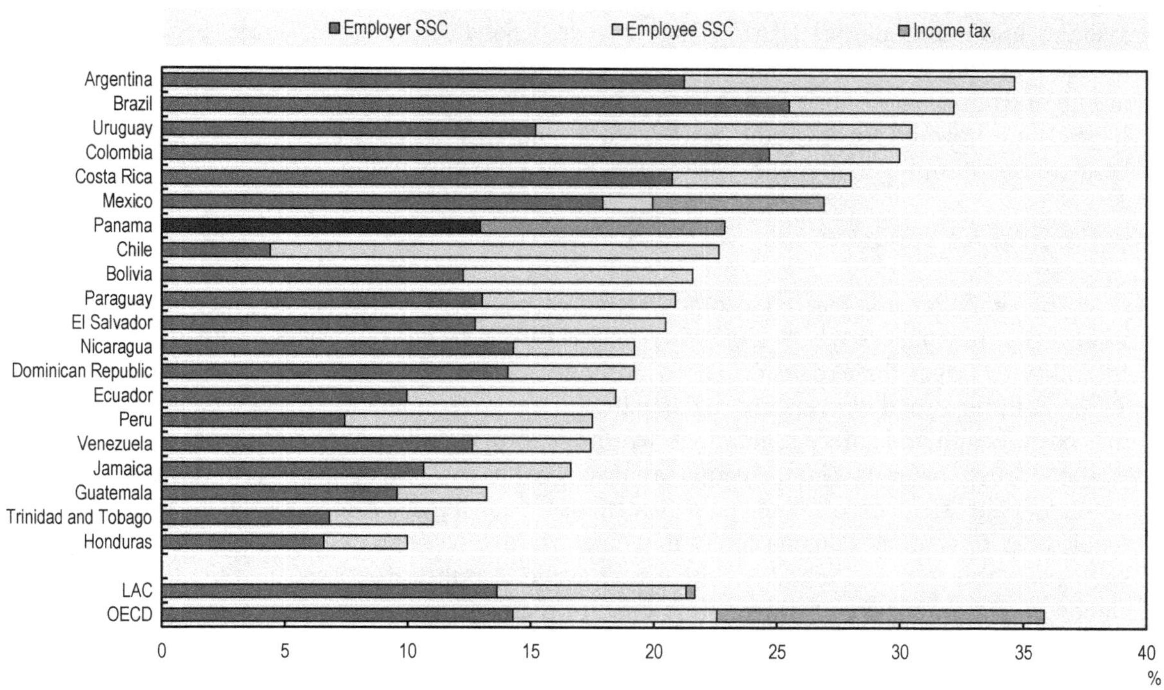

Source: OECD/CIAT/IDB (2016), *Taxing Wages in Latin America and the Caribbean*, http://dx.doi.org/10.1787/9789264262607-en.

StatLink http://dx.doi.org/10.1787/888933777034

Formalisation costs from labour taxes do not explain informality for most workers in Panama, especially those in the upper three quintiles of the income distribution. Overall, higher informality rates among wage earners do not relate to higher formalisation costs in Panama. This is a distinctive feature that differentiates Panama from the rest of the region. Theoretical formalisation costs are defined as the proportion of workers' income that grants them access to health care and pension savings. The interaction of average income levels and the existence of a legally mandated lower earning threshold to participate in these social security programmes increase their price in most countries in Latin America. Yet, the existing earnings threshold in Panama is low relative to reported income, making the formalisation cost for individuals proportional (23% of the worker's income) throughout the income distribution. On average, other factors might influence an individual's or employer's choice between formality and informality. These might include job security; labour regulations (i.e. monetary and non-monetary registration costs, firing costs, vacations); the value a person places on the programme or services; expectations of receiving future benefits; and a component of myopic behaviour by the individual or employer.

Introducing progressivity into SSCs and lowering SSCs temporarily for new low-paid workers could foster workers' formalisation. Although there is little evidence that overall labour informality in Panama is the result of the high tax wedge, as is the case in most Latin American countries (OECD/CIAT/IDB, 2016), this applies mainly to the mid-to-higher end of the income distribution. Firms find the contributions to social security programmes are too costly relative to informal worker's productivity at the lower end of the income distribution, since workers do not produce enough value-added to cover the costs of being hired formally. The total yearly SSCs for a single worker making an average minimum wage of PAB 423 per month adds up to more than three monthly average minimum salaries (PAB 1 334) a year. Likewise, the total yearly SSCs for a married worker with two children making an average minimum wage of PAB 423 per month adds up to more than four monthly average minimum salaries (PAB 1 775) a year. If SSCs are lowered for low-paid workers to promote formalisation, SSC ceilings should be increased to mitigate revenue losses and add progressivity to the system.

Adjust the pension system to increase the incentives of being a formal worker

Over the years Panama has reduced poverty and especially old-age poverty. An important issue for policymakers when addressing informality is to consider which dimensions of formality to target for expansion based on both workers' preferences and policy needs. When both firms and workers are registered with the government there is a greater chance that basic health and safety regulations will be enforced, and that workers receive higher wages, better benefits (i.e. pension savings, health insurance, contracts, termination notices, paid sick leave, and paid vacations) and legal protections than informal employees. Given that Panama offers universal health coverage, having access to pension savings in the future – together with better wages, further discussed in this chapter – stands out as an important pillar in the country's efforts to reduce poverty and decrease inequality.

Although pension coverage in Panama is better than in most Latin American countries, it is far from universal. Both in terms of the number of active workers – contributors (75%) and passive workers/pensioners (45%) – coverage lags behind OECD countries and needs to be extended to cover all the Panamanian population. Likewise, the *120 a los 65* ('120 at 65') non-contributory pension, which was created to protect Panamanians against old-age vulnerability and compensate for extensive informality – especially among women–, still has coverage gaps (Figure 2.21). As such, a progressive universal approach should be adopted by expanding pension coverage.

Progressive pension contribution subsidies for formal jobs, along with a social pension, diversified savings channels, and better enforcement, are promising ways to spur formality. Formality can be fostered with stronger monetary and non-monetary incentives, backed with new technologies. Although stopgap measures, such as the targeted benefits from '120 at 65' non-contributory pension, serve to alleviate old-age poverty; they are not the most appropriate tool for encouraging formalisation. Instead, a combination of traditional and innovative social, tax, and labour tools should be used to improve the incentives for businesses and workers to become formal. Increasing formality through pension contribution subsidies and new savings channels would at the same time increase saving, notably among the growing Panamanian middle class, and boost growth and equity (Melguizo, 2015).

Figure 2.21. Pension coverage in Latin American, 2015

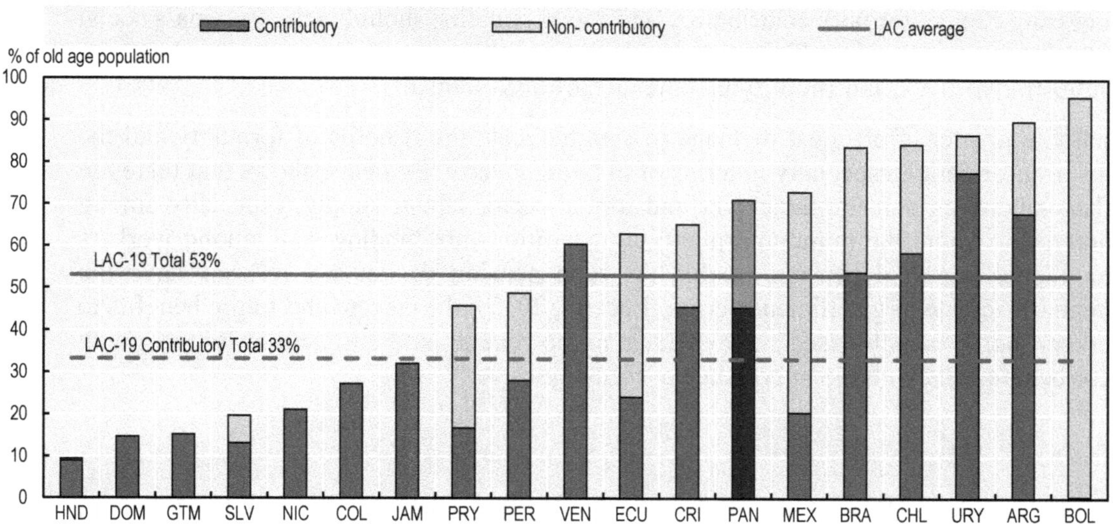

Source: IDB (2016), SIMS (Labour Markets and Social Security Information System) (database).

StatLink http://dx.doi.org/10.1787/888933777053

The first step towards a social security system that promotes labour formalisation is to integrate the '120 at 65' non-contributory pension and the contributory system (Pillar I of the CSS) into a unique pension scheme. The central requirement to qualify for the '120 at 65' non-contributory pension is not to have enough contributory pension savings to receive a contributory pension. This requirement discourages low-pay workers and those who regularly shift from formal to informal jobs from favouring formal jobs and saving. By integrating both systems, all savings would be recognised – no matter how small they are – towards a future pension benefit. As such, working in a formal job and making savings contributions would be always rewarded (Levy, 2008).

Contributory schemes need to be attractive, flexible and adapted to different forms of employment such as self-employed, domestic and temporary workers. Currently the CSS offers a special regime for domestic work, temporary agricultural work and self-employment under some circumstances. Providing alternative schemes to incorporate independent workers, domestic workers and temporary agricultural workers into the social security system is essential in order to bring a large share of the most vulnerable works into the contributory system. While contributions should be compulsory for all workers they should be accompanied by 1) possibilities for gradual incorporation to the system; 2) allowances for specific contribution patterns (e.g. less regular contributions); 3) unification of charges and services provided across all similar types of activities.

At the same time social protection programmes, subsidies and transfers can be made more efficient by creating a true social protection system, with shared tools and registries among contributory and non-contributory programmes, to mitigate the pervasive impact of informality. Panama has a large number of policies and programmes for social protection, offered by the CSS, Ministry of Education, Instituto para la Formación y Aprovechamiento de Recursos Humanos (IFARHU), Ministry of Social Development, Ministry of Labour and Ministry of Health. Integrating and co-ordinating the provision of services could significantly increase the effectiveness of social protection and the efficiency of social spending (World Bank, 2015). The creation of shared targeting instruments for multiple programmes, such as a unique social registry and one-stop processing centres for both contributory and social benefits, should make Panama's social protection system more efficient by reducing duplication of programmes, lowering administrative costs, and simplifying bureaucracy and payments.

Finally, a greater effort must be made to communicate the benefits of formality and the risks of informality, especially in terms of old-age poverty. Evidence shows that there are linkages between pension incentives and formal-sector labour supply, especially among workers for whom the minimum qualifying conditions are binding, and among workers with higher expected pension wealth. As such pension design and reforms have the potential to create large efficiency costs (Becerra, 2017); the current and future benefits to workers should be publicised and explained to the general public to familiarise them with these benefits and with the importance of formal jobs.

Invest in better and relevant skills

High informality and low skills reinforce each other in Panama. Higher skill levels lead to higher productivity levels, which in turn lead to better access to formal jobs and even to their creation. The correlation between the use of skills in the workplace and productivity is very significant (OECD, 2016a). Usually, informal workers not only have low skills but also have poor upgrade opportunities. Informal firms generally provide workers with fewer opportunities to accumulate human capital and are less productive (La Porta and Schleifer, 2014). This makes it hard to escape the low-productivity trap and find jobs that are a good fit for their abilities. In the context of informality, certain skills tend to deteriorate or remain limited to a low value-added range, and access to unemployment insurance and intermediation services is scarce for informally employed workers. All of this might thus pose an additional burden on the earnings and career advancement of the most vulnerable (OECD/CAF/ECLAC, 2016).

Low skills is one of the main barriers to formality

The available pool of skills in Panama has improved along the last decades but is still poor. As explained in the Multi-dimensional Country Review of Panama Volume 1, the composition of the labour force in Panama has changed significantly from 2004 to 2015 towards more skilled workers. The proportion of the labour force with a low level of education (i.e. less than eight years of education) decreased from 50% in 1990 to close to 30% in 2014 (OECD, 2017). Consequently, the gap with the proportion of highly educated workers has narrowed. In 2014, more than 25% of the labour force attained more than 13 years of education, compared to nearly 15% in 1990.

Additionally, the pool of skills in Panama is disconnected from the demands of the productive sector. Although most informal workers are self-employed with low earnings, they are not necessarily unqualified workers. In fact, almost two out of three informal workers are service, sales and trade workers (22%), skilled manufacturing, construction and mining workers (17%), professionals (12%) and technicians (10%); while only 18% are non-qualified workers (Figure 2.22). Hence, either medium-skilled workers are acquiring skills that are not demanded by the productive sector of Panama, or the quality of the training they receive is poor.

Figure 2.22. Composition of informal workers by skills level of their job in Panama, 2016

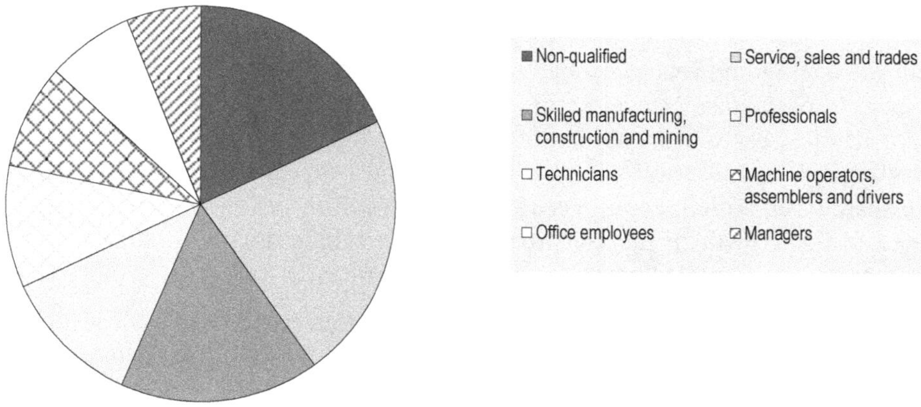

Note: Legal definition of informality: workers are considered informal if they do not have the right to a pension when retired.
Source: OECD calculations based on data provided by INEC.

StatLink http://dx.doi.org/10.1787/888933777072

A scarcity of engineers, technicians, and especially skilled-trade workers is a recurrent complaint of employers in Panama. Nearly 46% of Panamanian firms report difficulties finding the necessary skills to operate (ManPower Group, 2016). As in other countries in the region, Panama registers a wide gap between the available pool of skills and those skills that its economy and society require (OECD/CAF/ECLAC, 2014). This is due to two factors: the low coverage of secondary education and that most educated Panamanians obtain university degrees and work in industries with lower returns. Both patterns are slowly changing. While education coverage has expanded for secondary education, it is still low for a country that wants to position itself as a worldwide logistics and tradeable service hub.

Panamanian tertiary education students seem to have partially responded to the higher returns in some under-filled industries. In 2002, the six university careers with most students were business administration (21%), education (16%), humanities (12%) – which included religion and theology; language, literature and linguistics; history and archaeology; philosophy and ethics – economics (6.5%), engineering (6%) and public administration (6%). By 2015, while business administration (29%) and education (13%) are still among the top choices, engineering and IT (12%), health (8.5%), and architecture and construction (6%) – careers associated with high-return industries – gained students (INEC, 2017; Hausmann, Espinoza and Santos, 2016) as did law (7%). At the same time, both humanities and to a lesser extent education are less attractive to students, as their share of enrolment decreased 8 and 3 percentage points respectively between 2002 and 2015. Careers such as mathematics or environmental protection are still rarely chosen by students in Panama (INEC, 2017; Hausmann, Espinoza and Santos, 2016)

The size of the foreign workforce remains significant, owing to skills shortages across most economic sectors. This suggests scope for stronger investment in education to increase the number of secondary graduates, as well as a larger role of technical and vocational education and training (TVET) at all levels.

Box 2.5. Estimating education return differentials for informal and formal workers

Overall, the average returns to education have decreased during the last 15 years in Panama. In particular, Mincer earnings regression estimates show that the rate of return has decreased from around 10% in 2001 to less than 8% in 2015. A decrease of the average rate of return to schooling over time suggests that the relative scarcity of skilled labour has diminished. Yet, this decrease could be also attributed to the growth of the construction sector, which mostly hired workers with primary education (Hausmann, Espinoza and Santos, 2016).

Informal workers face lower average returns to education. When Mincer earnings regression estimates are calculated separately for formal and informal workers, they show that on average formal workers' rate of return is more than 1% higher than that for informal workers (Table 2.2).

Table 2.2. Mincer equation for formal and informal workers (maximum likelihood estimates)

	Formal workers		Informal workers	
	Coefficient estimate	Standard error	Coefficient estimate	Standard error
Years of education	0.079	(0.00018)	0.068	(0.00037)
Age	0.038	(0.00038)	0.060	(0.00080)
Age square	-0.0004	(4.91E-06)	-0.0007	(0.00001)
Women	-0.219	(0.00130)	-0.713	(0.00341)
Constant	4.561	(0.00774)	3.4373	(0.02520)
Fixed effects for 12 regions	included		included	
Fixed effects for 21 industries	included		included	
Observations	7 809		7 417	

Notes: $\ln(w_i) = \beta_0 + \beta_1\, years\ of\ education_i + \beta_2\, age_i + \beta_3\, age^2_i + FE + u_i$ where years of education is the number of years each individual reported, age serves as proxy for the years of experience, age^2 its square, regional fixed effects and industry fixed effects. The return of schooling is captured by the parameter $\beta 1$.

Source: OECD estimates based on microdata from *Encuesta de Propsitos Multilpes* of 2016 (INEC, 2016).

In addition, secondary education has lost value, whereas tertiary degrees are still high paying. Mincer earnings regression estimates to calculate the rate of return by level of education show that the return to secondary schooling has diminished from 3% in 2001 to 1% in 2015, while returns to primary school have increased between 3% and 4%. This might be the result of a supply-and-demand effect. On one hand, there has been an increase in the supply of secondary educated workers relative to workers who only completed primary school. On the other hand, the construction boom improved relative wages of workers who only completed primary education. Both effects make the time invested in pursuing a secondary degree unprofitable, except if students advance in their schooling careers to complete a tertiary degree. Indeed, though the number of workers with tertiary education increased, the return to tertiary schooling did so as well, from below 4% in 2001 to 5% in 2015 (Hausmann, Espinoza and Santos, 2016).

Upgrading skills of the population in general and improving their links to the production system can raise labour productivity levels. A secondary and a tertiary education curriculum better focused on developing technical, science, technology, engineering and mathematics and soft skills, and stronger connections between the education system and skill demands in the economy to support further productive developments, are critical to raising skill levels and productivity in Panama (OECD, 2016a). The recognition and certification of skills acquired in the informal sector is also important for policy action. Moving towards a national qualifications framework could be a relevant policy goal in the medium term to favour access to formal jobs.

Strengthening education and skills to upgrade the labour force

Shifting from infrastructure-driven growth to knowledge-driven growth will require an upgrade of the skills of the Panamanian population. Although the government has taken action in recent years by increasing expenditure and infrastructure, the educational attainment and skills of Panama's population are low by international standards. Despite progress at all levels, and especially at the primary and lower secondary levels, only 52% of the population aged 25-64 has completed secondary education, in contrast with the OECD average of 80% (INEC, 2016; OECD, 2016b). The main challenges to building a better skilled-labour force in Panama are to expand secondary education – which provides students with the minimum skills to participate in the labour markets – to strengthen TVET education at secondary and post-secondary levels, and spread educational benefits more fairly across the country.

Inequalities in the education system begin early (only 70% of pre-primary-age children are enrolled in education), but become most evident at the high-school level through low upper-secondary enrolment rates (Figure 2.23). Only 59% of the upper-secondary education population (14 to 17 years old) is enrolled in school, with almost 15% attending a lower grade than the one corresponding to their age cohort (MEDUCA, 2015). As a result, almost 300 000 Panamanians aged 15 to 29 – 35% of youths – have not completed secondary and are not enrolled in school. By the age of 25, less than one-quarter of those who come from poor families will have completed high school (OECD/CAF/ECLAC, 2016).

Figure 2.23. Enrolment rates are rising but are still low at upper secondary level

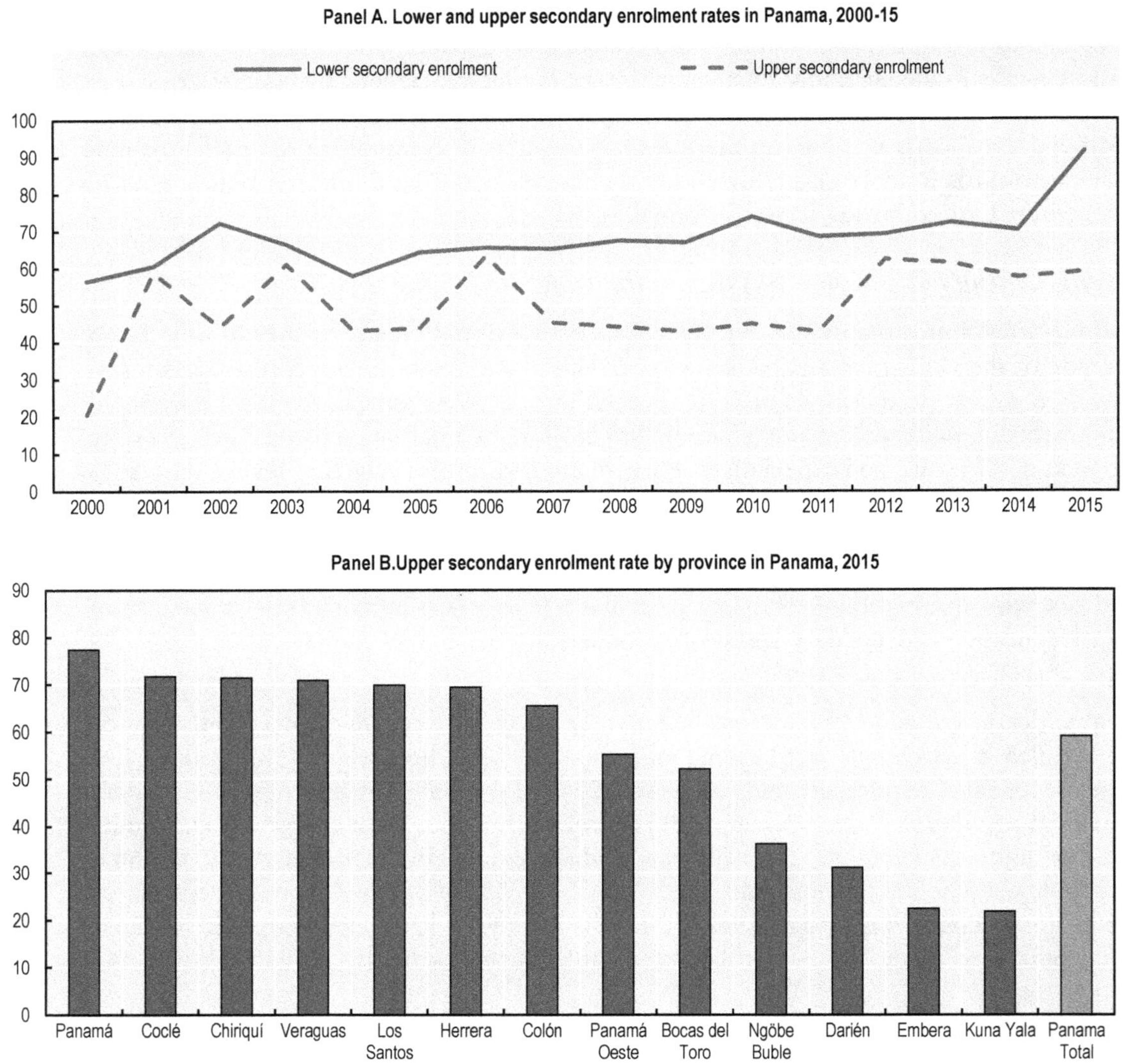

Source: OECD calculations based on data provided by INEC and the Ministry of Education of Panama (MEDUCA, 2017).

StatLink http://dx.doi.org/10.1787/888933777091

As coverage increases, the low quality of education becomes apparent. Panamanian students perform poorly in reading and mathematics compared with students in Latin America and OECD countries. While secondary and tertiary education attainments remain a challenge, low qualifications are not restricted to those who left the education system. The education system is the obvious tool for improving the skills of Panama's citizens. Performance in both OECD's Programme for International Student Assessment (PISA) and UNESCO's Third Regional Comparative and Explanatory Study (TERCE) is poor. TERCE scale ranks students across four proficiency levels. More than 90% of sixth-grade students performed in the lowest two levels of TERCE's mathematics proficiency test and more than 75% did so in the reading test in 2013, ranking among the lowest countries in the region. Likewise, 15-year-old Panamanians perform poorly in PISA 2009 (the latest PISA test in which Panama has participated), where students' proficiency in reading and mathematics are evaluated on scale of 600 points later converted into a six-level proficiency scale. In reading, one-third of Panamanian students did not achieve level 1, placing the country among the worst three countries out of the 75 participating in PISA 2009, and the worst Latin American country. In mathematics, 15-year-old students in Panama performed 136 points lower than the average OECD student and 33 points lower than the average Latin American student (OECD, 2010a). This is equivalent to more than three years and almost one year of schooling, respectively.

The large share of Panamanian students below a basic level of proficiency constitutes an obstacle to further development of more specific skills. According to the PISA test, more than 70% of young Panamanians enrolled in school do not acquire basic-level proficiency in reading, mathematics and science. These students often face significant disadvantages in their transition into higher education and the labour force. In the case of OECD economies, this occurs for a quarter of 15-year-old students (OECD, 2014b).

At the same time, the small number of top performers may hamper innovation and entrepreneurship, limiting productive transformation and upgrading. Knowledge-based and skills-based economies increasingly depend upon a broad base of technically skilled individuals, as well as a sizeable share of high performers who can produce new knowledge. Few Panamanian students perform at the top levels. Indeed, less than 1% of Panamanian students perform among the highest levels of proficiency – levels 5 or 6 – in mathematics, reading or science (OECD, 2010b). In contrast, 12% of students in OECD countries perform in the top two levels in mathematics, and 8.5% reach these levels in reading and science.

Low government investment in education is affecting both quality and coverage. Overall investment in education is low, especially compared to countries with similar per capita income. Government expenditure on education in Panama in 2016 was PAB 1 838 (equivalent to USD) per student, which represents 3.8% of GDP, below the regional average (INEC, 2017). Although overall spending has increased in absolute terms during the last decade, the annual expenditure per primary student relative to per capita GDP has remained constant, while the annual expenditure per secondary student relative to per capita GDP has increased slightly. Still, expenditures fall behind other Latin American countries and benchmark economies, especially those that rely on knowledge-driven growth, and are especially top-heavy if compared to university education spending (Figure 2.24). Spending is important in terms of education performance since PISA analysis has shown a positive relationship between spending per student and mean performance in reading, mathematics and science. As expenditure on educational institutions per student increases, so does a country's mean performance; but the rate of increase diminishes fast (Figure 2.24). Expenditure per student accounts for 30% of the variation in mean mathematics performance between PISA-participating countries/economies – and 17% of the variation in OECD countries – while it explains 54% of the variation in mean science performance between PISA-participating countries/economies – 38% of the variation in OECD countries (OECD, 2010a; OECD, 2014; OECD, 2016b).

Ensuring that a large base of the population acquires core literacy and numeracy skills is fundamental for the diffusion of knowledge and innovation that sustains economic growth. An increase of one standard deviation in cognitive skills (measured using PISA-type exams) is associated with approximately a 2% increase in annual growth of per capita GDP (Hanushek and Woessmann, 2012). Additionally, poor early basic skills acquisition is detrimental for the later acquisition of labour specific skills. Early performance in mathematics is correlated with job-relevant numeracy skills. The results from the 2012 Survey of Adult Skills (PIAAC) show that countries performing well in PISA tend to display a relatively high performance in PIAAC and vice versa. Students' performance in PISA will be at least partly reflected in their acquisition of job-related skills later in life. Part of the effect will depend upon the ability to pursue further education, the quality of post-secondary training in the different countries and the specialisation chosen (OECD, 2016d).

Box 2.6. Panama in PISA

The OECD has identified gaps in education participation, performance and outcomes as one of the most significant structural constraints to sustained growth in low- and middle-income countries. Progress on a range of economic indicators, including productivity, formal employment, economic diversification and reduced dependency on commodities, will be held back unless emerging economies can achieve better education outcomes, develop higher quality skills and widen their talent base.

To tackle this challenge of quality and participation in education, it is important to understand the factors that are associated with low student performance, poor attendance and dropout, especially at the secondary level. For this reason, OECD developed PISA, which aims to evaluate education systems worldwide by testing the skills and knowledge of 15-year-old students. In 2015 over half a million students, representing 28 million 15-year-olds in 72 countries and economies, took the internationally recognised two-hour test. Students were assessed in science, mathematics, reading, collaborative problem solving and financial literacy. PISA provides useful information to determine policies to improve students' performance (Avendaño, Barrera, Nieto-Parra and Vever, 2016).

Likewise, the PISA for Development (PISA-D) project aims to increase middle- and low-income countries' use of PISA assessments for monitoring progress towards nationally set targets, for the analysis of factors associated with student learning outcomes, particularly for poor and marginalised populations, for institutional capacity building and for monitoring international targets in the Education 2030 framework developed within the UN's thematic consultations.

Panama is participating in PISA 2018 as well as the out-of-school component of the PISA-D project. A key aim for Panama in participating in PISA 2018 and PISA-D is to collect better, actionable assessment and contextual data on 15-year-olds who are in and out of school. As well as providing internationally comparable data on Panamanian students' performance on tests of reading, mathematics and science, the PISA 2018 and PISA-D surveys will also provide valuable data on barriers to school attendance and factors that may impede students' progress through education. This information will be available at the end of 2019 and will be presented in a national report.

Figure 2.24. Spending in education and quality of education

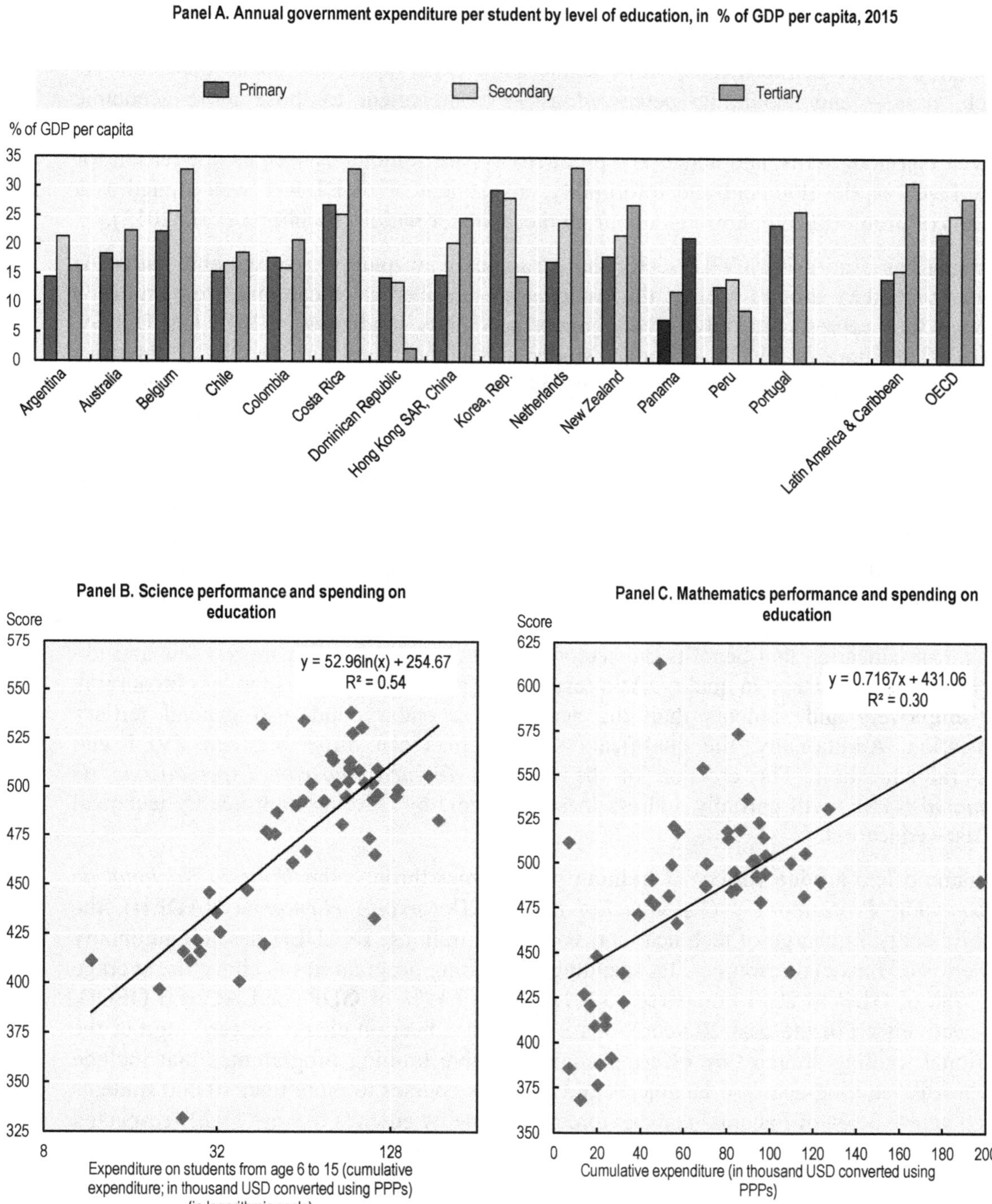

Notes: Panels B and C compare countries' actual spending per student, on average, from the age of 6 up to the age of 15, with average student performance in science and mathematics. Expenditure on students from age 6 to 15 (cumulative expenditure; in thousand USD converted using PPPs). In Panel B the cumulative expenditure is in a logarithmic scale.

Source: OECD; PISA 2012 and 2015 databases; OECD calculations based on data provided by INEC and the Ministry of Education of Panama (MEDUCA, 2017), and World Bank Development Indicators.

StatLink http://dx.doi.org/10.1787/888933777110

In this context, high quality TVET is crucial for developing a highly skilled labour force, with a range of mid-level trade, technical, professional and management skills alongside those high-level skills associated with university education (OECD, 2014c). In emerging and less-developed countries, TVET is increasingly perceived as a tool to respond to changing labour market needs, while at the same time supporting social cohesion. As such, it is – and should be perceived as –a complement to those more academic programmes typically found in universities or *bachillerato* (upper secondary education). Given that poor skills, and hence low productivity, are sometimes seen as one reason for low levels of development and informality, investment in TVET has been argued as a means of promoting a bottom-up labour market transformation (Eichhorst et al., 2012).

Panama has a mid-size TVET sector that struggles with quality, prestige and status. At upper secondary around half of the students are enrolled in vocational programmes – though they represented only 19% of upper secondary graduates in 2015 (MEDUCA, 2016). The share of TVET secondary students is higher than that for OECD countries where 26% of the population in secondary education are enrolled in TVET programmes, but aligned with the Netherlands where 48% are enrolled in TVET programmes (UNESCO, 2016). However, only less than 10% of tertiary education graduates – only 2 000 students a year – are instructed in TVET programmes which are in high demand in the country. The nature and duration of the programmes – most of them offered by private providers – vary from institution to institution. Moreover, quality is heterogeneous: high-quality schools that are highly respected and generate positive returns for students and employers coexist with low-quality ones. Although TVET represents an important source of innovation and experimentation in the design of technical education that benefits the sector as a whole, programmes are too few and too small to drive a change in quality. As a result, TVET is often looked upon less favourably by employers and students than the academic secondary and also general tertiary education. Additionally, the qualification of teachers can differ between TVET and general education. The creation of the *Instituto Técnico Superior Especializado de Panamá* (ITSE) will partially address these problems by offering high-quality technical tertiary education.

Panama offers a wide variety of training programmes through the *Instituto Nacional de Formación Profesional y Capacitación para el Desarrollo Humano* (INADEH), the public entity in charge of technical and vocational training. INADEH has full autonomy in terms of financial resources. Its spending on training programmes is above the average (0.17% of GDP in 2014 compared to 0.12% and 0.15% of GDP for LAC and OECD, respectively). For the past 20 years, this institute has been in charge of carrying out the national training strategy by offering comprehensive training programmes that include technical, learning-at-work, languages and business courses to more than 70 000 students each year – 3.6% of Panama's labour force. Yet, quality courses that are highly respected and generate positive returns for students and employers coexist with low-quality ones, adding to the quality and prestige struggle of the sector. Relatively few job seekers and workers with higher education participate in these programmes and INADEH struggles with quality, prestige and status among high-skilled workers. Job training and search measures need to support all jobseekers and informal workers as well as encourage the inactive by improving their employability and helping them find appropriate jobs. These programmes should help ensure that those out of work return to employment in the most appropriate job; likewise, they should help informal workers become more productive and find jobs which are a better fit for their skills.

Panama has recently strengthened its training programmes for youth, especially those from poor and vulnerable households. INADEH has developed *Nuevas Oportunidades de Empleo para Jóvenes* (New Employment Opportunities for Youth), a programme that offers job training and placement services to low-income youth in Panama City. Likewise, the Panama Ministry of Labour has recently developed a number of training and lifelong learning programmes for youth, particularly in less advantaged socio-economic groups and women. The *Pro Joven* (Pro Youth) programme, created in 2015, for example, promotes employability of youth through internships in enterprises. The beneficiaries are youth in the last year of technical and vocational programmes. Participating enterprises receive a government subsidy for hiring interns and are required to hire at least 50% of those young workers once their internship contracts ends. The programme started as a pilot with 1 000 beneficiaries and is now being scaled up. Furthermore, the *Autoridad de la Micro, Pequeña y Mediana Empresa*, the public entity in charge of promoting small and medium enterprise development, has also introduced a series of programmes to promote business training, with the goal of increasing formalisation among young entrepreneurs. Additionally, the *Desarrollo Financiero y Empresarial* (Financial and Business Development) and *Fondo Emprende* programmes aim to increase opportunities for entrepreneurship and promote the creation of new companies.

TVET should be better aligned with the demands of the labour market. Linkages between the TVET system and employers are relatively weak, illustrated by the low level of involvement of employers in overall TVET policy development. Although INADEH over the years has developed strong relationships with certain private sector firms, TVET must concentrate on developing the skills demanded in construction, trade, logistics, manufacturing and some retail. Courses in these sectors account for 15% of graduates, while 25% of the students graduate in low-paying trades such as agriculture, crafts, woodworking, upholstery, beauty, cosmetology and tailoring (INEC, 2017). Efforts should be made by all TVET institutions, as well as the upcoming ITSE, to develop better links with the modern tradeable service sector.

There is little co-ordination between upper secondary TVET programmes, tertiary TVET programmes, INADEH courses and the general education system. One of the main problems is that institutions operate in isolation, limiting students' ability to pursue different options. Moreover, degrees offered by the Ministry of Education and INADEH are not harmonised, and neither connects well with the higher education system. Additionally, skills acquired from TVET often go unrecognised by the traditional education system; many students are unable to proceed to higher levels of general education studies based on TVET certificates. For this reason, is very important that the ITSE co-ordinate its programmes and curricula with the existing TVET institutions of Panama, as well as with the general education programmes.

National Qualifications Frameworks classify qualifications by level based on learning outcomes, standardise qualifications in order to facilitate the evaluation and allow comparison of skills across systems. A few countries in Latin America have started implementing National Qualifications Frameworks to align TVET education with general secondary and tertiary education. ChileValora and the Ministry of Education in Chile; Instituto Nacional de Formación Técnico Profesional (INFOTEP) and several ministries including the Ministry of Education in the Dominican Republic; and Servicio Nacional de Aprendizaje and the Ministry of Education in Colombia, for example, have implemented these frameworks. Likewise, Costa Rica, Nicaragua and Ecuador are developing co-ordination mechanisms between TVET and general education programmes (OECD/CAF/ECLAC, 2016).

TVET schemes in Panama may enhance inequality. Students enrolled in TVET are more likely to be from poor or vulnerable households than those in general education programmes (OECD/CAF/ECLAC, 2014). As noted above, those with TVET certificates have greater challenges in pursuing higher education. As a result, TVET can perpetuate inequality by amplifying the discrepancies in opportunity between those with higher and lower socio-economic status. Additionally, TVET can amplify gender disparities: many of the higher-paying, technical tracks in TVET are male dominated, while, on average, women focus in low-paying trades (UNESCO, 2010). All of this calls for improving TVET programmes to help ease the associated stigma and contribute towards a more equal education, and better-quality jobs later in life.

Panama could benefit from strengthening TVET at secondary and post-secondary, given the low coverage of upper secondary education and the shortage of skilled workers with training to work in the modern service sector (MITRADEL, 2015). In LAC in general, TVET serves an important equity function. It caters to the needs of different segments of the population: school-leavers, students looking for more practical education and older individuals seeking to deepen their professional skills, make a sideways career move or return to work after an absence (Quintini and Manfredi, 2009). High-quality vocational education pathways, particularly in upper secondary education, can help those who have become disaffected with academic education to re-engage with the education system and improve graduation rates. And vocational and technical programmes at the tertiary level can provide those with no appetite for academic education with practical skills that respond to the needs of the job market, especially in an economy with a strong service sector such as Panama. At the same time, alternative training courses such as the one provided by INADEH can provide high school and tertiary education drop-outs with job skills training to increase their employability and access formal jobs (OECD/CAF/ECLAC, 2016).

Box 2.7. Work-based learning can be a powerful tool

Workplace learning plays an essential role in high quality vocational programmes. It is a powerful tool for developing both hard and soft skills, transitioning students into employment, engaging employers and linking the mix of programmes to employer needs. At the same time, it is too often neglected. On the one hand, education and training organisations find it easier to work on their own without having to involve employers. On the other hand, employers do not recognise the potential returns from offering work placements to students.

There should be a mandatory work-based learning component in every vocational programme

Evidence from a number of countries suggests that making work-based learning a mandatory element of vocational programmes is feasible and has multiple benefits. Many institutions tend to operate in isolation, and education and training institutions are no exception. Reaching out to employers means breaking out of this isolation. It also means overcoming the resistance of classroom teachers to the idea that students can learn much in the workplace that they cannot learn so readily in the classroom. Therefore, institutions need strong incentives to establish partnerships with employers for an effective workplace learning element in programmes. But employers also need incentives. Sometimes employers believe (often wrongly) that work placements are an unnecessary cost that they can reasonably avoid; they would prefer simply to recruit graduates of vocational programmes.

Against this background, making work placements mandatory can be a game-changer. It means that programmes will only be funded when training institutions develop and maintain the active partnerships that support work placements. Under these conditions, training providers will see employer partnerships as central to their mission. For their part, employers will see that, unless they are willing to offer work placements, their source of recruits may shrink or disappear; government funding may well shift to another sector or another region. Under these conditions, many currently reluctant employers will choose to offer work placements, assuming they value the training programmes.

International examples

It is striking that poorer countries with relatively weak infrastructure (Romania) and weak labour markets (Tunisia), countries with little history of employer engagement in the vocational system (Sweden) and countries with high rates of youth unemployment (Spain) have successfully implemented mandatory arrangements for work-based learning in some of their vocational programmes (OECD, 2014c).

In Romania, all upper secondary and postsecondary vocational programmes include work placements with quality assurance mechanisms (a workplace supervisor, student portfolio and a contract between the school and employers) (Musset, 2013). In Tunisia, vocational programmes under the Ministry of Vocational Training and Employment have a mandatory work-based learning component: about 11% of students are enrolled in apprenticeship programmes where they spend one day a week in a training centre and the remaining days in the workplace. The other 89% of students are enrolled in *programmes d'alternance* (a combination of school-based and work-based modules), in which the length of the work placement(s) varies, but is never less than one month. Likewise, more than nine out of ten vocational students in Tunisia benefited from some type of placement with employers in 2011 (OECD, 2015b). In Spain, in both upper secondary and postsecondary programmes, workplace training normally takes place through a compulsory three-month module at the end of the programmes (Field, Kis and Kuczera, 2012).

Such arrangements cannot be implemented overnight. In the early 1990s, for example, Spanish employers had to learn how to make use of students at work, and to appreciate the benefits to their firms (Field, Kis and Kuczera, 2012). South Africa developed tax credits to foster on-the-job training, as well as a simple process for employers to take trainees from vocational programmes (OECD, 2013a).

Developing active labour market programmes to reduce skills mismatch

Labour markets can become more inclusive and resilient when active labour market policies (ALMPs) are scaled up to satisfy the needs of all workers including youth, women, indigenous populations, the vulnerable and the middle class. ALPMs such as training, public employment services and incentives for job creation and entrepreneurship, that involve people in full-time activities, increase the employability of jobseekers and contribute to keeping workers productive in a cost-effective manner (OECD, 2015b). Many vulnerable workers, such as informal workers, fall out of these categories.

Panama performs well in offering training programmes in contrast to other countries in the region. Almost 0.17% of GDP is estimated to be concentrated in training programmes (Cerutti et al., 2013). OECD countries, in comparison, spend nearly 0.15% of GDP in training (Figure 2.25). Additionally, the proportion of formal wage workers offered formal public or privately financed training (68%) is relatively high for the region (62%), and higher than around the world (53%) (World Bank, 2010). However, current training programmes lack a proper evaluation mechanism and do not have a real monitoring framework. No impact evaluations have been implemented to assess the efficiency of training expenditure, and therefore evidence of their effectiveness is lacking.

Panama should increase its offer of labour market policies other than training and spread them across the country. Apart from training, there are very few programmes to help unemployed and informal workers find jobs that are a good match for their skills. Furthermore, the few existing programmes are concentrated in the large cities.

Figure 2.25. Although spending on training is high, overall labour-market policy spending is low

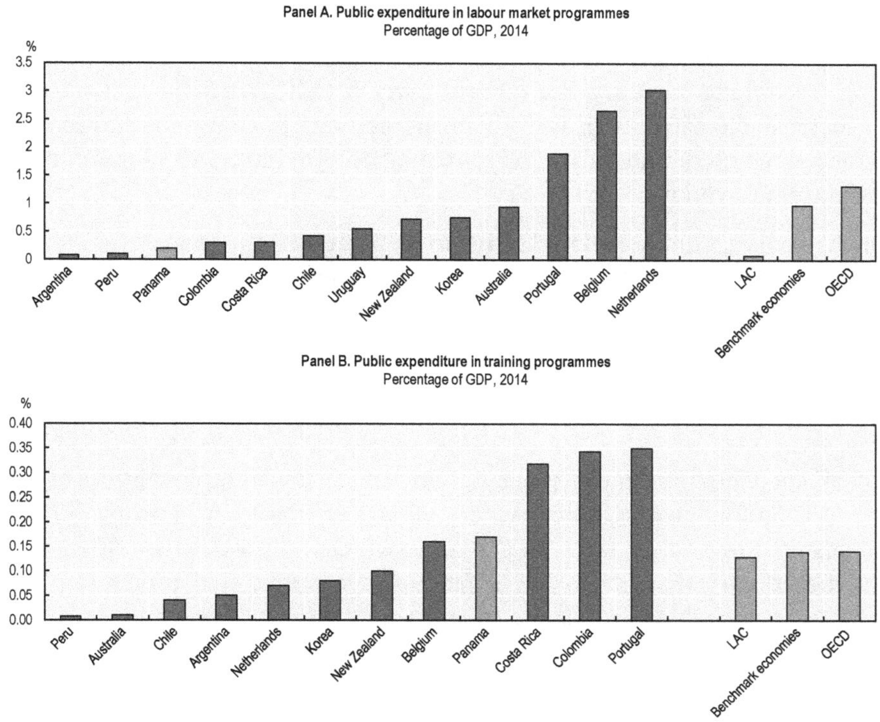

Notes: Panel A: Includes active, intermediary and passive policies. Data for Costa Rica and Guatemala are for 2012; Nicaragua, for 2013; Argentina, Australia, Belgium, Brazil, Chile, Honduras, Korea, Netherlands, New Zealand, Panama, Portugal and OECD average for 2014. The LAC average includes Argentina, Bolivia, Brazil, Chile, Colombia, Costa Rica, Dominican Republic, Ecuador, El Salvador, Granada, Guatemala, Honduras, Mexico, Nicaragua, Panama, Peru and Uruguay. Panel B: Data for Argentina, Australia, Belgium, Brazil, Chile, Korea, Netherlands, New Zealand, Panama, Portugal and OECD average is from 2014; Costa Rica, Guatemala, Nicaragua and Peru is from 2013, Dominican Republic, Honduras and Mexico is from 2012, Ecuador is from 2011, and Colombia is from 2010. The LAC average includes Argentina, Brazil, Chile, Colombia, Costa Rica, Dominican Republic, Ecuador, Guatemala, Honduras, Mexico, Nicaragua, Panama and Peru.
Source: OECD (2015b) and World Bank (2016), *ASPIRE: The Atlas of Social Protection Indicators of Resilience and Equity* (database), http://datatopics.worldbank.org/aspire/.

StatLink http://dx.doi.org/10.1787/888933777129

Better supervision and enforcement of labour laws

The role of institutions in performing inspections and setting up enforcement mechanisms may also explain informality levels in Panama. Informal employment within the formal sector is particularly significant in Panama. Both informal workers working for formal firms and domestic workers account for almost a quarter of the informal worker population. These two groups are the 'low-hanging fruit' of formalisation policies (INEC, 2016). The authorities exercise little control over the working conditions of salaried workers. In 2017, the Ministry of Labour carried out 5 131 inspections, of which only half were labour related. Enforcement mechanisms through inspection and penalties are insufficient to encourage firms to formalise their workers.

The level of formality could increase by improving the Ministry of Labour's supervising and law-enforcement capacity. In order to improve the supervisory capacity of the Labour Ministry, it must be given more and better qualified inspection personnel, and must improve its co-ordination with the other institutions guaranteeing labour rights, such as the CSS, and those responsible for business formalisation such as AMPYME and the *Mecanismo Independiente de Consulta e Investigación* (MICI). At the same time, it is necessary to increase the capacity of the labour inspectorate to address issues of safety at work for informal workers and firms by providing information and counselling about labour rights to formal workers.

Likewise, the Ministry of Labour should strive to be perceived by firms as non-tolerant of labour informality. To do so, it should work on making the conciliation and sanction process more effective, for instance by reducing the number of conciliation procedures and increasing the number and cost of fines.

Conclusions and policy recommendations

The scarcity of good quality employment opportunities, poor employability of a large share of the population and informality are persistent issues in Panama. The dual economy has resulted in a dual employment market which in turn largely explains income inequality in the country. On one hand, Panama has a strong and productive modern tradeable service sector which has steered the country's recent economic growth. This sector is mainly composed of skill-intensive activities that create relatively little employment. On the other hand, the less-productive service sector, agriculture and in some measure the manufacturing sector, in which own-account workers and micro-productive units have proliferated, offers subsistence and informal jobs to most workers.

The spike in non-residential construction that promoted employment for low-skilled workers has started to slow down. The demand for infrastructure from the transport and financial sectors has offered a large share of low-skilled workers from the agriculture sector formal and more productive jobs, reducing informality, raising salaries and ultimately reducing poverty and inequality. The demand for infrastructure and construction is expected to decelerate significantly and employment opportunities might be reduced for this group of workers.

At the same time, labour informality remains high. Although between 2003 and 2011, high economic growth contributed to reducing the informality rate; since 2012, as the modern tradeable service sector slowed down, informality increased and two out of three new jobs created were informal jobs. As emphasised in this chapter, informality poses a triple interrelated threat representing large losses for workers, for firms and the wider economy.

To promote more formal jobs and mitigate the negative effects of informality, public policy should identify and combine 1) a short-term agenda to deal with proximate causes of informality, including poor enforcement, and encourage formalisation of firms and workers, 2) a long-term agenda to address structural causes of informality such as insufficient productive development, slow labour productivity growth in sectors that create large employment and poor skills and 3) an effort to address and mitigate the consequences of informality across a number of areas, especially in social protection coverage (OECD, 2016a). Five main policy areas for action are recommended to promote formal, better quality jobs and formal economic activities in Panama.

In order to successfully use policy as a lever to create better employment opportunities, address informality, increase productivity and reduce inequality, Box 2.6 presents the main policy recommendations of this chapter.

Box 2.8. Key recommendations for building better skills and creating formal jobs for all Panamanians

Create better conditions for productive development

- Co-ordinate institutional efforts to increase economic transformation in most of the provinces with the development of the agro-industry sector and the upgrade of services linked to logistics and connectivity sector.
- Set efforts for job creation and formalisation as a key item within the broader national development strategy to co-ordinate action across line ministries and agencies.

Boost the formalisation of MSMEs and independent workers

- Consider a simplified tax system for independent workers and micro-productive units.
- Adapt CSS contributions for independent workers (frequency and payment method) and enforce the mandatory contribution of independents to the CSS.
- Disseminate and extend the use of incorporation and tax regimes for MSMEs.
- Reduce red tape and administrative/recurrent costs associated with formal status, especially at the municipal level, and the compliance costs of formally operating.
- Facilitate the use of the existing one-stop shops for business creation and licensing procedures.
- Establish more clear and simple schemes to determine minimum wages as well as future indexations which include objective productivity criteria.
- Introduce progressivity into social security contributions and lower social security contributions temporarily for new low-income workers.

Adjust the pension system to increase the incentives of being formal

- Move towards universal coverage by first expanding the '120 at 65' programme's beneficiary set.
- Integrate the '120 at 65' non-contributory pension and the contributory system (Pillar I of the CSS) into a unique pension system.
- Guarantee that the pensions of all the workers who contributed to the CSS are larger than the non-contributory pension of workers who never contributed.
- Provide alternative schemes to incorporate independent workers, domestic workers and temporary agricultural workers into the social security system, which should be compulsory but accompanied by 1) possibilities for gradual incorporation to the system, 2) allowances for specific contribution patterns (e.g. less regular contributions), and 3) unification of charges and services provided across all similar types of activities.

- Provide financial education and foster the creation of savings and insurance instruments for vulnerable groups (e.g. insurance against occupational hazards, crop insurance, etc.).
- Communicate the benefits of formality and the risks of informality, especially in terms of old-age poverty (including in secondary school).

Invest in better and relevant skills for the labour force to accompany the productive development of Panama

- Increase secondary education (including adult education) and strengthen the mechanisms to support students at risk of dropping out.
- Enhance the quality of technical secondary education and incorporate current and future needs of the productive sectors into the curricula.
- Increase the involvement of employers in the design of education curricula, technical programmes and workplace education.
- Increase educational offerings and quality in technical careers (including non-university degrees and alternative training diplomas), especially in the provinces.
- Provide reliable and free information about employment options, wage levels in different industries, and labour market status by degree and university.
- Generate links between academic and technical education by implementing a national qualifications framework to align technical and vocational education with general education and allow students to easily transit across academic and technical schools as well as INADEH, ITSE and all tertiary institutions.
- Include business training earlier in the educational curriculum (accounting, finance, management and supervisory, etc.).
- Reinforce active labour market policies by strengthening employment services and youth training programmes to prevent young people from entering into informal jobs.
- Establish a policy of lifelong learning that includes regular on-the-job training.

Supervise and enforce labour laws

- Improve the links between different institutions guaranteeing labour rights (MITRADEL, CSS) and those responsible for business formalisation (MICI, AMPYME).
- Increase efforts to supervise firms by endowing the MITRADEL with more and better qualified inspection personnel, and improving its co-ordination with the CSS.
- Increase fines and make the sanctioning power of the MITRADEL more effective.
- Make the processes of conciliation and sanctions more efficient for instance by reducing the number of procedures.
- Increase the capacity of the labour inspectorate to address issues of safety at work for informal workers and firms through the provision of information and counselling about labour rights to workers.

Notes

[1] Assuming constant employment elasticity of growth and keeping the employment-to-population ratio at 61% and unemployment at 6%.

[2] The *Centro Nacional de Competitividad* (CNCs) and the AMPYME classify MSMEs by gross income: firms that have revenues of PAB 2.5 million per year or less.

References

Agosin, M.R. et al. (2014), *Rethinking Productive Development: Sound Policies and Institutions for Economic Transformation*, Inter-American Development Bank, Washington, DC.

Avendaño, R. et al. (2016), "Understanding student performance beyond traditional factors: Evidence from PISA", *OECD Development Centre Working Papers*, No. 331, OECD Publishing, Paris, http://dx.doi.org/10.1787/5jlz7n7bxn0p-en.

Becerra, O. (2017), "Pension incentives and formal-sector labor supply: Evidence from Colombia", Document CEDE No. 2017-14, Universidad de Los Andes, Bogota, http://dx.doi.org/10.2139/ssrn.2922105.

Bosch, M. and W.F. Maloney (2010), "Comparative analysis of labor market dynamics using Markov processes: An application to informality", *Labour Economics*, Vol. 17/4, pp. 621-631.

Bosch, M., A. Melguizo and C. Pagés (2013), *Better Pensions, Better Jobs: Towards Universal Coverage in Latin America and the Caribbean*, Inter-American Development Bank, Washington, DC.

CEDLAS (Centro de Estudios Distributivos, Laborales y Sociales) and World Bank (2016), *SEDLAC (Socio-Economic Database for Latin America and the Caribbean)* (database), Centro de Estudios Distributivos, Laborales y Sociales, Universidad Nacional de La Plata, La Plata, Argentina, http://sedlac.econo.unlp.edu.ar/eng/ (accessed 1 February 2018).

Cerutti, P. et al. (2013), "Social assistance and labor market programs in Latin America: Methodology and key findings from the social protection database", *World Bank Social Protection and Labour Discussion Papers*, No. 1401, World Bank, Washington, DC.

Céspedes, N., P. Lavado and N. Ramírez Rondán (eds.) (2016), *Productividad en el Perú: Medición, Determinantes e Implicancias* (*Productivity in Peru: Measurement, Determinants and Implications*), Universidad del Pacífico, Lima, http://repositorio.up.edu.pe/handle/11354/1083.

CNC (Centro Nacional de Competitividad) (2010), "La informalidad en Panama" [Informality in Panama], CNC, Panama, http://www.cncpanama.org/cnc/.

ECLAC (Economic Commission for Latin America and the Caribbean)/ILO (International Labour Organization) (2016), *Employment Situation in Latin America and the Caribbean: Recent Improvements and Persistent Gaps in Rural Employment*, No. 14, May 2016, UN Publication, Santiago, Chile, http://repositorio.cepal.org/bitstream/handle/11362/40098/S1600315_en.pdf?sequence=1&isAllowed=y.

González, D. (2006), "Regimenes Especiales se Tributación para Pequeños Contribuyentes en America Latina" [Special tax regime for small taxpayers in Latin America], Inter-American Development Bank, Washington, DC.

González-Páramo, J. and A. Melguizo (2012), "Who bears labour taxes and social contributions? A meta-analysis approach", *Journal of the Spanish Economic Association*, Vol. 4/3, pp. 247-271.

Hanushek, E.A. and L. Woessmann (2012), "Do better schools lead to more growth? Cognitive skills, economic outcomes, and causation", *Journal of Economic Growth*, Vol. 17/4, pp. 267-321.

Hausmann, R., L. Espinoza and M.A. Santos (2016), "Shifting gears: A growth diagnostic of Panama", *Center for International Development Working Papers*, No. 325, Center for International Development at Harvard University, Boston.

IDB (2016), *SIMS* (*Labor Markets and Social Security Information System*) (database), Inter-American Development Bank, Washington, DC, available at https://data.iadb.org/ (accessed 1 February 2018).

ILO (2017), *Minimum wage policy guide: A summary*, International Labour Organization, Geneva.

ILO (2016), *Key Indicators of the Labour Market*, 9th Edition (database), International Labour Organization, Geneva, http://ilo.org/global/statistics-and-databases/lang--en/index.htm (accessed 1 March 2017).

IMF (2017), *World Economic Outlook* (database), International Monetary Fund, https://www.imf.org/external/pubs/ft/weo/2017/02/weodata/index.aspx (accessed 1 February 2018).

INEC (2017), *Sistema Integrado de Indicadores para el Desarrollo* (*SID*), Instituto Nacional de Estadística y Censo (National Institute of Statistics and Census), Panama, http://estadisticas.contraloria.gob.pa/redpan/sid/que_es_el_sid.html (accessed 20 February 2018).

INEC (2016), *Encuesta Continua de Hogares [National Household Survey*], INEC, Panama, https://www.contraloria.gob.pa/inec/.

Islam, I. and S. Nazara (2000), "Estimating employment elasticity for the Indonesian economy", International Labour Office, Jakarta.

Kucera, D. and L. Roncolato (2008), "Informal employment: Two contested policy issues", *International Labour Review*, Vol. 147/4, pp. 321-348.

La Porta, R. and A. Shleifer (2014), "Informality and development", *Journal of Economic Perspectives*, Vol. 28/3, pp. 109-126.

Lehmann, H. and A. Muravyev (2012), "Labor market institutions and informality in transition and Latin American Countries", in Frölich, M. et al. (eds), *Social Insurance and Labor Markets: How to Protect Workers while Creating Good Jobs*, Oxford University Press, pp. 375-410.

Levy, S. (2008), *Good Intentions, Bad Outcomes: Social Policy, Informality, and Economic Growth in Mexico*, Brookings Institution Press, Washington, DC.

ManPower Group (2016), *Talent Shortage Survey: Research Results*, ManPowerGroup, Milwaukee, Wisconsin.

Melguizo, A (2015), "Pensions, informality, and the emerging middle class", Article No. 169, IZA World of Labor, https://wol.iza.org/articles/pensions-informality-and-emerging-middle-class/long.

MITRADEL (Ministerio de Trabajo y Desarrollo Laboral de la República de Panamá) (2017), *Sistema Integrado de Indicadores de Educacion*, Ministerio de Educación de Panamá, Panama.

OECD (Organisation for Economic Co-operation and Development) (2017), *Multi-Dimensional Review of Panama: Volume 1: Initial Assessment*, OECD Publishing, Paris, http://dx.doi.org/10.1787/9789264278547-en.

OECD (2016a), *Multi-dimensional Review of Peru: Volume 2. In-depth Analysis and Recommendations*, OECD Development Pathways, OECD Publishing, Paris, http://dx.doi.org/10.1787/9789264264670-en.

OECD (2016b), *PISA 2015 Results (Volume I): Excellence and Equity in Education*, OECD Publishing, Paris, http://dx.doi.org/10.1787/9789264266490-en.

OECD (2016c), *PISA Products* (database), https://www.oecd.org/pisa/pisaproducts/ (accessed 1 March 2017).

OECD (2016d), Survey of Adult Skills (PIAAC) (The Programme for the International Assessment of Adult Competencies) (database), http://www.oecd.org/skills/piaac/ (accessed 1 June 2016).

OECD (2015a), *Multi-dimensional Review of Peru: Volume I. Initial Assessment*, OECD Publishing, Paris, http://dx.doi.org/10.1787/9789264243279-en.

OECD (2015b), *OECD Employment Outlook 2015*, OECD Publishing, Paris, http://dx.doi.org/10.1787/empl_outlook-2015-en.

OECD (2014), *PISA 2012 Results: What Students Know and Can Do (Volume I, Revised edition, February 2014): Student Performance in Mathematics, Reading and Science*, PISA, OECD Publishing, Paris, http://dx.doi.org/10.1787/9789264208780-en.

OECD (2012), *PISA 2012* (database), http://www.oecd.org/pisa/pisaproducts/pisa2012database-downloadabledata.htm.

OECD (2010a), *PISA 2009 Results: What Students Know and Can Do: Student Performance in Reading, Mathematics and Science (Volume I),* PISA, OECD Publishing, Paris, http://dx.doi.org/10.1787/9789264091450-en.

OECD (2010b), *PISA 2009 Results: Equity in Learning Opportunities and Outcomes (Volume II)*, PISA, OECD Publishing, Paris, http://dx.doi.org/10.1787/9789264091504-en.

OECD/CAF (Development Bank of Latin America)/ECLAC (2018), *Latin American Economic Outlook 2018: Rethinking Institutions for Development*, OECD Publishing, Paris.

OECD/CAF/ECLAC (2016), *Latin American Economic Outlook 2017: Youth, Skills and Entrepreneurship*, OECD Publishing, Paris, http://dx.doi.org/10.1787/leo-2017-en

OECD/CAF/ECLAC (2014), *Latin American Economic Outlook 2015: Education, Skills and Innovation for Development*, OECD Publishing, Paris, http://dx.doi.org/10.1787/leo-2015-en

OECD/CIAT (Inter-American Center of Tax Administrations)/IDB (2016), *Taxing Wages in Latin America and the Caribbean 2016*, OECD Publishing, Paris, http://dx.doi.org/10.1787/9789264262607-en

Perry, G. et al. (2007), *Informality: Exit and Exclusion*, Latin American and Caribbean Studies, World Bank, Washington, DC.

Quintini, G. and T. Manfredi (2009), "Going separate ways? School-to-work transitions in the United States and Europe", *OECD Social, Employment and Migration Working Papers*, No. 90, OECD Publishing, Paris, http://dx.doi.org/10.1787/221717700447.

Schwab, D. (2016), "Employment protection and the labor information of the youth: Evidence from India", *Institute for Economic Development Working Papers Series from Boston University Department of Economics,* No. dp-280, Department of Economics, Boston University, Boston, http://econpapers.repec.org/paper/bosiedwpr/dp-280.htm.

UNESCO (United Nations Educational, Scientific and Cultural Organisation) (2016), *Education and Literacy* (database), UNESCO Institute for Statistics, Montreal, http://uis.unesco.org/ (accessed 1 March 2017).

UNESCO (2015), *Informe de Resultados TERCE. Tercer Estudio Regional Comparativo y Explicativo. Factores Asociados* (*TERCE Results Report: Third Regional Comparative and Explanatory Study, Associated Factors*), UNESCO, Santiago, Chile, http://unesdoc.unesco.org/images/0024/002435/243533s.pdf.

World Bank (2017), *World Bank World Development Indicators* (database), Washington, DC, http://data.worldbank.org/ (accessed 1 March 2017).

World Bank (2016), *ASPIRE: The Atlas of Social Protection Indicators of Resilience and Equity* (database), World Bank, http://datatopics.worldbank.org/aspire/ (accessed 1 March 2017).

World Bank (2015), *Social Protection for the Harder Road Ahead: Containing the Social Costs of Lower Growth in Latin America and the Caribbean,* World Bank Group, Washington, DC, http://documents.worldbank.org/curated/en/582321468188664832/Social-protection-for-the-harder-road-ahead-containing-the-social-costs-of-lower-growthin-Latin-America-and-the-Caribbean/.

World Bank (2010), *World Bank Enterprise Survey 2010* (database), World Bank, Washington, DC, www.enterprisesurveys.org/data (accessed 1 March 2017).

Chapter 3. Strengthening regional development policy to boost inclusive growth

This chapter explores how regional development can be a lever to help Panama continue on its growth trajectory and achieve more inclusive socio-economic outcomes. It discusses Panama's current multi-level governance architecture, identifying where it should be strengthened to better support the design and implementation of regional development policy. In addition, it evaluates the need for a more strategic approach to regional development and greater capacity in subnational finance, institutional co-ordination, and quality public service delivery, at all levels of government. A special focus is placed on Panama's local authorities in light of specific resource challenges and the 2014 decentralisation reform. Finally, the chapter looks into what would be necessary to achieve a strategic shift towards a "place-based" policy approach for regional development, and provides recommendations for action.

Regional development is a policy lever for sustainable and inclusive growth in Panama. To better meet national objectives of sustained development with greater inclusiveness, a number of territorial challenges should be addressed (OECD, 2017a). These include ensuring more equal access to public services across regions, reducing the level of labour market informality, and strengthening the mechanisms that can finance development. A regional development strategy that is built around the unique and competitive attributes of each region – a "place-based" approach – supported by effective multilevel governance mechanisms could help Panama achieve more inclusive socio-economic outcomes.

This chapter is dedicated to exploring regional development as a policy lever for Panama to better meet its sustainable growth and inclusiveness aims, and focuses on the need to improve strategic planning and implementation frameworks. It begins by reviewing Panama's multilevel governance structures as they relate to regional development, explores the benefits associated with a "new paradigm" approach, and identifies multi-level governance tools, particularly with respect to co-ordination, that could strengthen institutional capacity to realise regional development aims. It concludes with a series of recommendations for regional development.

Why a national-level regional development policy matters

A national level policy establishes the guiding principles for decision making and action with respect to a specific sector (e.g. education, transport, energy) or a multisector concern (e.g. regional economic development, labour markets, social inclusion). In a regional development context, the purpose and value of a national regional development policy is several fold. First, it sets the guidelines for decision making and action in a complex, multistakeholder policy area. Second, when well designed, executed and monitored, a national-level regional development policy can help align priorities and build greater coherence and complementarity among the various actors involved, particularly since sector priorities and approaches may differ among them. When regional development is approached in terms of a policy package (rather than individual sector interventions), there is less potential for the unintended and undesirable effects that can arise when policy measures are undertaken in isolation (OECD, 2012). Third, it facilitates capitalising on cross-sector policy synergies that can better promote inclusive and sustainable growth.

Regional development is a key multisector policy area that promotes well-being and economic prosperity. Taking a regional perspective, including an aim to promote growth in all regions, rather than focusing on high or low performance regions, is likely to yield economies that are less vulnerable to external shocks (OECD, 2012). At the same time, there is increasing agreement that the quality of governance structures (institutions and frameworks) plays a significant role in the ability to generate sustained increases in wellbeing and economic prosperity (EC, 2017a). Regional development policy contributes to inclusive and sustainable growth by acting as a framework for action at the national and subnational level.

Approaches to regional development in OECD countries

Investing in regions, including the less-performing ones, is beneficial for sustainable growth. While there is no question why governments should invest in regions that are engines of growth, policy makers and the public can question why it is just as important to invest in regions that are less dynamic. Regions that underperform can be costly to national budgets. Missed growth opportunities go hand in hand with lower tax revenues, and ensuring adequate public service delivery can be very expensive. In addition, if the decline is not reversed, political pressures can lead to expensive policies dedicated to sustaining communities and living standards through transfers, which in time can lead to conflict (particularly as wealthier regions tire of paying for such support) (OECD, 2012).

Shifting from an approach that focuses on transfers and subsidies as generators of wellbeing and growth to one that concentrates on identifying and building the productive potential of each region can contribute to regional dynamism and national inclusive growth (OECD, 2012). Over the past few decades, OECD countries have done precisely this, using regional development policy to promote more integrated and market-oriented approaches in order to solve national growth challenges. This has resulted in a "new paradigm" driving the design and implementation of regional development policy (Table 3.1), where effort and resources are concentrated on building competitive regions by bringing together actors and targeting key local assets rather than ensuring the redistribution from leading to lagging regions (OECD, 2009a; OECD 2009b).

Table 3.1. Old and new paradigms of "place-based" regional development policy

Action	"Old" Paradigm	"New" Paradigm
Objectives	"Balancing" economic performance by compensating for spatial disparities	Tapping underutilised regional potential for competitiveness
Strategies	Sector-driven approach	Integrated development projects
Tools	Subsidies and state aid	Development of soft and hard infrastructure
Actors	Central government	Different levels of government
Unit of territorial analysis	Administrative regions	Functional regions
Focus	Redistribution from leading to lagging regions	Building competitive regions by bringing together actors and targeting key local assets

Source: OECD (2009b), *Regions Matter: Economic Recovery, Innovation and Sustainable Growth,* OECD Publishing, Paris, http://dx.doi.org/10.1787/9789264076525-en.

The goal of regional development policy is to ensure that different types of regions are able to thrive and offer a high quality of life for their residents (OECD, 2016a). Introducing such a policy in and of itself will not automatically generate growth or inclusiveness. It serves as a framework to guide the implementation of sector and cross-sector policies and programmes that can – in the short, medium and long term – contribute to the performance of a country and its regions. It needs to be complemented not only by effective sector policies that support infrastructure, labour markets, and innovation, but also by effective multilevel governance structures – the institutions and frameworks supporting relationships, decision making, and implementation processes between national and subnational levels of government, including subnational development planning.

Panama's multilevel governance structures supporting regional development

The design and execution of regional development policy relies heavily on the successful interaction of multiple levels of government, government sectors, actors and interests. It must align national and subnational objectives and priorities, and its implementation depends on the capacity, including human, financial, and infrastructure endowments, of all levels of government. Its success also relies on empowered, accountable, and properly resourced subnational governments, both regional and local. Panama's multilevel governance structures (i.e. the institutions and frameworks) that support regional development are centralised and top-down, not fully able to promote a "place-based" or "new paradigm" approach. This is further limited by the minimal role that subnational governments play in the country's economic and social development.

Panama's territorial administrative structures

Panama is a presidential republic of over four million inhabitants. Compared to OECD member countries, it is similar in population to Ireland, New Zealand and Norway. In total area it is slightly smaller than the Czech Republic. It is a unitary country with two levels of government established constitutionally: national and municipal. At the subnational level, administration is divided into two administrative tiers, with municipalities divided into submunicipal units (Table 3.2).

Table 3.2. Panama: Subnational administrative bodies

Tier 1: Provincial level	*Provincias*	10
	Comarcas	3
Tier 2: Municipal level	*Distritos*	77[1]
	Indigenous settlements[2]	2 101
Submunicipal level	*Corregimientos*	679

Notes: [1] Within the context of the decentralisation law and in order to ensure government transfers, Panama counts 78 municipalities with the 78th municipality being the combination of three *comarcas:* Madugandí, Wargandí and Guna Yala.

[2] Panama's three *comarcas* have a total of 2 073 populated areas broken down as follows: Kuna Yala (117), Emberá (82), Ngäbe Buglé (1 874). The two indigenous groups that are embedded in provinces, Kuna de Wargandí and Kuna de Madungandí, have 5 and 23 populated areas, respectively. Note that for these last two areas, data is in anticipation of the census in 2020, for the others data is from February 2018.

Sources: Adapted from: OECD (2017a), *Multi-dimensional Review of Panama: Volume 1. Initial Assessment*, OECD Development Pathways, OECD Publishing, Paris, http://dx.doi.org/10.1787/9789264278547-en; editorialox (n.d.), "Panama" available: http://www.editorialox.com/panama.htm; Data for indigenous settlements provided by Panama from INEC (National Institute of Statistics and Census of Panama).

Provinces are deconcentrated entities of the central government. Each is led by a presidentially appointed governor and administered by a *Junta Territorial* composed of representatives from each line ministry. An indirectly elected Provincial Council[1] acts as an advisory body to the governor. Provinces do not have revenue-generating capacity, and are responsible for implementing the plans and programmes developed by the national government. *Comarcas* with provincial status are semi-autonomous, and have traditional, "communal" structures (Box 3.1). They can generate their own revenues, often from tourism, fishing, and crafts that are transferred into a community treasury or fund. Other *comarca* revenues come from state transfers and from remittances to family by community members living and/or working outside the *comarca.*

Each province is divided into autonomous municipalities (*distritos*), which themselves are divided into subunits – *corregimientos.* Municipalities are led by democratically elected mayors and have municipal councils comprised of two representatives from each *corregimiento.*

Box 3.1. *Comarcas*: Panama's indigenous territories and communities

Approximately 12% of Panama's population is a member of one of seven indigenous groups. The majority live either in one of three semi-autonomous *comarcas* or in indigenous territories embedded in provinces. Combined, these territories cover about 24% of the country's total land mass. Functioning as collectives, the communities are governed by local leaders. Additionally, there are 10 General Congresses and two General Councils, representing the maximum authority for the indigenous population of Panama. *Comarcas* are represented in Panama's National Congress. Each *comarca* has its own organic (constituting) law, which recognises the right of the communities to hold collective property (within the *comarca*), and contains specific references to natural resources, government, justice, economy, culture, education, and health. While not always the case, poverty levels are generally higher and wellbeing outcomes are generally lower in the *comarcas* than in Panama's non-indigenous provinces.

Sources: UNDP (2014), *Imaginando un Futuro Común: Plan de Desarrollo Integral de los Pueblos Indígenas de Panamá*, United Nations Development Programme, New York, available http://www.pa.undp.org/content/panama/es/home/library/poverty/sistematizacion-plan-desarrollo-indigena.html; OECD (2017a), *Multi-dimensional Review of Panama: Volume 1. Initial Assessment*, OECD Development Pathways, OECD Publishing, Paris, http://dx.doi.org/10.1787/9789264278547-en.

First-tier outcomes and growth patterns can reinforce territorial disparities

There is a large gap between provinces and *comarcas* in terms of wellbeing outcomes. Residents of *comarcas* are much more likely to live in poverty and report lower levels of satisfaction about their living conditions. They are also at greater risk of having an informal job, or not having access to drinkable water in their dwelling. The lowest level of electricity coverage in Panama is among the indigenous population. However, low outcomes in material and living conditions are also evident in the provinces as well, generally those that are rural, and regardless of whether they have a high percentage of indigenous residents (Figure 3.1) (OECD, 2017a).

A strategic approach to regional development, supported by a policy for its implementation, can help mitigate a risk of *ad hoc* growth and development, and better ensure the ability to successfully address inequalities. Projections indicate that provincial population growth between 2010 and 2020 is expected to range from a low of 1.6% in Los Santos, to 33.5% in Bocas del Toro. The population of Panama City is expected to increase by over 20% in this same 10-year period, a growth level also expected of the three *comarcas*[2] (Controlaría del Gobierno de Panamá, 2010). In light of this, there are two points that should be underscored. First, the population is expected to grow most in some of the least-advantaged territories, where quality of life/wellbeing outcomes are already low, particularly in the *comarcas,* Bocas del Toro, and Los Santos (OECD, 2017a). Second, Panama City is also expected to grow significantly and the challenge will be to ensure adequate infrastructure, housing, amenities, and service delivery capacity to keep up with growing demand, while also maintaining or improving quality of life. While appropriate spatial and land-use planning is fundamental to meet the challenges represented by such growth, they complement and contribute to a regional development policy; they do not replace it.

Figure 3.1. Quality of life by regions

Standardised scores

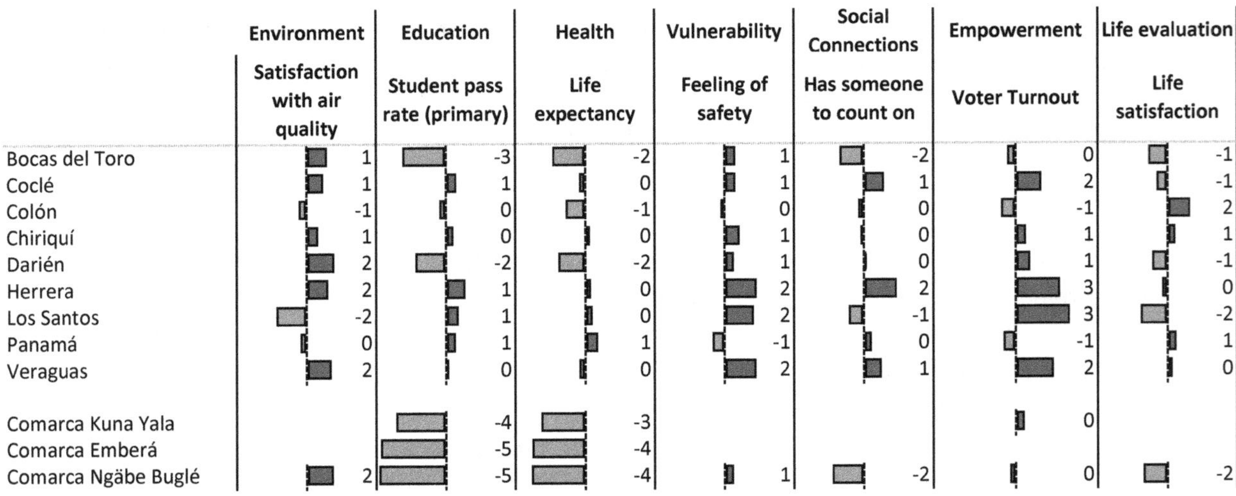

Notes: This analysis looks at the original province of Panamá, although Panamá and Panamá Oeste recently split. Z-score or standard score stands for the signed number of standard deviations by which the regional outcome is above or below the national average. This normalisation enables an assessment of how much a region's performance is deviating from that average.
Source: OECD (2017a), *Multi-dimensional Review of Panama: Volume 1. Initial Assessment*, OECD Development Pathways, OECD Publishing, Paris, http://dx.doi.org/10.1787/9789264278547-en.

Normative and institutional frameworks for the subnational level

Territorial administration is governed by a series of laws, some of which date to the 1970s, and others which were recently introduced. These include the Constitution; *Ley N9-106 Sobre Regimen Municipal* from 1973 which establishes municipal categories, autonomy and structure; Law No. 37 of 2009 *Que Descentraliza la Administración Pública* – Panama's first decentralisation law; and Law No. 66 of 2015 *Que Reforma la Ley 37 de 2009,* which updates and amends Law No. 37 of 2009. In addition, a national policy for land use with a horizon to 2030 (*Política Nacional de Ordenamiento Territorial)*, together with an action plan establishing priorities, is under preparation by the Ministry for Housing and Land Use (*Ministerio de Vivienda y Ordenamiento Territorial)*.

Planning frameworks for regional development could be better targeted

Regional development in Panama is guided by successive government programmes, currently the *Plan Estratégico de Gobierno 2015-2019* (PEG) (Box 3.2). The document outlines the president's objectives and approach for the country's development, including at the subnational level. It is implemented by sector-driven projects and programmes. However, this plan does not guide regional development in the long term. Rather, regional development is a central level process guided by government strategies that are limited to a period of five years. Implementation depends on the plans of each line ministry, as well as the articulated needs of local authorities that emerge from provincial government bodies. Panama is also developing a 12-year national development plan, the *Plan Estratégico Nacional con Visión de Estado – Panamá: 2030*, which can be a valuable longer-term strategic document to embed broader national objectives, although it does not specifically refer to regional or territorial development.

Box 3.2. The territorial dimension to Panama's Government Strategic Plan, 2015-2019

In the current government programme – the *Plan Estrategico de Gobierno 2015-2019* (PEG) – the overall ambition is to promote greater sustainability and equality, increased competitiveness and more effective investment throughout the country. In order to achieve this, the PEG calls for a national "master plan" for land use and territorial development supported by a new legal framework, greater citizen and business participation in territorial and urban interventions, and building institutional capacity at all levels of government. It includes a section dedicated to modernising the public sector that focuses on public finance and investment effectiveness, as well as on taking a more strategic approach to public management, promoting civil service reform, and advancing the decentralisation agenda.

Source: Gobierno de la República de Panamá (2014), *Un Solo País: Plan Estratégico de Gobierno 2015-2019*, Gobierno de la República de Panamá, Panama, available: http://www.mef.gob.pa/es/Documents/PEG%20PLAN%20ESTRATEGICO%20DE%20GOBIERNO%202015-2019.pdf

There are several concerns with this approach to regional development planning and implementation. First is the lack of a link to a larger strategy, one built using longer-term strategic foresight, solid evidence bases, and which establishes clear outcome objectives. This means that there is limited guidance for decision making and action by line ministries and their relevant agencies, and little that can be used to support monitoring, evaluation and government accountability. Second is the limited time horizon (five years) for implementation – it corresponds to one presidential term and is not tied to a longer term vision or investment strategy (OECD, 2017a). This is particularly challenging as the concrete results stemming from a strategically-based regional development policy can take longer to materialise. Third, there is no requirement that sector plans be binding in terms of implementing regulatory or investment policies to achieve objectives set in the government plan (OECD, 2017a).

OECD and non-OECD countries use a variety of mechanisms to ensure their regional development strategies have a longer-term dimension, and link to sector and subnational planning. For instance, some countries use a legal framework to support strategic regional development planning and implementation at a central or subnational level. This is the practice in Finland (Act on Regional Development, 2014), Slovenia (Law on the Promotion of Balanced Regional Development), Switzerland (Federal Law on Development Policy, 2006), and Ukraine (Law on Fundamentals of State Regional Policy, 2014) (OECD, 2016b; Verkhovna Rada, 2015) while others use white papers (e.g. Australia, UK), state strategies for regional development (e.g. Sweden) or other framework documents such as state-region planning contracts (e.g. France) or regional growth programmes (e.g. New Zealand) specifically dedicated to the task (OECD, 2016b). In addition, some countries dedicate funds to regional development planning in their national budget codes or through dedicated special funds.

At the subnational level, development planning instruments are gradually being introduced and focus on the municipal level. Article 13 of the original law on decentralisation (No. 37) included a hierarchy of planning instruments, beginning with the government plan, followed by a national land-use plan, provincial development plans, municipal development plans and finally ending with *corregimiento* development plans

(República de Panamá, 2009). As the law was suspended and then reintroduced, this planning hierarchy appears to have been modified. The amended decentralisation law requires municipal development planning in the form of district strategic plans (*Planes Estratégicos Distritales* – PED). These are combined development and land-use plans (República de Panamá, 2015) that are intended to link back to the Strategic Government Plan 2015-2019 (PEG) and the National Strategic Plan 2030 (*Plan Estratégico Nacional con Visión de Estado-Panamá: 2030)*. Prior to this, it is reported that local level development planning was under the responsibility of the central government, based upon identified needs that were communicated upward by local authorities, and for which the central government would design the corresponding plan.

Institutional responsibility for regional development is fragmented

Responsibility for regional development is fragmented across sectors in Panama. The Ministry of Economy and Finance (*Ministerio de Economía y Finanzas* – MEF), and specifically its Direction for Public Policy, and Department for Regional Planning within the Direction for Investment Programming, play important roles. Line ministries with a territorial logic, such as the ministries of Agriculture, Education, Employment and Labour Force Development, Health, Housing and Land Use, Social Development, and the Vice-ministry for Indigenous Affairs, as well as relevant agencies, are also involved, realising their objectives through a variety of plans and programmes. In addition, the Ministry of Government and its Department for Planning and International Co-operation also have a hand in the cross-sector co-ordination of subnational initiatives that support productive development. Finally, the Secretariat for Decentralisation will likely play an increasingly visible role with respect to local development and development planning.

This institutional framework underscores two issues. First, responsibility for regional development is highly fragmented, within institutions as well as among actors across sectors. Second, there is no government body exclusively dedicated to regional development in terms of its design, implementation, co-ordination, monitoring and evaluation. When confronted with this degree of fragmentation, institutional co-ordination becomes fundamental and inter-ministerial co-ordination is an important ingredient for success, given the complexity and cross-sectoral nature of regional development policy.

Centre-of-Government (CoG) bodies are often responsible for ensuring co-ordination across government, for instance in the area of regional development. Cross-government co-ordination committees, in turn, can delegate the oversight of the policy's implementation to a specific ministry, which can be vital to success. In Panama, however, the level of influence that the CoG has over line ministries to encourage co-ordination is relatively low – limited to expressing its views rather than potentially executing sanctions. Also, there appears to be limited to no responsibility on the part of the CoG to organise cross-government policy co-ordination committees. Panama together with Paraguay belong to the few countries in the region where this is the case. In the others, there is responsibility for such organisation on at least one level (OECD, 2016c).

In sum, regional development in Panama could be strengthened through more targeted normative and institutional frameworks. Currently, two frameworks lead the regional development process, the PED and the Law on Decentralisation, the implementation of which are supported by the individual strategies and plans of line ministries and other government bodies. A dedicated national regional development policy could help bring these pieces together and ensure continuity over the medium term (see sections below).

Generating regional level growth depends on greater subnational capacity

Panama's subnational governments face financial challenges and constraints in administrative and management capacity that can limit successful regional development and the implementation of place-based plans and programmes. The law on decentralisation could help address these, however it is in its early stages and so it is too soon to assess its real or potential impact.

Subnational fiscal and financial frameworks

As currently structured, Panama's financing and investment frameworks do not easily support a "place-based", regionally-driven approach to development. This is true at the provincial and municipal levels, where governments play a limited role in public expenditures, supposing a high degree of centralisation (Figure 3.2).

Figure 3.2. Subnational government expenditure is low in Panama (2014)

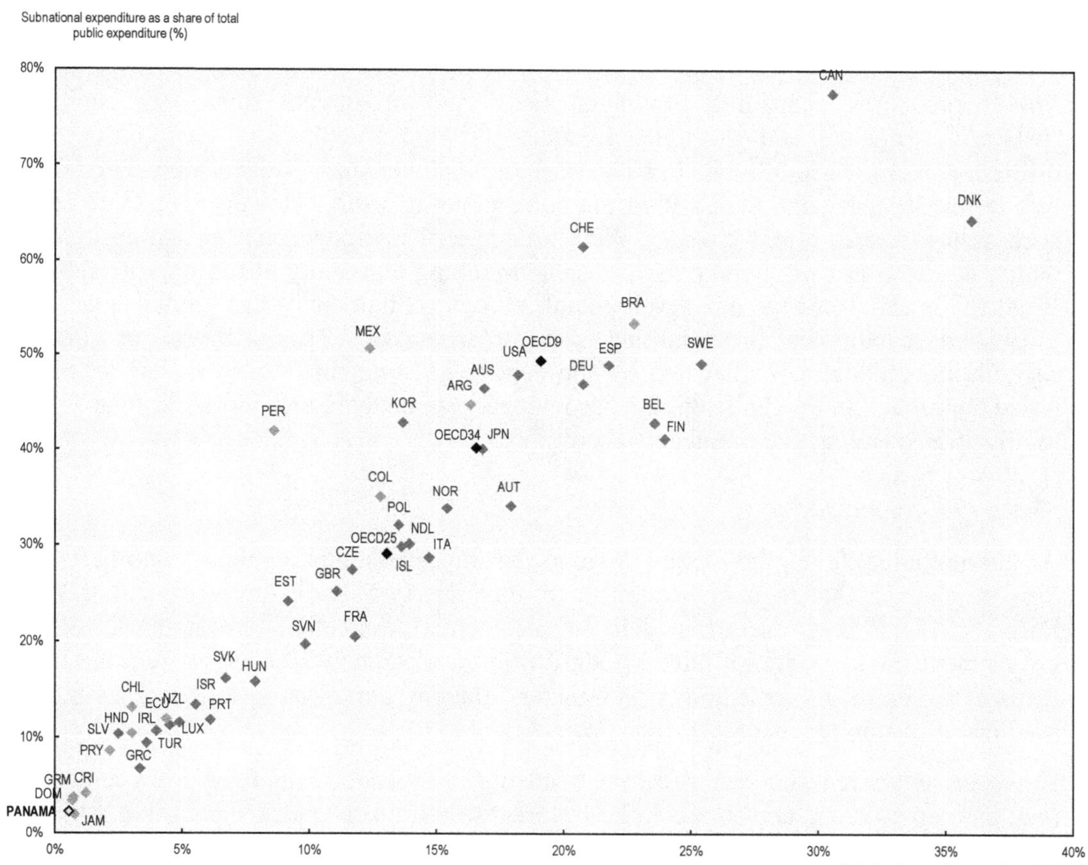

Notes: Data for Panama are for 2016. Subnational government calculations for Panama reflect expenditure by municipalities and Juntas Comunales, because provincial expenditure is counted as part of central government expenditure. Panama is highlighted in bold, Latin American countries in grey, OECD countries in blue.
Source: OECD calculations from Contraloría General de la República – Dirección General de Fiscalización, Municipalidades de la República y Ministerio de Economía y Finanzas Dirección de Presupuesto de la Nación (DIPRENA); OECD (2017b), *Making Decentralisation Work in Chile: Towards Stronger Municipalities*, OECD Multi-level Governance Studies, OECD Publishing, Paris, http://dx.doi.org/10.1787/9789264279049-en.

StatLink http://dx.doi.org/10.1787/888933777148

Provincial frameworks

Provincial governments have no own-source revenue, and their expenditures are financed directly from the central budget. Their fiscal frameworks are limited to the immediate budget year (i.e. there is no multi-annual budgeting), and are frequently not formula based. Instead, line ministries are responsible for financing their sector's subnational responsibilities, and funds are assigned annually after the ministries have defined their budgets with the Ministry of Economy and Finance. Once funds are allocated, each sector redistributes funds down the line (i.e. to the province and from there to specific areas such as schools or hospitals) based on identified local needs and projects. Funding gaps arise, and if there are insufficient funds one year, then programming waits until the next year's budget round. Panama's time span for fiscal projections is up to five years – a time span common to a majority of Latin American and Caribbean countries. There is no requirement for the budget to be based on long-term fiscal projections – as practised by 70% of countries in the region – nor must it take demographic change into account (OECD, 2016c). Fiscal projections can be useful for identifying future expenses in light of expected demographic and economic change, and can contribute to the reform agenda (OECD, 2016c).

This approach to managing provincial fiscal and investment funds can challenge sustainable regional and local development. Provincial authorities have little to no discretion over the use of funds in a cross-sectoral manner since budgets are handed down by the line ministry and kept within the corresponding sector. However, in some cases, such as healthcare, recent changes allow a degree of interchangeability within a sector which is a step toward greater fiscal decision-making autonomy at the provincial level. What this means for regional development, though, is that funds are limited unless the associated development programming is sector driven, or a special budget or fund for regional development is allocated by the central government. It also makes a "place-based" approach more challenging as provincial governments are limited in their ability to prioritise spending needs and act accordingly.

Municipal frameworks

At the municipal level, the picture is somewhat more complex, as there is no particular legal framework that regulates central level transfers to municipal governments (World Bank, 2013). These are often left to presidential discretion. In addition, central government transfers do not have standard frameworks, such as rules or formulas. This lends a degree of unpredictability to transfers, thereby contributing to a lack of budget predictability among local authorities (World Bank, 2013).

However, municipalities can generate own-source revenue from fees, fines and taxes (e.g. municipal taxes, tax on alcoholic beverages, and on livestock [abattoirs], which is paid to the municipality of the animal's origin), income from public lands, properties or municipal assets; duties on the extraction of a variety of natural resources (e.g. wood, sand, stone, clay, coral) and on public performances (e.g. concerts) (Gobierno de Panamá, 1972/2004). Despite their autonomous status, however, municipalities have few attributed responsibilities. Those that they do have are heavily concentrated on general urban amenities and education with some additional services in public health, transport, recreation and culture (Annex A) (Ministerio de Economía y Finanzas, 2002). This links to the limited weight of municipalities in general government expenditure, estimated at 2.2% in 2016, representing around 0.5% of GDP (Figure 3.3). This is significantly different from the OECD average where municipal governments represent 40% of public expenditure and 17% of GDP. It is also far from many other Latin American countries.

While municipal revenue levels remain low, they have been rising since 2014 (Figure 3.3), as a result of the reintroduction of the Law on Decentralisation. In addition, municipal revenue is starting to grow faster than expenditure, which may reflect the impact of the law's injection of funding for investment that has not yet been matched by an increase in the level of responsibilities that require spending. Despite these upward trends, however, Panama's municipalities generate very limited revenue and have low expenditure levels as a percentage of GDP and as a percentage of total general government revenue. In Chile, for example, one of the OECD's most centralised countries, subnational government revenue represented 3.6% of GDP and 15.5% of general government revenue in 2016 (OECD, 2017c), compared to Panama's 0.7% of GDP and 3.0% of general government revenue.

Figure 3.3. Municipal expenditure as a percentage of GDP and total general government revenue

2009-16

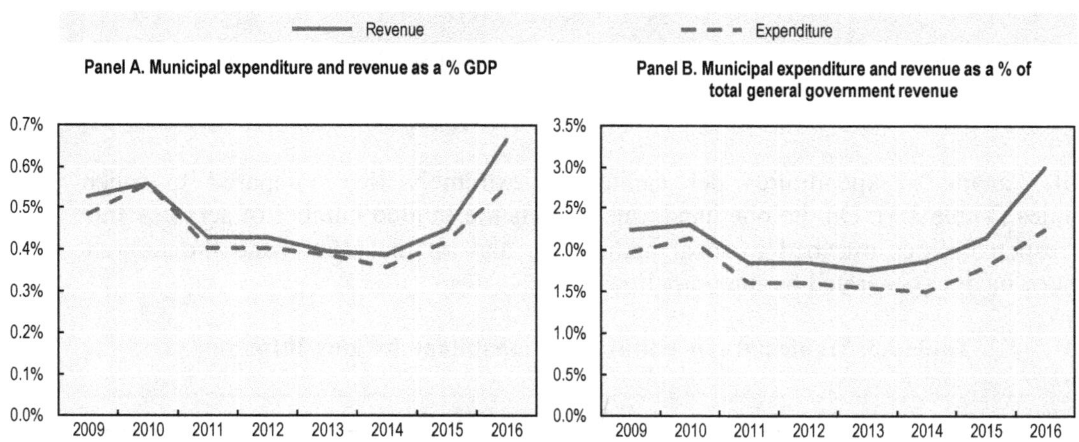

Source: OECD calculations from Contraloría General de la República – Dirección General de Fiscalización, Municipalidades de la República y Ministerio de Economía y Finanzas Dirección de Presupuesto de la Nación (DIPRENA).

StatLink http://dx.doi.org/10.1787/888933777167

Despite these positive shifts in municipal financing, municipal expenditure is unevenly distributed across municipalities. For example, municipalities in the province of Panamá were responsible for 62% of all municipal expenditure in 2016, underscoring large differences in the ability of local authorities to deliver quality public services and effectively administer a municipality. Disparities are also evidenced by municipal expenditure per capita, which in 2016 ranged from an average of PAB[3] 14 in the communities of Ngäbe Buglé to an average of PAB 112 in those located in the province of Panamá (Figure 3.4).

Figure 3.4. Per capita municipal revenues and expenditures, 2016 (USD)

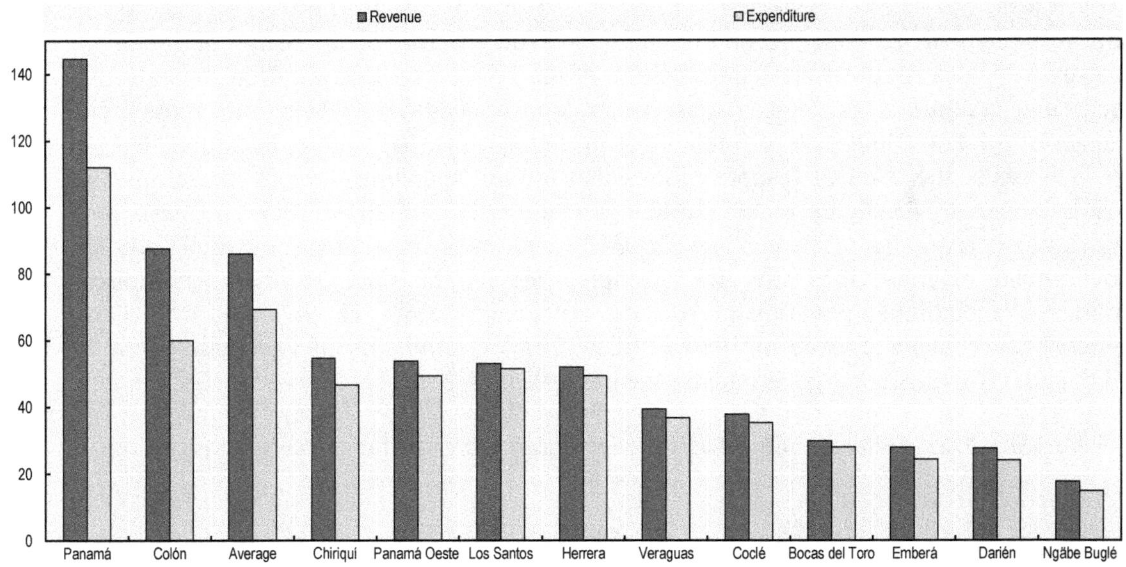

Source: OECD calculations based on data from Contraloría General de la República –DIPRENA.

StatLink http://dx.doi.org/10.1787/888933777186

Overall, Panama's expenditures per capita are extremely low compared to other economies (Table 3.3). On the one hand, this reflects the limited number of services and other responsibilities ascribed to local authorities, and on the other hand the limited amount of income generated by municipalities.

Table 3.3. Municipal expenditures per inhabitant are low, 2016

Country	Municipal expenditures		
	per inhabitant (USD)	as % GDP	As % general government expenditure
Panama	70	0.5%	2.2%
Chile	648	3.0%	13.0%
Greece	894	3.3%	6.7%
Turkey	706	4.0%	11.0%

Note: PAB 1 = USD 1.
Sources: OECD calculations based on data from Contraloría General de la República – DIPRENA; OECD (2017c), "Subnational governments in OECD countries: Key data" (brochure), www.oecd.org/regional/regional-policy (database: http://dx.doi.org/10.1787/region-data-en).

Of importance to regional – and local – development is the ability for subnational governments, including municipalities to invest. In 2016, 11.6% of municipal expenditure, on average, was dedicated to direct investment in infrastructure and large facilities. This is a level close to the OECD average (11.2%). This ability among Panamanian municipalities is relatively new, as in 2012 and 2015 direct investment accounted for only 4% and 6% of their expenditure, respectively. There are, however, large disparities across municipalities. In three provinces (Herrera, Bocas del Toro, Darién) and one *comarca* (Emberá), direct investment represented less than 1% of municipal expenditure in 2016 (Figure 3.5, Panel A). In the same year, among the municipalities located in Panamá province direct investment represented 15% of municipal expenditure and overall accounted for 88% of total municipal direct investment (Figure 3.5, Panel B). It should be remembered, however, that the share of municipalities in total public direct investment remains extremely low – 1.6% compared to the OECD average of 59.3% (Contraloría General de la República, 2018). Overall, municipal investment is very low, and concentrated mainly in Panama City.

Figure 3.5. Investment at the provincial level (2016)

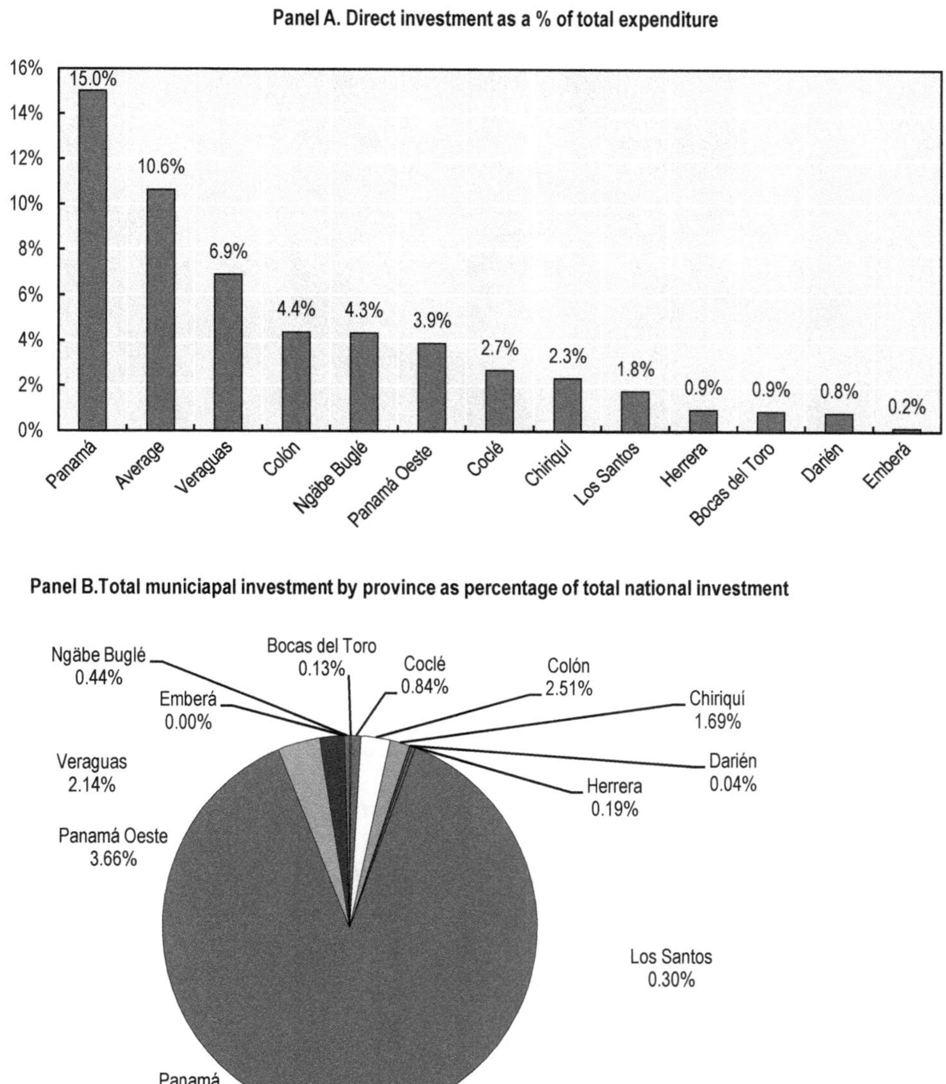

Source: OECD calculations based on data from Contraloría General de la República –DIPRENA.

StatLink http://dx.doi.org/10.1787/888933777205

On the revenue side, taxes are the main source of municipal income. While since 2014, and especially 2015, municipal revenue has been increasing as a percentage of GDP and total general government revenue (Figure 3.4), taxes have decreased as a share of municipal revenue since 2015 when municipalities started to receive grants linked to the decentralisation reform (Figure 3.5). The result is a significant increase in the weight of grants, and especially current grants, in municipal budgets. On the one hand, this can mean that the proportion of municipal budgets generated by taxes and other own-revenue sources is declining, thereby limiting fiscal autonomy. Central government transfers are often linked to specific uses, while own-source revenue can be used at municipal discretion and is associated with greater spending autonomy. On the other hand, it also means a more diversified and, in this case, balanced financing system for local authorities.

Figure 3.6. Changes in municipal revenue 2012-2106

% of total municipal revenue

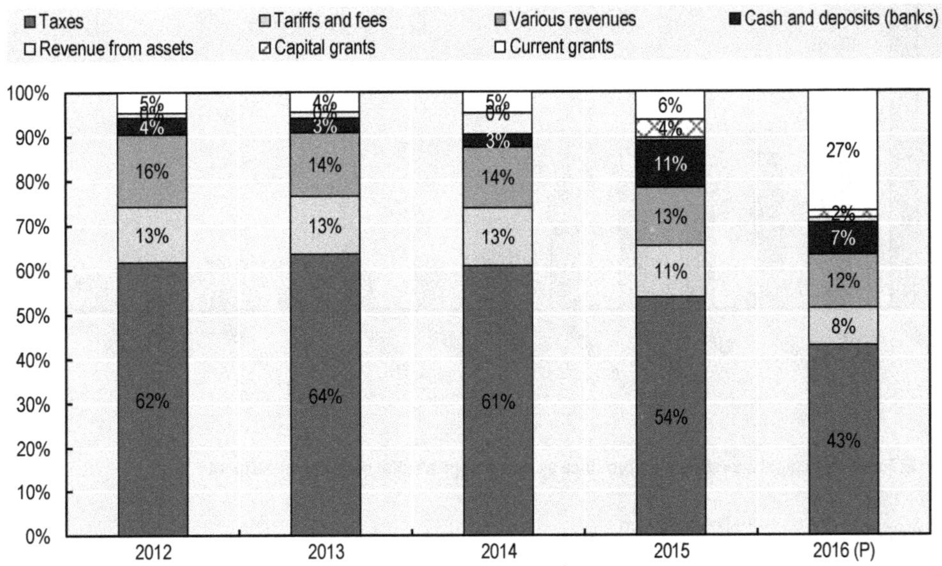

Note: 2016 figures are projected.
Source: OECD calculations from Contraloría General de la República –DIPRENA.

StatLink http://dx.doi.org/10.1787/888933777224

In addition to disparities among municipalities in terms of expenditure levels, there are also disparities in terms of revenue generation (Figure 3.6). For instance, while in Ngäbe Buglé only 7% of municipal revenues came from taxes, in Bocas del Toro, taxes represented 69% of municipal revenues. Meanwhile, grants contributed only 2% to the revenues of Panamá Oeste's municipalities, but 67% to the communities of Ngäbe Buglé. This can signal a significant discrepancy in the capacity to raise revenue, and also indicates highly different degrees of dependence on central government support.

The province of Panamá and its municipalities are the leading generators of municipal revenues – accounting for 65% of total municipal revenue in 2016. They also received 77% of all central government transfers, and accounted for 59% of municipal tax revenue in 2016. This creates a territorial disparity in terms of financial resources that can be translated in differences regarding the quality of public services provided.

Figure 3.7. Municipal revenue by category in 2016 (%, provincial level)

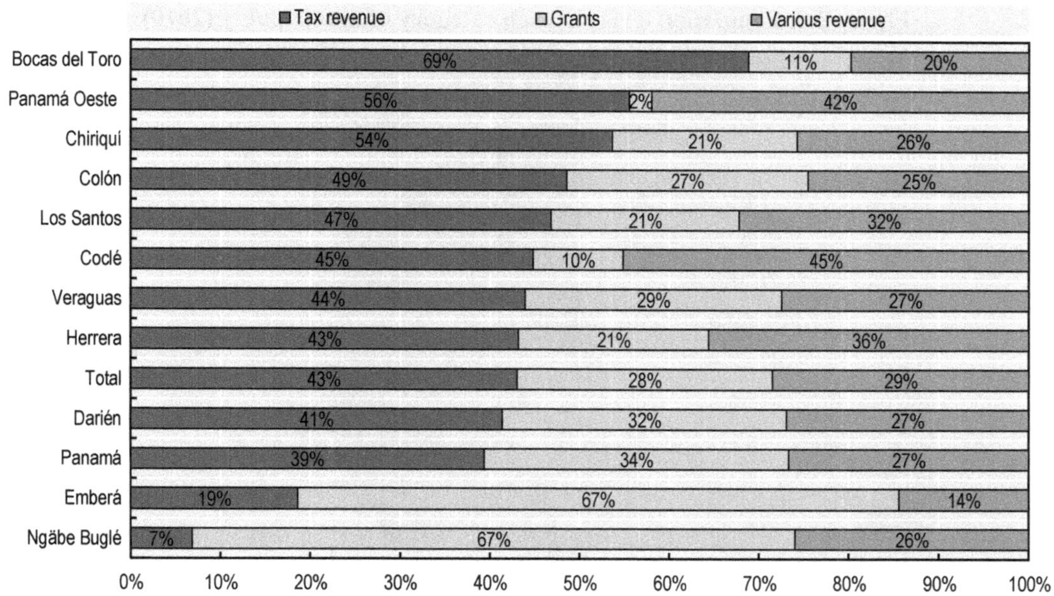

Source: OECD calculations from Contraloría General de la República –DIPRENA.

StatLink http://dx.doi.org/10.1787/888933777243

Municipal administrative and management capacity is constrained

As autonomous entities able to generate own source revenue, local authorities are expected to cover their operating and administrative costs, as well as deliver services and invest in development. However, this does not appear to be the case for the majority. It is currently estimated that 77% of Panama's municipalities are receiving state subventions for operating and administrative costs. In some provinces all or all but one municipality require support from the central government (AMUPA, unpublished). This challenge can be linked to various factors including size (population and territory) and demographic makeup – those with higher levels of poverty, and/or a lower percentage of an active population in the formal labour market – will have greater difficulty generating sufficient resources to meet their operational costs.

A population imbalance across municipalities can further impact disparities in municipal capacity, including in management and administration, service delivery and development planning. While municipal (administrative) fragmentation appears to be limited in Panama, population levels are not evenly spread across the territory, and thus there is a certain degree of imbalance.[4] This is reflected, at least in part, by the discrepancies in revenue and expenditure between Panama (city and province) and other parts of the country.

Panama's system of municipal classification may be compounding territorial disparities at the local level and contributing to resource challenges. Panama's four-category classification of municipalities[5], identifies the bulk of municipalities as semi-urban (51 in total), with an additional 10 being rural, 15 urban, and two metropolitan (Figure 3.7). However, this system may not reflect each territory's actual economic and social dynamic, which can undermine the ability to develop territorially appropriate policies and plans, and to identify the actual costs of service delivery as well as opportunities for revenue generation. A functional area analysis often more accurately captures the economic, social and connectivity factors contributing to a territory's productivity.

Figure 3.8. Population levels in each category of municipality (2010)

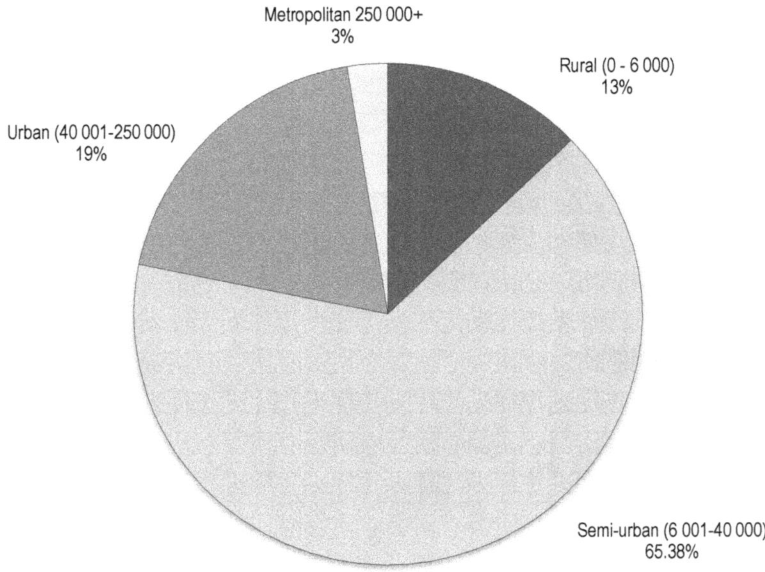

Note: Data from 2010, last official census.
Source: Authors' calculations based on data from Controlaría del Gobierno de Panamá (2010), "Boletín 16: Estimaciones y Proyecciones de la Población Total del País, por Provincia, Comarca Indígena, Distrito y Corregimiento, según sexo y edad: años 2010-2020", Instituto Nacional de Estadística y Censo, Panamá, Panama, available at:
https://www.contraloria.gob.pa/inec/Publicaciones/Publicaciones.aspx?ID_SUBCATEGORIA=10&ID_PUBLICACION=556&ID_IDIOMA=1&ID_CATEGORIA=3.

StatLink http://dx.doi.org/10.1787/888933777262

The classification system raises two concerns with respect to regional development. First is the large percentage of rural plus semi-urban municipalities (79%). This can exacerbate intermunicipal and interregional disparities based on revenue generation capacity, and affects capacity and outcomes in municipal delivery. In addition, if one considers the differences in minimum wage paid in urban versus rural municipalities, the system may be supporting segregation between urban and rural communities (see Chapter 2). Ultimately, this undermines greater inclusiveness.

The second concern is the subdivision of municipalities into smaller units, the *corregimientos*. Submunicipal administrative units are more frequent in countries with very populous municipalities, such as Ireland, Korea, Japan, New Zealand or the United Kingdom, where average municipal populations range from a low of almost 70 000 in New Zealand to a high of almost 223 000 in Korea (OECD, 2017c; OECD, 2017d). Panama certainly has populous municipalities. However, these are not the majority and *corregimientos* are characteristic of all municipalities, not just the larger ones. This can fragment municipal decision making, as each *corregimiento* has its own leadership. *Corregimientos* are represented on the municipal council as well as on the provincial council (*Consejo Provincial*), giving them a fair amount of representative power. This is not negative but the co-ordination mechanisms within municipalities need to be sufficiently strong to ensure adequate and effective prioritisation and decision making across the municipal territory.

Municipal administrative and management capacity is also challenged by human resource limitations. This is evidenced first by the number of inhabitants per municipal staff – on average there are 420 people per civil servant. However, as with financial capacity, there are significant disparities – ranging from a ratio of 73:1 in Taboga to 1 370:1 in La Pintada (Figure 3.8). Low staffing levels could reflect the limited tasks assigned to municipalities, of the difficulties to meet administrative costs which then limits hiring, and also of a skills gap, i.e. an inability to recruit staff with the necessary skills.

Figure 3.9. Number of inhabitants per municipal staff member, 2013

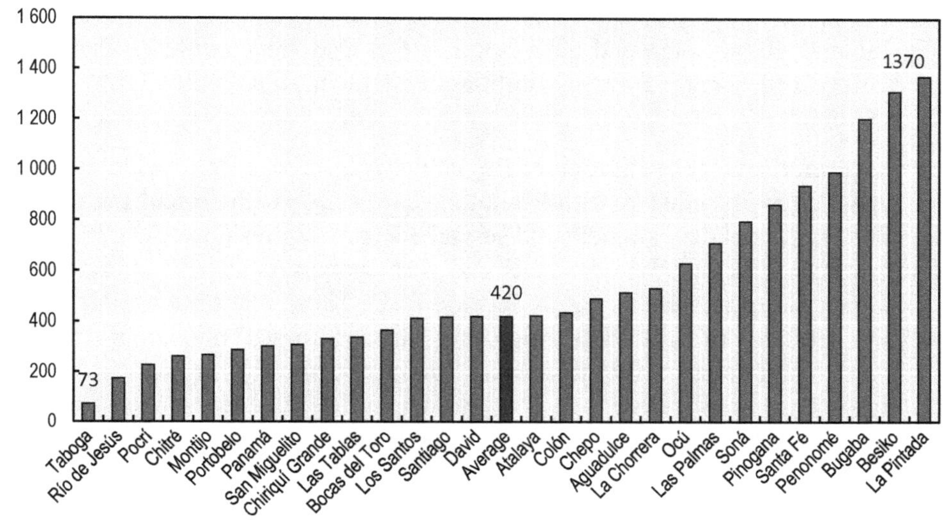

Note: For reasons of legibility, this figure is limited to a representative sample of municipalities and provincial capitals.
Source: OECD calculations based on data from the national statistics office.

StatLink http://dx.doi.org/10.1787/888933777281

Sufficient financial capacity is needed to guarantee the high skills of public servants. The law on decentralisation (discussed below) stipulates that all municipalities must employ a municipal engineer, a legal advisor, an administrator, a planner, a person responsible for citizen services, and a person responsible for municipal services. This should address some specific capacity issues. However, it may not be enough if the quantity and variety of responsibilities increase with the advancement of the decentralisation process. Thus, sufficient financial capacity will be fundamental to ensure that remuneration levels are appropriate to recruit subnational public servants with the right skills and experience.

Panama's Law on Decentralisation

Decentralisation is a tool that contributes to realising national and subnational government objectives by transferring a range of powers, responsibilities and resources from central government to elected subnational governments in three interconnected areas (OECD, 2017d):

1. Political decentralisation: involves a new distribution of powers (including how subnational administrators are selected) with the objective of strengthening democratic legitimacy.

2. Administrative decentralisation: involves a reorganisation and clear assignment of tasks and functions between territorial levels to improve the effectiveness, efficiency and transparency of national territorial administration.
3. Fiscal decentralisation: involves delegating taxing and spending responsibilities to subnational tiers of government. The degree of decentralisation depends on both the amount of resources delegated and the autonomy in managing such resources (e.g. decisions on tax bases, tax rates and the allocation of spending).

Decentralisation can more actively involve subnational authorities in the development of their territories, while also building accountability for performance, quality and results. In addition to the "traditional" reasons for introducing decentralisation[6], some countries, such as Chile and Mexico, use decentralisation reforms to fight against poverty and large territorial disparities, or to preserve historical, linguistic and cultural specificities (e.g. in Belgium, Finland, Italy, Spain and the UK). There is also some evidence that countries with more devolved spending responsibilities tend to have a higher GDP per capita (OECD, 2017d).

Panama's Law on the Decentralisation of the Public Administration (the Decentralisation Law) as amended is intended to build municipal capacity so that local authorities can better assume municipal development and service responsibilities (Box 3.3). It establishes the administrative structure for *comarcas* and local governments. In addition, the law requires municipalities and *comarcas* to develop PED. These plans are to link directly to the relevant sections of the PEG. The law also increases municipal funding by establishing two municipal level investment funds and foresees a gradual transfer of responsibilities once it is determined that municipalities have been accredited by the Secretariat for Decentralisation and show they have the capacity to meet such responsibilities.

Box 3.3. Panama's Laws on the Decentralisation of the Public Administration

Law No. 37 of 2009 on the Decentralisation of the Public Administration (Ley No. 37 Que Descentraliza la Administración Pública) was introduced in 2009. It defines the principles and objectives of decentralisation and local governance, establishes categories of municipalities according to population and density, foresees a development planning hierarchy, classifies, defines and lists the responsibilities to be delegated to local authorities, and establishes a multistakeholder, autonomous government entity to oversee the process. It takes a gradualist approach to decentralisation, permitting the transfer of competences to local authorities once their competence has been accredited, and they have completed an application process. This law was suspended by the subsequent government before it was fully implemented.

In 2015, Law No. 66 was passed, updating and amending the original legislation. Law No. 66 maintains the gradualist approach and the concept of accreditation before assignment of responsibilities. However, it amends the original law (Law No. 37) with the objective of improving local investment capacity by supporting the Ministry of Economy and Finance's capacity to collect property and real estate tax, create an intermunicipal solidarity fund, target investment funding, improve citizen participation and transparency and promote local development and land-use planning. In addition, Law No. 66 stipulates the responsibilities that can be attributed to municipalities funded by resources from the collection of the property and real estate tax. Broadly these include:

maintenance and improvement of education, healthcare, recreation, and sports facilities; basic public services to homes (e.g. aqueducts, street lighting, waste management and recycling services); infrastructure for public safety; construction and maintenance of social service facilities; construction and maintenance of infrastructure for tourism and culture; construction and maintenance of infrastructure for socio-economic development (e.g. urban and public infrastructure, water landings, municipal markets, infrastructure for municipal microenterprises, and support for the agricultural sector).

Sources: República de Panamá (2009), Ley No. 37 Que Descentraliza la Administración Pública, República de Panamá, Gaceta Oficial Digital, Panama, available at: http://www.organojudicial.gob.pa/cendoj/wp-content/blogs.dir/cendoj/ADMINISTRATIVO/ley_37_de_2009_que_descentraliza_la_administracion_publica.pdf; República de Panamá (2015), Ley No. 66, Que Reforma la Ley 37 Que Descentraliza la Administración Pública, República de Panamá, Gaceta Oficial Digital, Panama, available at: https://www.gacetaoficial.gob.pa/pdfTemp/27901_A/GacetaNo_27901a_20151030.pdf.

Panama's decentralisation process is just getting started. However, care will need to be taken that it does not fall short of its intentions in three critical ways.

First is the limited extent of fiscal autonomy it appears to offer. The financial capacity component of the reform provides municipalities with two investment-financing sources. The first fund derives from the property and real estate tax. Of the funds transferred into this investment budget by the central government, urban municipalities can use 90% for investment in hard infrastructure in areas outlined by the law (e.g. public works such as roads, lighting, water, electricity, etc.) and municipal services (see Box 3.3) and 10% for increasing their administrative budgets. All other classifications of municipalities can dedicate 75% of the funds for investment in hard infrastructure and 25% for administrative capacity (República de Panamá, 2015). The intention of this fund is twofold. First it aims to give municipalities more opportunity to finance development projects, particularly in infrastructure; and second it is a way to support local authorities which have had difficulty covering their operating and administrative costs in the past. This increase in funding is welcome and it appears to be having some effect on local revenues, as discussed above. It could be made even stronger if it were accompanied by greater spending autonomy by local governments. As it now stands, local authorities are limited in how the development funds are spent, and they have no ability to increase the property or real estate tax rate to grow the fund. The second investment fund is an equalisation mechanism, the Solidarity Fund – *Fondo de Solidaridad* – which can be used to finance service and "soft-infrastructure" projects and programmes. It is a common pool fund with a redistribution formula, part of which is based on population. There is general agreement that this fund needs to be reformed. The Public Works and Municipal Services programme (*Programa de Obras Públicas y de Servicios Municipales)* transfers USD 110 000 to each *junta comunal* (the representative body of each *corregimiento*), of which 70% can be used for investment projects (subject to citizen consultation) and the remaining sum can be dedicated to administrative or operational functions (República de Panamá, 2015). Certainly the introduction of these funds is a large shift from the past when priorities and spending were centrally managed. However, the funds are in essence central level transfers and not a delegation of fiscal responsibilities. Thus, fiscal decentralisation through the law is limited.

Second, administrative decentralisation requires further clarification in the criteria of selection, funding and transfer of responsibilities. Service and administrative responsibilities will be delegated to accredited municipalities that have proven capacity to manage their investment funds based on their investments and results achieved. Accreditation requires a completed PED, and each municipality must apply to receive delegated responsibilities. It is expected that in 2018 the Secretariat for Decentralisation will begin the process of determining municipal capacity, classifying municipalities according to ability, and then identifying which responsibilities will be transferred. It is a form of asymmetric decentralisation which can be successful for ensuring improved service delivery by municipalities. However, there is a need to clarify: a) the criteria that will be used to determine capacity and/or eligibility for the responsibilities; b) how municipal classifications will be matched to responsibilities – will responsibilities be grouped into sets, or will it be a pick–and-choose approach; c) how the new responsibilities will be funded, if through a central level transfer or through greater revenue-generating capacity at the local level; and d) how to ensure a balanced transfer of responsibilities across the territory and across sectors. There is a risk of generating incoherence in the degree of decentralisation and even greater subnational inequality, particularly if smaller municipalities do not have the capacity to take on additional responsibilities.

Third, the success of decentralisation may depend on addressing municipal capacity. There is a resource gap at the local level. In some countries this is due to scale and excessive fragmentation (too many small municipalities). In other cases it is due to limited municipal revenues. In Panama, only a very small percentage of municipalities have less than 5 000 inhabitants (Figure 3.9), and so the problem is more likely to be due either to the cost of service delivery or to low revenue-generating capacity rather than fragmentation. Given the limited service responsibilities attributed to municipalities, the former is not likely to be a significant factor. The latter, low revenue-generating capacity, however, is highly probable. Diverse factors can contribute to the resources shortfall, including the high levels of labour force informality, which then impacts tax revenue (see Chapter 4). However, for such a reform to be successful subnational authorities must have the administrative capacity and revenue-generating base to meet the responsibilities which they are assigned. While the current decentralisation law provides them with additional funds in the form of transfers, it does not necessarily solve the problem in the long run because it is not increasing their capacity to meet cost obligations, by either reducing expenditures or increasing revenues.

It is still too early to determine if the decentralisation law will lead to a more decentralised approach and, through this, will better support regional development at the local level. Its success will rest on, among other things, the capacity of municipalities to manage their revenues in light of new expenditure responsibilities (e.g. generate more revenue or reduce costs), the responsibilities that are transferred down, and the degree of autonomy local authorities have with respect to municipal management, prioritising investment, delivering services and using their resources. Panama may wish to consider the guidelines for effective decentralisation that the OECD has developed as these can help governments identify where and how they can strengthen their approach to decentralisation (e.g. through a clear, coherent and balanced decentralisation process, sufficient subnational capacity, adequate co-ordination mechanism and room for pilots or experimentation) (Annex C).

Figure 3.10. Municipal population levels by number of inhabitants

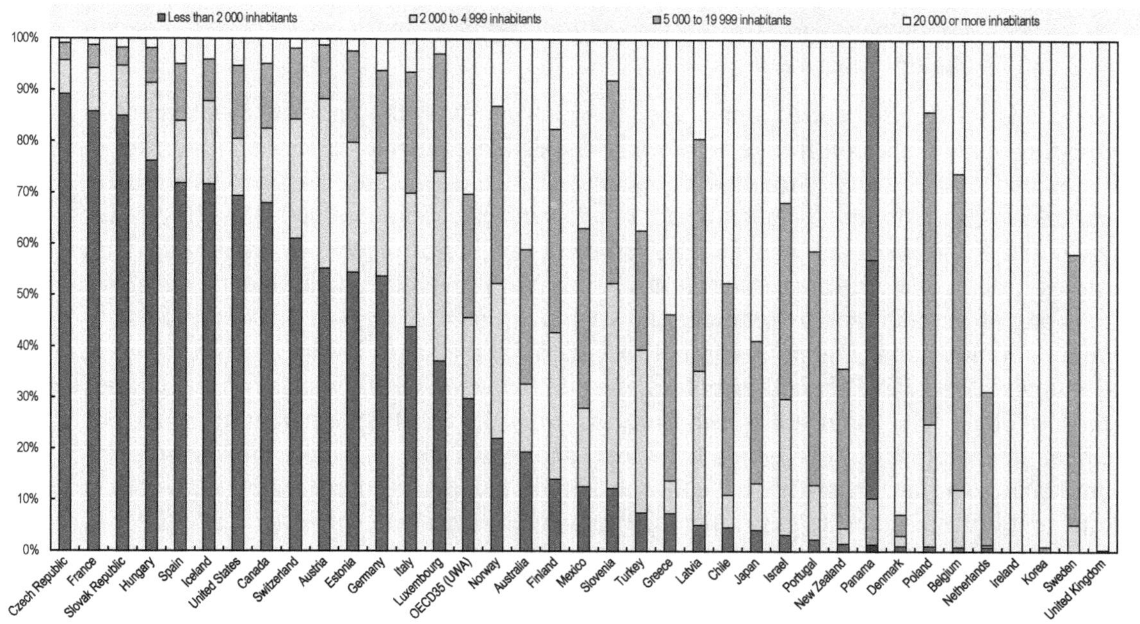

Note: Data for Panama comes from 2010 census.
Source: Controlaría General de la República de Panamá (2010), https://www.contraloria.gob.pa/inec/Publicaciones/Publicaciones.aspx?ID_SUBCATEGORIA=10&ID_PUBLICACION=556&ID_IDIOMA=1&ID_CATEGORIA=3; OECD (2017c), "Subnational governments in OECD countries: Key data" (brochure), www.oecd.org/regional/regional-policy (database: http://dx.doi.org/10.1787/region-data-en).

StatLink http://dx.doi.org/10.1787/888933777300

Taking a "new paradigm" approach to regional development

There are several forces affecting Panama's capacity for more inclusive territorial development. The first is strong socio-spatial segregation at the regional level that separates non-indigenous and indigenous, as well as urban and rural communities. This is mirrored by socio-economic segregation at the local level, particularly within large urban and metropolitan areas. Socio-spatial segregation, particularly of residences, by ethnicity, class or race, combined with an uneven spatial distribution of quality public services, results in limited opportunity for a percentage of the population (Greenstein et al., 2000). While this is particularly true in cities, it is certainly applicable to regions as well. Addressing this, requires strongly integrated activity across ministries and levels of government to build programmes and design service delivery that can begin to break down the barriers (horizontal co-ordination), and a clear policy path outlined in a national level document dedicated to regional development and supported by subnational (provincial and *comarca*) plans (vertical co-ordination).

The second is a policy of wealth redistribution based mainly on social transfers. Although they are well targeted, territorial differences in Panama's wellbeing outcomes remain high (OECD, 2017a). Some consideration should be given to how to increase the sustainability of regions and communities so that such transfers are less necessary. There is a strong need for subnational governments to be able to generate wealth, and ideally manage at least some of it. This is closely linked to making sure the provinces, *comarcas*, cities and other categories of local communities are attractive places to live and offer opportunities for employment, which itself is linked to subnational development. The risk with Panama's approach, particularly over the long term, is that it does not help lagging regions adjust their productive capacities.

The third is insufficient subnational capacity to partner with the national government in addressing social cohesion from a territorial perspective. Panama's approach to territorial development has been "top-down", expressed through successive government programmes, and driven by social and other transfers. This has left little room for subnational – and especially local – governments to build experience in dealing with complex policy matters in a "bottom-up" fashion. Provincial governments do so as extensions of the national government and its line ministries, *comarca* governments are semi-autonomous and thus not expected to undertake the same initiatives as provinces, and municipalities have limited resources, despite being where the impact of inequalities is most strongly felt. The result is a capacity gap at all levels of government in the area of regional development. This being the case, and given the principle of subsidiarity, subnational governments should have the capacity in terms of resources (financial, human capital and infrastructure) to play a stronger role in development of their territories.

Panama's approach to regional development has focused on addressing economic disparities through subsidies and state aid transferred by the central government to provinces and *comarcas*, as well as redistributive policies and the funding of sector-driven projects. Given the socio-economic challenges, Panama may wish to consider shifting away from its traditional approach toward the "new paradigm" highlighted at the beginning of this chapter. From a strategic perspective, a "new paradigm" approach could help subnational authorities (e.g. provinces, *comarcas*, metropolitan areas) maximise their capacity to improve wellbeing outcomes. It can offer a more sustainable approach, and has the advantage of allowing greater flexibility in addressing and harnessing the unique opportunities offered by Panama's different provinces and *comarcas*. It would mean, however, developing an explicit regional development policy at the national level, taking an integrated approach to policy and programming, developing effective performance measurement systems to generate accountability by government to citizens, and building stronger partnerships with subnational governments and other stakeholders to collectively identify unique competitiveness factors and capitalise on local assets.

A national regional development policy to improve co-ordination across different levels of governments

An explicit national-level policy for sustainable regional development and growth would be beneficial in Panama as it could clearly articulate national territorial objectives and priorities, and build vertical co-ordination and co-operation mechanisms between relevant stakeholders across different levels of government. It could also engender greater coherence in the implementation of sector strategies and support policy and programming prioritisation at the subnational level. A policy of this kind can guide actors with diverse interests on how to proceed, while reinforcing and clarifying accountability of input and of results. Its success, however, depends on clear strategic direction on the part of the central government, as well as strong bottom-up involvement in order to build ownership between central and subnational authorities, the private sector, civil society organisations, and citizens (Cuadrado-Roura and Güell, 2008).

A general strategic framework for regional development is based on a clear hierarchy, in which each tier cascades down from the one above (Figure 3.10). The first tier sets the vision and should transcend political parties and election cycles, reflecting societal aspirations for the country. Tier 2 provides the roadmap for realising the larger ambitions, and finally the Tier 3 offers the practical dimension of implementation. In Panama, and specifically with respect to regional development, Tier 1 could correspond to a vision for a more inclusive society, supported by a national regional development policy with clearly articulated objectives (Tier 2), including, for example, poverty reduction among indigenous communities and rural areas, and realised through Tier 3 sector and subnational policies, programmes and projects that contribute to reducing poverty (e.g. healthcare, education, economy, labour, housing, public works).

Figure 3.11. The policy cascade: a schematic using a vision based on inclusiveness

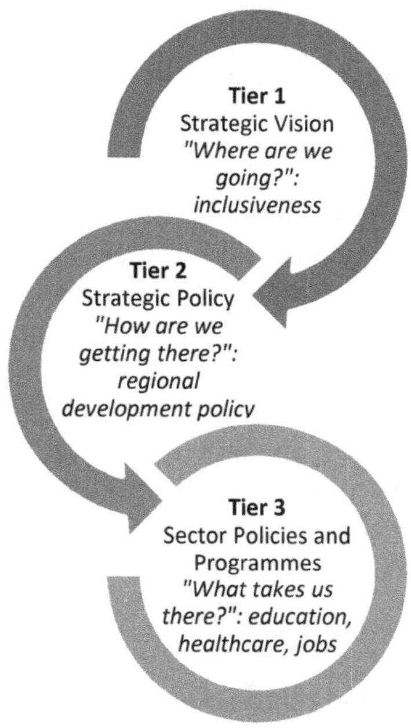

Source: Adapted from OECD (2016f), *OECD Territorial Reviews: Córdoba, Argentina,* OECD Publishing, Paris, http://dx.doi.org/10.1787/9789264262201-en.

A formalised national regional development policy would be valuable for supporting development goals, and for guiding relevant policy development and implementation among line ministries in the short and medium terms. One of the obstacles in Panama's policy process, however, is a lack of technical capacity. Strengthening technical capabilities within ministries is on the government's agenda and could improve planning and evaluation. To do so, however, additional in-work training is important, as well as building the professionalisation of Panama's civil service through a more stringent and transparent admission process (OECD, 2017a).

Approaches to formalising regional development in selected countries

The formalisation of regional development strategies varies across countries. Some countries develop explicit long- or medium-term strategic documents (e.g. Ireland and Sweden), while others, such as Mexico, create a specific plan linked to the government programme, and still others use intergovernmental contracts (e.g. France and Colombia) (Box 3.4). Regardless of the approach, the majority of OECD countries, including the Czech Republic, Estonia, Iceland, Ireland, Italy, New Zealand, Norway and Switzerland, follow an explicit regional development strategy defined in one or several documents. Those that do not have an overarching strategic policy include federal countries (e.g. Belgium, Germany and the United States). On average, countries have two strategic documents – in some cases a legal framework complemented by a more regularly updated plan (e.g. seven years is common in European Union (EU) countries to correspond with the EU policy cycle). This permits them to strike a balance between policy stability over time and flexibility to adapt to changing circumstances (OECD, 2016a). In all cases, however, formalised strategies and/or policies help co-ordinate the diverse interests involved in regional development. In addition, they can provide some guidance for dedicated urban and rural development policies.

Box 3.4. Formalising regional development strategies: examples from select countries

Long- and medium-term regional development strategies: Ireland and Sweden

The National Spatial Strategy for Ireland 2002-2020 was developed to guide more balanced regional development. It aims to improve the spread of job opportunities throughout the country, improve the quality of life, and improve the places where people live. It examines the country's economic and spatial structure, identifies how the various regions can contribute to realising the strategy's objectives, and takes an integrated approach by indicating the role that policies promoting economic development (e.g. employment, tourism), housing, quality of life (e.g. social infrastructure, service delivery, urbanism), and the environment play in building and ensuring competitive regions. It also includes guidelines on implementation, clearly designating a ministry responsible for co-ordinating the plan's implementation, setting an implementation time frame, and building ownership among subnational governments through the preparation and adoption of statutory regional planning guidelines.

Sweden's National Strategy for Sustainable Regional Growth and Attractiveness 2015-2020 serves as a guideline for regional authorities, state agencies, government offices, non-governmental organisations and other actors involved in regional growth efforts. The strategy aims to help actors prioritise regional-level activities, such as sectoral programming at the national level and regional-level development strategies. It is also used to support spending evaluations, specifically of national grants, and it monitors and steers the use of central government appropriations for regional growth measures. The strategy elaborates priorities for regional growth and how meeting these can help address societal challenges, and identifies policy tools for the strategy's implementation. The document also highlights the role of regions in meeting the strategy's objectives and the importance of subnational regional development strategies.

A dedicated regional development policy linked to the government programme: Mexico

Within the framework of its 2013-2018 National Development Plan, Mexico developed a Regional Development National Policy. It focuses on regional, urban and rural development, and includes infrastructure, competitiveness, social inclusion and environmental sustainability. The Ministry of Agrarian, Territorial and Urban Development complements the national policy with regional programmes for development covering to the north, south-southeast and central regions of the country, which are countersigned by 15 ministries.

A contractual approach to regional development: France and Colombia

France promotes its regional development and investment priorities through a series of planning contracts – *Contrats de Plan Etat-Région* – signed between the state and its regions on six- to seven-year cycles. In these planning contracts, the state and subnational authorities of all levels identify priorities and develop a common strategy to promote territorial competitiveness and attractiveness. In the current cycle, the six priority areas for investment are multimodal mobility; higher education, research and innovation; the environment and energy transition; digital technologies and very high-speed broadband; innovation, industries and factories of the future; and regions, with employment being the transversal priority linking the rest. In order to ensure equality between territories within regions, contracts mobilise specific resources for priority areas (i.e. urban priority neighbourhoods, vulnerable areas undergoing major economic restructuring, rural areas and others facing a deficit of public services, metropolitan areas and the Seine Valley).

Colombia has developed the *contratos plan* between the national government and departments to facilitate their interaction and to help deliver regional development policy. The *contrato plan* is a multiyear binding agreement between them and co-ordinates their investment agendas. Contracts focus on improving road connectivity, poverty reduction and support for regional competitiveness. The *contrato* allows departments and municipalities to co-ordinate different sources of revenues from different levels of government.

Sources: Republic of Ireland, *National Spatial Strategy for Ireland 2002-2020: People, Places and Potential*, Government of Ireland, Stationary Office, Dublin, Ireland, available at: http://nss.ie/pdfs/Completea.pdf; Sweden, Ministry of Enterprise and Innovation (n.d.), *National Strategy for Sustainable Regional Growth and Attractiveness, 2015-2020 – Short Version*, Government offices of Sweden, Ministry of Enterprise and Innovation, Stockholm, Sweden, available at: http://www.government.se/information-material/2016/04/swedens-national-strategy-for-sustainable-regional-growth-and-attractiveness-20152020---short-version/; OECD (2016a), *OECD Regional Outlook, 2016: Productive Regions for Inclusive Societies*, Country Notes, OECD Publishing, Paris, available at: http://www.oecd.org/regional/oecd-regional-outlook-2016-9789264260245-en.htm; France, Ministère de la Cohésion des Territoires (2015), *Les Contrats de Plan Etat-Région: Présentation Générale*, Ministère de la Cohésion des Territoires, Paris, France, available (in French) at: http://www.cohesion-territoires.gouv.fr/les-contrats-de-plan-etat-region; OECD (2016d), *Making the Most of Public Investment in Colombia: Working Effectively across Levels of Government*, OECD Multi-level Governance Studies, OECD Publishing, Paris, http://dx.doi.org/10.1787/9789264265288-en.

An overall regional development policy with a framework to support comarca *development*

Incorporating the *comarcas* as a strategic component to national development would be an important step toward addressing the challenges posed by socio-spatial segregation. However, as part of the policy's implementation, Panama may also wish to include a framework dedicated to the development of the *comarcas* to better work with and support the unique opportunities and complex challenges facing indigenous communities. Canada has taken this approach with its Federal Framework for Aboriginal Economic Development (Box 3.5). In addition, Canada's Department for Indigenous and Northern Affairs[7] explicitly links its sustainable development objectives with the federal sustainable development strategy through its departmental plan. This plan also articulates a series of performance indicators that either contribute to a goal or target or are specific programme activities that support sustainability outcomes, for example clean drinking water, effective action on climate change, sustainable food, and safe and healthy communities (Government of Canada, 2017).

Box 3.5. Canada's Federal Framework for Aboriginal Economic Development

Introduced in 2009, the Federal Framework for Aboriginal Economic Development is a roadmap for the government's actions and activities (i.e. legislation, partnerships and programmes) dedicated to increasing the participation of Canada's First Nations, Inuit and Métis people in the Canadian economy, and to improve economic action for indigenous peoples throughout the country. The Framework emphasises strategic partnerships with indigenous groups, the private sector, provinces and territories. The Framework seeks to maximise federal-level investment by: i) strengthening entrepreneurship; ii) enhancing the value of indigenous assets; iii) building new and effective partnerships to maximise economic development opportunities; iv) developing indigenous human capital; v) more effectively focusing on the role of the federal government. Its aim is to build indigenous communities that are able to seize economic development opportunities, to achieve viable indigenous businesses and that have a skilled indigenous workforce.

Through a process of extensive engagement with indigenous communities the Framework has been adjusted since its introduction to reduce administrative burdens and programme duplication. The result is a streamlined set of five programmes dedicated to increasing the participation of indigenous communities in Canada's economy and to help indigenous peoples pursue new opportunities for employment, income and wealth creation. To support this effort the government has integrated land management with economic development to facilitate support to communities as they build their economic base.

Sources: Government of Canada (2015), "Lands and Economic Development", Indigenous and Northern Affairs Canada, Ottawa, Canada, available at: www.aadnc-aandc.gc.ca; Government of Canada (2010), "Federal Framework for Aboriginal Economic Development", Indigenous and Northern Affairs Canada, Ottawa, Canada, available at: www.aadnc-aandc.gc.ca.

In 2013-14, Panama embarked on a similar path with an integrated development plan for indigenous communities (*Plan Nacional de Desarrollo Integral de Pueblos Indígenas de Panamá)*, articulated in conjunction with the UNDP. The plan was based on a dialogue process between Panama's indigenous communities, the government, the United Nations and the Catholic Church. The process called for establishing a National Council for the Development of Indigenous Communities in Panama (*Consejo Nacional de Desarrollo de los Pueblos Indígenas de Panamá),* which would oversee the Plan's implementation and be responsible for designing and implementing future economic, social and cultural development strategies for indigenous communities (UNDP, 2014). A draft law establishing the Council and its responsibilities, including the integrated development plan, was presented to the National Assembly but failed to garner sufficient votes to be approved. As of 2018, the government is revisiting this Plan and has established a timeline for launching its implementation. In addition, a USD 80 million loan from the World Bank was announced in March 2018, specifically for this initiative (World Bank, 2018). As a complement to this plan and in direct support of its objectives, Panama may wish to consider this idea of a territorial development strategy for *comarcas* as part of a larger regional development policy, which could also help embed the action across electoral cycles. This should be accomplished with the active involvement of the *comarcas* and supported in its realisation through *comarca* development plans elaborated at the community level.

Introducing regional development planning at the provincial and comarca level

There is a need to reconcile national and subnational level development priorities. While at the national level priorities may be highly "macro" (e.g. inclusiveness), at the subnational level they are imminently practical (e.g. sanitation, schools and healthcare). These two perspectives are not mutually exclusive but rather mutually supportive. To capture the potential synergies, a link needs to be made between government aims and subnational priorities. Without such links regional development risks remaining a series of sector and *ad hoc* programmes and projects at the national and local levels that may not be complementary and therefore have difficulty effectively contributing to meeting development objectives in a coherent and integrated fashion.

Intermediate level plans could help bridge Panama's goals and the immediate and highly practical development needs of subnational governments. Subnational regional development planning – including at the metropolitan level – can lead to greater responsibility being taken by the provinces and *comarcas*, particularly when the plans are designed, implemented and monitored at the subnational level and in dialogue with the central government. It would, however, require that each intermediate authority play an active role in identifying its development objectives and the mechanisms to realise them.

The capacity and capability challenges in planning seen at the central level are even more acute at the subnational level. Thus a focused effort on training and support for planning among subnational leaders would have to be made. Building the capacity among subnational officials to develop such plans, however, will be critical. This was the approach taken with the majority (73 of 77) of local authorities when developing their PED, for example. In these cases, the Direction for Investment Programming, through the Department for Regional Planning in the Ministry of Economy and Finance, developed a methodological guide and worked with local planners and in consultation with civil society and other stakeholders, to develop the PED. A similar approach could be taken if deciding to introduce regional-level development plans. In addition, consideration should be given to first developing a national-level policy which can subsequently be used to guide the design of subnational plans. This requires a region's perspective of its priorities, strengths and weaknesses, and combines both top-down and bottom-up elements in development planning.

In addition, consideration should be given to building financial capacity as well. Regional development policies, plans and programmes are stronger when associated with funding. For instance, a regional development fund could be established as a fixed line item in the national budget and then distributed on a formula-based allocation system. Another option would be to combine a formula-based budget with a national development fund. This would provide each province with its own budget, affording greater budget visibility and decision-making flexibility, and would shift away from the current system of earmarked grants transferred by individual line ministries to a block operating, service and investment grant. Uruguay has adopted this method for financing its provincial tier and promoting regional and local development (Box 3.6).

Box 3.6. Subnational financing mechanisms for development in Uruguay

Uruguay's constitution establishes that 3.33% of total annual government income be transferred to its departmental (provincial) governments. The system is constructed so that subnational governments share in the economic success of the country and in case of economic difficulties the risk of budget shortfalls is somewhat mitigated as provincial governments know they will be guaranteed a certain amount of funding. If a provincial government does not meet its performance agreement as established with the national government, it does not receive its full portion of the 3.33% set aside. Thus, not only is there a monitoring mechanism built into the system, but also an incentive for responsible fiscal management and performance.

The Interior Development Fund (*Fondo de Desarrollo del Interior*) is the second main source for subnational financing in Uruguay, and is also guaranteed by the constitution (article 298). All provinces (except Montevideo), receive a portion of this fund which is financed by national taxes collected outside of the capital. Of the total fund, two-thirds are used for implementing sectoral policies that support decentralisation and the remaining one-third goes to provincial governments to support projects co-financed with municipal own-source revenues.

Source: Michalun, M.V. (2018), *Diagnostico de Desarrollo Territorial de Uruguay,* Estudio no. 24, Serie: Analysis, Area: Descentralización, Programa EUROsociAL, Madrid, Spain

In some provinces, the gap in regional development planning at the intermediate level is being filled by the private sector through non-profit competitiveness centres (*Centros de Competetividad*). These function in a manner similar to regional development agencies, but they are directly sponsored by the private sector, rather than being funded by the government as is more commonly the case. By late 2017, four centres had been opened, including in a *comarca*, and the trend is expected to continue. They promote and bring together financing for projects in targeted and competitive areas such as agriculture, logistics, and tourism, combining private and public initiatives. These centres are also working with international financial institutions such as the Inter-American Development Bank and the Latin American Development Bank (*Banco de Desarrollo de America Latina*) to identify and implement development projects and to develop long-term development plans for their provinces (e.g. *Vision Chiriquí 2025*), and neighbourhood master plans including for those for modernisation.

The centres play a vital role in ensuring more dynamic territories and are positive contributors to their provinces. However, they also point to a gap in planning and planning capacity at the central and subnational level. In general, the private sector plays a fundamental role in regional development, for instance through investment, as well as in identifying and generating new areas for productive growth and innovation. However, it may be valuable to support regional development agencies in a private plus government partnership-based manner. This is an approach taken in Poland (Box 3.7). Polish regional development agencies were established in the early-to-mid-1990s, whose shareholders are the government of the region, and can include banks, regional institutions and regional or local enterprises. They launch initiatives to promote regional development, taking regionally differentiated approaches.

Box 3.7. Regional Development Agencies in Rzeszow and Torun, Poland

The Rzeszow Regional Development Agency supports improving the quality and standard of life for residents, and works to promote the region as a modern, innovative and economically developed area as well as a tourist destination. Its activities include training for entrepreneurs, managing EU-funded projects, co-ordinating a Technology Transfer Centre and managing an Enterprise Development Centre, among other things.

In Torun, the Agency for Regional Development (64% of which is owned by the regional government) aims to support small and medium enterprises and co-operate with local authorities and stakeholders in order to strengthen regional development. It prepares feasibility studies and business plans for investment projects, offers training, seminars, and conferences, and acts as a financing agency for EU programmes in the region. Among its primary activities are implementing EU structural funds, offering advisory services, and managing regional cluster projects. It is also the driver behind the Torun Technology Park which aims to attract investment and create favourable conditions for entrepreneurship.

Source: OECD (2018 – forthcoming), *Maintaining Momentum of Decentralisation in Ukraine's Decentralisation*, OECD Multi-level Governance Studies, OECD Publishing, Paris.

Using monitoring and measuring performance to track success and build accountability

Performance measurement systems, including indicator systems, policy and programme monitoring and evaluation, and spending reviews contribute to building government capacity in designing and implementing more effective policy, support evidence bases and evidence-based policy making, and help co-ordination efforts. They can also be powerful tools for building government accountability.

Panama can improve public policy evaluation, which affects accountability to citizens and results in less effective government spending (OECD, 2017a). In Panama's current frameworks, individual ministries, agencies or governments are responsible for provincial level performance measurement, establishing performance indicators, and programme reviews. It is reported, however, that this is not systematically practised, but it may be changing in some ministries. The Ministry of Education, for example, is undertaking an extensive reform of its provincial reporting practices that could help improve data collection, availability, and contribute to higher-quality evidence bases for policy making and monitoring. Municipal governments are responsible for their own monitoring and evaluation practice, but here too, there are limitations due to capacity, which is not uncommon.

Performance measurement and indicator systems for regional development

Building indicator systems for regional development and investment could be a step forward in evaluating policies and measuring progress. Performance indicators can address information asymmetries that arise between levels of government or between government and stakeholders, including citizens. They are also effective tools for reinforcing accountability at all levels of government by improving transparency. When carefully coupled with specific incentive mechanisms and realistic targets, indicators can stimulate and focus actors' efforts in critical areas. Consequently, they help focus on priorities, and promote capacity development and good management practices (Mizell, 2008).

When developing indicators, it is important to get as much input from all relevant stakeholders as possible. This is especially true if policy success depends on the participation of multiple actors with complex relationships and divergent interests. There are a diversity of monitoring practices among OECD countries, but most often they are applied at the national, regional and metropolitan levels (Box 3.8). The OECD is also developing a series of multilevel governance indicators of the use of formal co-ordination mechanisms specifically with respect to public investment, allowing for a comparison among countries (OECD, 2016d).

Box 3.8. Examples of indicator systems for the national, provincial and local levels

In **Chile**, the National System of Municipal Indicators provides over 150 standardised indicators for each of the municipalities in Chile. This initiative introduced by the Subsecretaria de Desarrollo Regional y Administrativo (SUBDERE) offers accessible information to the general public. Its data make it possible to compare the performance of all Chilean municipalities and help different stakeholders to make informed decisions. The system offers information dating from 2001 onward.

In 2000, the Province of Ontario, Canada, introduced the Municipal Performance Measurement Program (MPMP) as an accountability mechanism and to help local authorities make more informed decisions; and its use became mandatory in 2001. Ontario's 444 municipalities – regardless of their size – are all responsible for reporting on 12 core service areas, resulting in 54 measures of efficiency and effectiveness. The MPMP has not only improved reporting, it has also given provincial and local authorities a solid database of information, supporting multiyear trend analysis and budgeting processes. Municipalities report performance data annually.

New York City's strategic development plan – OneNYC – is supported by a series of performance indicators aligned with the city's four-pronged strategic vision. Each one clearly states the indicator, the performance target and data for the most recent year as a baseline. For example, "sustainable city" objectives are supported by a goal to improve air quality, which in turn has three indicators and associated targets. Details regarding the lead agency responsible for accomplishing each initiative, funding status and source are also available. Citizens can find information on how the city is performing with respect to its stated goals, make comments, and download reports.

Sources: OECD (2009), *OECD Territorial Reviews: Chile 2009*, OECD Publishing, Paris, http://dx.doi.org/10.1787/9789264060791-en; OECD (2010X), *OECD Territorial Reviews: Sweden 2010*, OECD Publishing, Paris, http://dx.doi.org/10.1787/9789264081888-en; Buckstein, J. (2009), "Municipal Performance Indicators are gaining in stature and efficiency across Canada", *CGA Magazine*, Chartered Professional Accountants, Canada, Ottawa, Canada, accessed: 15 April 2016, available at: www.cga-canada.org/enca/AboutCGACanada/CGAMagazine/2009/May-Jun/Pages/ca_2009_05-06_bsin_feature.aspx; Government of Ontario (2015), "Municipal Performance Measures", Ministry of Municipal Affairs and Housing, Government of Ontario, Ontario, Canada, accessed: 15 April 2016, available at: www.mah.gov.on.ca/Page297.aspx; City of New York (n.d.), *One New York: The Plan for a Strong and Just City*, City of New York.

As an ongoing activity and when effectively communicated, performance measurement mechanisms, and particularly indicator sets, can show citizens how government is meeting its stated objectives, how it is using its resources, and how its policies are performing. While acknowledging their value, many governments are challenged to establish effective performance measurement systems, in part due to difficulty in building meaningful indicators. Among the obstacles they encounter are the lack of a strategic objective; organisational cultures which inhibit broad-based co-ordination and building ownership; insufficient appreciation of the relationship and links between strategies, policies, targets, outputs and outcomes; policies that are not clearly articulated; and indicators that are imprecise. Scotland's experience with performance measurement is a good example of how indicator systems support government policy making over time, and can be communicated in an easy, accessible way for citizens (Box 3.9).

Box 3.9. Government performance and development indicators in Scotland

In 2007, the Government of Scotland set out to streamline government resources and improve overall territorial performance. To do so, it aligned the government around five strategic objectives which established a series of national outcomes articulating what Scotland wished to achieve over the subsequent ten years. It then established a set of indicators that cut across many of the national outcomes, helping decision makers and policy designers identify policy complementarities, and helping citizens identify where progress could be made.

Performance in each indicator was easy to interpret as it was based on an arrow – up, down or horizontal – to indicate improvement, decline or no change over time. The importance and current status of each indicator was explained on the website, together with the indicator measure, what influenced change, the government's role, how Scotland was performing in the indicator over time, criteria for change, partners engaged in creating change, and any related strategic objective. Scotland constantly monitors its performance, updating its objectives and indicators accordingly.

Source: Adapted from The Scottish Government (2014), "Scotland Performs", www.scotland.gov.uk/About/Performance/scotPerforms.

Moving forward, Panama may need to consider formalising and communicating an indicator set for regional development. Establishing stronger evidence bases and setting targets for regional development activities would be critical first steps. If the development of a national regional development strategy is pursued, it is recommended to associate it with output and outcome indicators[8] that are realistic and measurable. This could also be applied at the municipal level, particularly among large cities and metropolitan areas, as illustrated in the boxes above. In all cases, desired outcomes should be widely communicated within government and to citizens in order to enhance transparency and accountability of government.

Enhancing institutional co-ordination to better support regional development

Ensuring sustainable growth and greater inclusiveness requires the concerted effort of a large array of ministries and agencies, as well as the co-operation of diverse subnational stakeholders – public and private. Results are likely to be stronger and more sustainable if the ministries work with each other to identify the policy links and sectoral synergies that need to be harnessed, and with communities to determine realistic implementation parameters to achieve better territorial outcomes. Success, therefore, depends on a co-ordinated approach among ministries with highly diverse portfolios and interests, and between national and subnational governments, not only in the planning stage, but at the implementation stage, as well.

There are good examples of interministerial co-ordination for promoting the government programme and its development agenda. The Ministry of Agriculture, for example, works with the Ministry of Social Development (*Ministerio de Desarrollo Social* – MIDES) for advancing rural development and reducing informality, and it works with *comarcas* to commercialise their products. MIDES has a number of successful programmes that depend on cross-sector, cross-agency involvement. For instance, its programme Plan Panama – Everyone's Country-Zero Poverty (*Plan Panamá – el País de Todos-Cero Pobreza*) depends on eight state institutions and a co-ordination secretariat. It is currently implemented in a number of regions and piloted in municipalities, and has ambitions to be nationwide. Another MIDES programme implemented at the regional level aims at improving productive development in agriculture and livestock, tourism, fishing, and crafts. It involves 15 state institutions, as well as local governments. One of the most extensive and formalised interministerial co-operation mechanisms is the *Gabinete Social* (Box 3.10). The Secretariat of the Presidency (*Secretaría de la Presidencia*) also plays a strong role in co-ordinating cross-sector and multistakeholder initiatives with a potential regional impact – for example a programme is underway with the Ministry of Labour and the International Labour Organisation to better support technical education. A variety of co-ordination tools are used to formalise interministerial agreements. At the presidential level these include Memoranda of Understanding and decrees. At the ministerial level, one-on-one agreements (*convenios)* between ministries are often used. MIDES has signed a series of such contracts, for example with the Secretariat for Decentralisation, the ministries of agriculture and of housing and land use, as well as with the tourism agency.

Box 3.10. Panama's *Gabinete Social*

Panama's *Gabinete Social* (Social Cabinet) is an unfunded, high-level interministerial body that co-ordinates programmes and projects focused on promoting social cohesion. Regulated by presidential decree, it is chaired by the Vice President, and includes the participation of eight ministries and a secretariat that is co-ordinated by MIDES.

Much of the *Gabinete*'s co-ordination work takes place at the institutional level, while it also supports programme implementation at the provincial and municipal levels. Consideration is being given to establishing provincial-level *gabinetes sociales* to facilitate a more integrated approach to programme implementation, and build greater social cohesion at the subnational level, particularly where there is a *Cero Pobreza* initiative underway.

Source: OECD interviews in Panama.

There appears to be no lack of co-ordination mechanisms or of interministerial interaction to advance sectoral development interests in support of the PEG. There are two points to consider, however. First, Panama's co-ordination approach for regional development is focused on horizontal interaction at the national level. Second, while mechanisms are well formalised, they are not firmly institutionalised. In other words, the co-ordination mechanisms work because of the government in place and its existing relationships, rather than because the co-ordinating body or mechanism has proven its value over time and through electoral cycles. This in turn may affect the sustainability of regional development.

A number of mechanisms that support a more co-ordinated approach to regional development have already been discussed or highlighted in this chapter, including a regional development policy, subnational regional development plans, and performance measurement and indicator systems. To further strengthen Panama's multilevel governance practices in regional development, enhancing institutional co-ordination for regional development would be valuable.

Dedicating an entity to co-ordinate regional development

To successfully use regional development as a policy lever for addressing territorial development, identifying a responsible body to champion the effort would be beneficial. As discussed, national-level strategies and/or policies can be strong horizontal and vertical co-ordination mechanisms, and are often used as such. Contracts and agreements are also useful tools. However, these mechanisms can be even more effective when championed by an entity responsible and accountable for ensuring that regional development objectives are met and priorities acted upon.

A cross-sectoral, integrated approach to regional development can be easier to realise with the support of a high-level institutional body. Such bodies – be they full ministries, interministerial committees or specialised agencies – can bring together stakeholders to identify objectives and ensure the alignment and realisation of policy priorities at the national and subnational levels. There are a number of different approaches governments take to strengthen cross-sectoral co-ordination of regional development. These include:

- A ministerial approach, where a specific ministry for regional development is established. These ministries have broad responsibilities and powers that encompass traditionally separate sectors. Some positive implications of the concentration of different responsibilities within the same authority include a more open and coherent perspective, a concentration of expertise and the possibility of a more integrated approach. This has been the case in Chile, the Czech Republic, Poland, the Slovak Republic, Slovenia and Colombia (Box 3.11). A less resource-intensive but still high-level alternative is to introduce departments for regional development within a relevant ministry. Other countries appoint regional ministers who must take into account the territorial aspects of the programmes and policies of their portfolios. In France and the Netherlands a minister is appointed who represents the interest of the leading region in the country, i.e. the State Secretary for the Development of the *Ile de France* and the Minister for *Randstad*.
- Co-ordinating structures can be established, such as interministerial committees and commissions. These are simpler than a ministerial approach as they are based on the existing government structure, and bring together representatives from the various ministries with a territorial logic. They are frequently chaired by a prime minister, president or vice president and generally mandate a ministry to act as the co-ordinating body. Examples include the Ministerial Committee for Regional Policy in Denmark, the Presidential Committee on Regional Development in Korea, and the Cabinet Subcommittee on Rural and Regional Policy in Norway.

- Special units or agencies provide planning and advisory support to facilitate policy coherence across sectors at the central level. High-level "special units" can ensure consistency among sectors. The closer such units or co-ordinators are to a chief executive, the greater the incentive for co-operation across sectoral ministries. Examples include the French General Commission for the Equality of Territories (*Commissariat Général à l'Egalité des Territoires* – CGET) (formerly DATAR), which is linked to the Office of the Prime Minister, and the Austrian Conference on Spatial Planning under the auspices of the Federal Chancellery. Special units under line ministries include the National and Regional Planning Bureau of the Ministry of Land, Infrastructure, Transport and Tourism in Japan and the Spatial Economic Policy Directorate of the Ministry of Economic Affairs in the Netherlands.

Box 3.11. Colombia's Department of National Planning

In Colombia, the Department of National Planning (*Departamento Nacional de Planeación*) has a ministerial rank and is in charge of cross-sectoral, vertical and horizontal co-ordination, in particular for the design and implementation of the National Development Plan. In 2012 the Department created a General Deputy Direction for Territorial Affairs and Public Investment (*Subdirección General Territorial y de Inversión Pública*) in charge of fostering links between national and territorial planning, between sectors, across government levels, and among financing sources, as well as to support subnational capacity for development and investment financing. The design of the National Development Plan involves a National Planning Council (*Consejo Nacional de Planeación*), established in 1991. The Council gathers representatives of the central government, departments, municipalities, the private sector and civil society. It is not involved, however, in the plan's implementation, or in performance monitoring.

Source: OECD (2016d), *Making the Most of Public Investment in Colombia: Working Effectively across Levels of Government*, OECD Multi-level Governance Studies, OECD Publishing, Paris. http://dx.doi.org/10.1787/9789264265288-en.

An interministerial co-ordinating body for regional development, modelled for example after existing cross-sectoral bodies, such the *Gabinete Social* or the Secretariat for Decentralisation could help advance and ensure the sustainability of a national regional development policy, and ensure national, sectoral and territorial priorities align and objectives are met. Such bodies are well placed to support coherent policy implementation, and can sponsor ongoing dialogue among relevant stakeholders. This helps identify what works and what does not, potential risk factors, as well as relevant – and ideally more integrated and innovative – solutions. Consideration could also be given to including representatives from the Association of Panama's Municipalities (*Asociación de Municipios de Panamá* – AMUPA) on such a committee.

An interministerial co-ordinating body could complement and support the current activity of the Ministry of Economy and Finance. However, consideration might be given to uniting the Department for Regional Planning (*Departamento de Planificación Regional)* and the Department for Regional Development (*Departamento de Desarrollo Regional),* creating one specific unit responsible for the full regional development policy cycle, and limiting additional fragmentation in this policy field. Whatever is established, the regional development objectives and perspectives should be clearly articulated and as relevant to the provinces as to the *comarcas*. It is important to highlight, however, that line ministries, agencies and other regional development stakeholders remain responsible for successfully contributing to regional development. An interministerial commission and a stronger internal regional development policy unit, as outlined above, should guide and co-ordinate the regional development policy cycle in order to ensure territorial objectives are met. Their existence does not exempt other institutions with a territorial logic from responsibility or action.

Strengthening dialogue bodies for more effective vertical co-ordination

Vertical co-ordination between national and subnational actors is particularly important for realising regional development objectives and establishing priorities because it is at the lower levels of government where programmes and plans are implemented and ultimately where objectives are realised.

If Panama's local authorities are to play a more active role in the development of their territories and communities, including through development planning, then success will depend on a clear communication of objectives and priorities both top-down and bottom-up. Reinforcing vertical co-ordination mechanisms, particularly those that foster a relationship based on partnership among levels of government rather than hierarchy will become increasingly important.

Formal dialogue bodies can be effective instruments for aligning interests and priorities among actors and levels of government. Panama's AMUPA already plays a role here with its convening and lobbying capacities. However, dialogue can be taken even further with an institutionalised body that brings together representatives from all levels of government on a regular basis, specifically to discuss regional development concerns and how to advance the country's regional development agenda. Ideally, this type of mechanism should be as much part of the political level as the administrative or technical level, gathering civil servants from different levels of government. In Italy, for example, political dialogue and vertical co-ordination is ensured through the State-Region Conference which plays a role in influencing the decision-making processes on regional issues (OECD, 2016d). In Sweden, the Forum for Sustainable Growth and Regional Attractiveness maintains a continuous dialogue among a wide array of stakeholders and is part of the implementation of Sweden's National Strategy for Sustainable Regional Growth and Attractiveness: 2015-2020 (OECD, 2017e).

If Panama decides to move forward with a dedicated regional development policy (a co-ordination mechanism in and of itself), expanding its current practices to "softer" levers such as an interministerial committee for regional development, and a dialogue body that brings together relevant stakeholders from different levels of government, would be valuable. Panama currently uses many "hard" levers – contracts, agreements, decrees, memoranda of understanding – to ensure the co-ordination and implementation of multisector programming. "Softer" levers could help strengthen the institutional dimension to regional development policy co-ordination and introduce a more multilevel perspective into the planning and implementation process. In addition, they could help align priorities, support stronger programme sequencing, and build ownership and capacity to ensure regional development objectives are met across sectors and by all levels of government.

Enhancing horizontal co-operation at the local level

Greater local capacity is fundamental for development in a "new paradigm" approach to regional development as the local level is just as important an actor as the central level. This makes local development planning as important as higher tier planning, and it is where the Law on Decentralisation plays a strong role with its required PEDs. For these reasons it is in the interest of all levels of government to ensure that Panama's local authorities build administrative, management and service capacity. More widespread intermunicipal co-operation could be a valuable mechanism in this respect, and it could be a strong complement to the Law on Decentralisation.

Strengthening intermunicipal co-operation to build scale and capacity

The law *Sobre Régimen Municipal* foresees a governance structure for associations between municipalities which includes a council, an administrative structure, and a treasury (*hacienda intermunicipal*) (República de Panamá, 1973). How often such arrangements are used among other municipalities is not clear. However, given the resource challenges and the few large-scale service responsibilities attributed to municipalities, its application may be limited.

Panama may wish to begin encouraging more intermunicipal co-operation (IMC) to build local capacity for meeting decentralised responsibilities. IMC can also help manage costs for expensive services or administrative requirements. For example, such agreements could help smaller municipalities to meet the requirements of specialised staff by sharing the cost of the expertise. It could also be useful for strengthening the capacity of indigenous communities. *Comarca* communities are known to co-operate with each other for ensuring education and health-care services, for example, but co-operation appears limited between indigenous and non-indigenous communities. Some consideration could be given to building co-operative arrangements between the two as a means to address common concerns, build capacity, and generate greater opportunities for development. To this end, the Federation of Canadian Municipalities and Canada's Council for the Advancement of Native Development Officers launched a First Nations Municipal Collaboration Programme which encompasses opportunities for joint economic development, and for infrastructure, particularly waste management (FCM 2017).

Intermunicipal co-operation can be particularly valuable to help municipalities fulfil compulsory service (or other) requirements that arise from shifts in task attribution and/or decentralisation reform. In a few countries, IMC has become compulsory for small municipalities and/or for specific services. In Iceland, for example, IMC became compulsory for municipalities of under 8 000 inhabitants following the decentralisation of social services for disabled persons, and it is required in Greece for waste management (OECD, 2017d). In the Netherlands, co-operative arrangements have gained momentum with the decentralisation of a number of additional responsibilities to local governments, particularly in the areas of employment and social welfare services. To comply with these new and complex responsibilities and to improve financial management, many Dutch municipalities created new co-operative structures, for example intermunicipal social services.

IMC's popularity rests on a number of factors including potential efficiency gains and cost savings. In Spain clear benefits were observed in the case of joint management of waste collection, especially for small municipalities where cost savings were estimated to be 20% in towns with less than 20 000 inhabitants and 22% in towns with less than 10 000. In England, the Local Government Association has reported that 416 shared-service arrangements among councils resulted in efficiency savings of GPB 42 million (as of September 2015) (OECD, 2017d). Results associated with IMC extend to better local public services, including improved processing times; more innovative, high-tech or specialised services (e.g. through the application of shared technologies); increased staff performance; and access to expertise, especially in remote locations with a skills shortage (Local Government New Zealand, 2011; OECD, 2017d).

The downsides to IMC include high transaction costs and the generation of externalities. It can be difficult to measure, faces transparency challenges, and can engender political, organisational and operational difficulties. In the end, the efficiency of IMC depends on a range of factors, including the number of participating municipalities, the extent of the transaction costs and the characteristics of the public good in question (Bartolini and Fiorillo, 2011; OECD, 2017d).

Despite these challenges, OECD countries are continuing to refine their approaches for encouraging the use of IMC among local authorities. For example, most OECD countries have passed laws in support of intermunicipal co-operation. In some cases, existing legal frameworks have been adjusted to reinforce IMC by encouraging or requiring that municipalities participate in co-operative agreements. This was seen in Austria in 2011, in Chile in 2011, in New Zealand in 2013, and in the Slovak Republic in 2012 and 2013 (OECD, 2017d).

In light of the challenges facing Panama's municipal governments, particularly fiscal and human resource gaps, and considering the benefits that can be associated with IMC, Panama may wish to strengthen intermunicipal co-operative practices and introduce incentive mechanisms that promote its use. This could be equally beneficial for the development of undercapacitated municipalities and for *comarcas*, as it could be for metropolitan areas where individual municipalities are reported to act on their own rather than in concert. Incentive mechanisms to encourage co-operative arrangements among communities are frequently financial. They include special grants, a special tax regime (applied in France), additional funds for joint public investment proposals (seen in Estonia and Norway), or bonus grants for municipalities that generate savings through co-operation (practised in Spain). Incentive structures can also be nonfinancial, such as the provision of consulting and technical assistance. Some governments have introduced new types of contracts and partnership agreements to encourage IMC. Poland and its territorial contracts are an example, as are Portugal's multilevel contracts (OECD, 2017d). There appears to be ample room for greater IMC in Panama, and there are a variety of areas in which greater formal co-operation between communities could help subnational governments manage capacity challenges. It could be a complementary mechanism to the decentralisation reform, and allow municipalities to build their service-delivery capacity, while limiting costs.

Conclusions and policy recommendations

Panama is growing rapidly, and with this comes increasing pressure on governments of all levels to better ensure continued growth while also promoting greater inclusiveness and wellbeing. To realise its dual territorial objective, a clearer and stronger approach to regional development would be valuable as well as adjustments to its multilevel governance practices. An explicit regional development policy – one that supports a strategic vision for how Panama would like its territory to look for the next generation – would be a positive step forward.

Consideration should be given to strengthening the normative and institutional frameworks supporting regional development. Currently, there is no overarching strategy to guide regional development in the long term, nor is there an explicit regional development policy to serve as a road map in the medium term. The implementation of regional development initiatives is spread across line ministries with a territorial logic, each introducing and executing its sector objectives and plans. This renders regional development a fragmented and sector-driven exercise, with limited visibility as to overall effectiveness and concrete results.

If regional development is to have an impact, a "place-based" or "new paradigm" approach is increasingly being considered good practice, and success rests in part on subnational decision-making ability and resource capacity. Subnational governments play a very limited role in Panama's economic and social growth. The revised Law on Decentralisation could have a positive impact, but additional clarity may be needed regarding how responsibilities will be transferred to municipal authorities, and to ensure them greater capacity – financial and human resource – in a sustainable manner.

To develop a policy that can successfully help Panama manage its territorial challenges, strengthening evidence bases and monitoring and evaluation mechanisms will be critical.

Enhancing institutional co-ordination is fundamental to support regional development. While there are strong horizontal co-ordination practices at the national level, these are less evident with respect to vertical co-ordination between levels of government. This is particularly important given what is perceived as a gap between "macro" level national priorities, such as ensuring greater inclusiveness, and "micro" level local priorities, such as education, healthcare, and transport/connectivity. While these are not mutually exclusive, work needs to be done to bridge the gap and help subnational authorities translate national priorities into initiatives that meet local needs. This, ultimately, is one of the fundamental roles of regional development policy at the national and subnational levels.

Box 3.12 summarises the main policy recommendations and requirements for each area covered in this chapter.

Box 3.12. Key recommendations for regional development policy

Strengthen multilevel governance practices to better support regional development:

- Consider supporting and adjusting normative and institutional frameworks for regional development, including:

– Taking a more strategic, long-term approach to regional development, inspiration could be drawn from practices in Finland and Slovenia (legal frameworks), the United Kingdom (white papers), Sweden (state strategies), France (state-region planning contracts) or New Zealand (regional growth programmes).

– Building evidence bases to manage territorial growth and development, particularly in light of expected population growth and the pressures placed on services, infrastructure, jobs, and administration.

– Reinforce the Law on Decentralisation by ensuring:

a) Clarity in competence attribution among levels of government, and transparency in the transfer of responsibilities.

b) Carefully monitoring and evaluating its contribution to municipal financial and administrative capacity and its impact on local administrative and fiscal prioritisation and decision-making autonomy.

- Build subnational capacity and resources, especially at the municipal level, by:
  - Enhancing subnational fiscal autonomy in decision making and budget management.
  - Considering a new municipal classification system based on functional areas rather than population and density.
  - Ensuring training for local public servants, including in skills in planning, budgeting, municipal management, and administrative service delivery.

Support a "new paradigm" approach to regional development

- Develop a national regional development policy that clearly articulates national territorial development objectives and priorities. Countries such as Colombia, France, Ireland, Mexico and Sweden have taken diverse approaches to formalising their regional development strategies.
  - Consider including a specific development framework for the *comarcas* within the policy's framework, and possibly reintroducing a multistakeholder, cross-sectoral body dedicated to promoting *comarca* development. Canada has adopted a similar mechanism.
- Introduce provincial and *comarca* regional development plans, elaborated by the corresponding subnational authorities, in order to better address subnational priorities and harness the unique opportunities corresponding to each area.
- Introduce regional development funding mechanisms that include a degree of predictability for the intermediate level. This can be either through a dedicated budget line or a special development fund. Uruguay may provide a useful example.
- Build performance measurement systems to better understand policy and programme effectiveness and build evidence bases at the national and subnational levels (seen in Canada, Chile, Scotland and the United States, for example), including:
  - Output and outcome indicator sets, and programme reviews to measure the effectiveness and impact of a national regional development policy, and subnational development plans.
  - Communicate objectives and intended targets to citizens, updating results on a predictable basis (e.g. biannually), in an easy and accessible format to understand advances, challenges and actors involved in these targets.
- Consider stronger partnership between the public and private sector when launching future regional development agencies. Poland's approach to regional development agencies may be of value.

Enhance horizontal and vertical co-ordination capacity

- Create a high-level interministerial body for guiding regional development policy, its priorities and performance, in an integrated, cross-sectoral manner.
- Form a dedicated unit for regional development policy to act as a steward, guiding and co-ordinating the policy design and implementation process on a day-to-day basis.
- Build vertical dialogue mechanisms at the political and potentially civil servant level to better understand priorities, capacities and the synergies that can arise from sectoral programming. Ensure that they meet regularly, have a clear agenda, and can point to results. Sweden's Forum for Sustainable Regional Growth and Attractiveness offers a successful example.
- Promote intermunicipal co-operation as a horizontal co-ordination mechanism to overcome capacity challenges in service delivery and local administration. Countries as diverse as Chile, Greece, Iceland, the Netherlands, New Zealand and Ukraine have mechanisms to support such co-operation.

Notes

[1] Provincial council members are not directly elected to the Council, but are (elected) representatives from each *corregimiento* in the province (República de Panamá, 1972).

[2] It is estimated that between 2010 and 2020 the population in Kuna Yala will have grown 22.2%, in Emberá 21.7% and in Ngäbe Bulgé 29.7%.

[3] The official currency in Panama is the Panamanian Balboa (PAB). This currency has been tied to the United States Dollar since 1904; 1 PAB equals 1 USD (US dollar).

[4] The OECD measures administrative fragmentation as the number of municipalities per 100 000 inhabitants.

[5] Panama classifies its municipalities in four groups based on population and density per km^2: metropolitan (over 250 000 inhabitants), urban (40 001-250 000 inhabitants and a density of 101-200 inhabitants per km^2), semi-urban (6 001-40 000 inhabitants and a density of 41-100 inhabitants per km^2), and rural (6 000 inhabitants) (República de Panamá, 2009).

[6] These tend to centre on increased democratic governance and participation, public services that are better adapted to a population's need, and increased transparency and accountability to citizens.

[7] This Department is in the process of dissolution and will be replaced by Indigenous Services Canada and a department for Crown-Indigenous Relations and Northern Affairs Canada.

[8] An output indicator is defined as an indicator to measure progress with an activity. It should be measurable, which implies that it must be quantitative – can be expressed numerically (i.e. physical or monetary units) – and time bound (i.e. limited to the lifetime of the corresponding activity). An outcome indicator can be broken down into two types: intermediate and final. Intermediate outcome indicators can be more directly attributed to public-sector activities than final outcome indicators which, while they significantly reflect the intended or unintended results of government actions, are also a function of other factors less within government control (OECD, 2013c).

References

Allain-Dupré, D. (forthcoming), "Assigning responsibilities across levels of government: Challenges and guiding principles", *OECD Regional Development Policy Working Papers*, OECD Publishing, Paris.

AMUPA (Asociación de Municipios de Panamá) (n.d.), "Datos Generales de los Municipios", AMUPA, Ciudad de Panamá, Panama.

Bartolini, D. and F. Fiorillo (2011), "Co-operation among local councils for the provision of public goods" *Rivista Italiana degli Economisti,* Vol. 16/ 1, pp. 85-108.

City of New York (n.d.), *One New York: The Plan for a Strong and Just City*, City of New York, New York, www.nyc.gov/html/onenyc/downloads/pdf/publications/OneNYC.pdf.

City of Seattle (n.d.), "Welcome to performance Seattle", Performance Seattle, Seattle, Washington, https://www.seattle.gov/performance.

Controlaría del Gobierno de Panamá (2010), "Boletín 16: Estimaciones y Proyecciones de la Población Total del País por Provincia, Comarca Indígena, Distrito y Corregimiento, según sexo y edad: años 2010-20", Instituto Nacional de Estadística y Censo, Panamá, Panama, https://www.contraloria.gob.pa/inec/Publicaciones/Publicaciones.aspx?ID_SUBCATEGORIA=10&ID_PUBLICACION=556&ID_IDIOMA=1&ID_CATEGORIA=3.

Controlaría General de la República (2018), Dirección General de Fiscalización, Municipalidades de la República y Ministerio de Economía y Finanzas Dirección de Presupuesto de la Nación (DIPRENA), https://www.contraloria.gob.pa/inec/Publicaciones/Publicaciones.aspx?ID_SUBCATEGORIA=27&ID_PUBLICACION=847&ID_IDIOMA=1&ID_CATEGORIA=4.

Cuadrado-Roura, J.R. and J.M. Fernández Güell (2008), "Metropolitan areas and the challenges of competitiveness", in Rojas, E., J.R. Cuadrado-Roura and J.M. Fernández Güell (eds.), Metropolitan Governance: Principles and Cases, Inter-American Development Bank, Washington, DC, and David Rockefeller Center for Latin American Studies, Harvard University, Cambridge, MA.

EC (European Commission) (2017a), *My Region, My Europe, Our Future: Seventh Report on Economic, Social and Territorial Cohesion,* Directorate General for Regional and Urban Policy, EC, Brussels, http://ec.europa.eu/regional_policy/en/information/cohesion-report/.

EC (2017b), "Rzeszow Regional Development Agency", Growth: Internal Market, Industry, Entrepreneurship and SMEs webpage, EC, Brussels, https://ec.europa.eu/growth/tools-databases/regional-innovation-monitor/organisation/rzeszow-regional-development-agency.

EC (2017c), "Torun Agency for Regional Development", Growth: Internal Market, Industry, Entrepreneurship and SMEs webpage, EC, Brussels, https://ec.europa.eu/growth/tools-databases/regional-innovation-monitor/organisation/torun-agency-regional-development.

Editorialox (n.d.), "Panamá", http://www.editorialox.com/panama.htm.

FCM (Federation of Canadian Municipalities) (2017), "First nations-municipal Community Economic Development Initiative," Federation of Canadian Municipalities, Ottawa, https://fcm.ca/home/programs/community-economic-development-initiative.htm.

Gobierno de la República de Panamá (2014), *Un Solo País: Plan Estratégico de Gobierno 2015-2019,* Gobierno de la República de Panamá, Panama, http://www.mef.gob.pa/es/Documents/PEG%20PLAN%20ESTRATEGICO%20DE%20GOBIERNO%202015-2019.pdf.

Government of Canada (2017), "2017-2020 departmental sustainable development strategy", Indigenous and Northern Affairs Canada, Ottawa, www.aadnc-aandc.gc.ca.

Government of Canada (2015), "Lands and economic development", Indigenous and Northern Affairs Canada, Ottawa, https://www.aadnc-aandc.gc.ca/eng/1100100032790/1100100032794.

Government of Canada (2010), "Federal framework for aboriginal economic development", Indigenous and Northern Affairs Canada, Ottawa, www.aadnc-aandc.gc.ca.

Greenstein, R., F. Sabatini and M. Smolka (2000), "Urban spatial segregation: Forces, consequences, and policy responses," *Land Lines*, November 2000, Lincoln Institute of Land Policy, Cambridge, MA, http://www.lincolninst.edu/publications/articles/urban-spatial-segregation.

Local Government New Zealand (2011), "Shared services for local government", Local Government New Zealand, Wellington, http://www.lgnz.co.nz/assets/Uploads/Shared-services.pdf.

Ministère de la Cohésion des Territoires (2015), *Les contrats de plan Etat-Région*: *Présentation générale,* Ministère de la Cohésion des Territoires, Paris, http://www.cohesion-territoires.gouv.fr/les-contrats-de-plan-etat-region.

Ministerio de Economía y Finanzas (2002), *Guía sobre Organización Municipal y Participación Popular*, Dirección de Desarrollo Institucional del Estado, Departamento de Fortalecimiento Institucional, Ministerio de Economía y Finanzas, Gobierno de Panamá, Panama, http://www.mef.gob.pa/es/servicios/Documents/Guia%20sobre%20Organizacion%20Municipal%20y%20Participacion%20Popular.pdf.

Ministry of Enterprise and Innovation (n.d.), "Sweden's National Strategy for Sustainable Regional Growth and Attractiveness, 2015-2020" (short version), Government Offices of Sweden, Stockholm, http://www.government.se/information-material/2016/04/swedens-national-strategy-for-sustainable-regional-growth-and-attractiveness-20152020---short-version/.

Mizell, L. (2008), "Promoting performance – Using indicators to enhance the effectiveness of sub-central spending", *OECD Working Papers on Fiscal Federalism*, No. 5, OECD Publishing, Paris, http://dx.doi.org/10.1787/5k97b11g190r-en.

OECD (Organisation for Economic Co-operation and Development) (2017a), *Multi-dimensional Review of Panama: Volume 1. Initial Assessment*, OECD Development Pathways, OECD Publishing, Paris, http://dx.doi.org/10.1787/9789264278547-en.

OECD (2017b), *Making Decentralisation Work in Chile: Towards Stronger Municipalities*, OECD Multi-level Governance Studies, OECD Publishing, Paris, http://dx.doi.org/10.1787/9789264279049-en.

OECD (2017c), "Subnational governments in OECD countries: Key data" (brochure), OECD Publishing, Paris, www.oecd.org/regional/regional-policy (database: http://dx.doi.org/10.1787/region-data-en).

OECD (2017d), *Multi-level Governance Reforms: Overview of OECD Country Experiences*, OECD Multi-level Governance Studies, OECD Publishing, Paris, http://dx.doi.org/10.1787/9789264272866-en.

OECD (2017e), *OECD Territorial Reviews: Sweden 2017: Monitoring Progress in Multi-level Governance and Rural Policy*, OECD Publishing, Paris, http://dx.doi.org/10.1787/9789264268883-en.

OECD (2016a), *OECD Regional Outlook 2016: Productive Regions for Inclusive Societies*, OECD Publishing, Paris, http://dx.doi.org/10.1787/9789264260245-en.

OECD (2016b), *Regional Outlook, 2016: Productive Regions for Inclusive Societies, Country Notes,* OECD Publishing, Paris, http://www.oecd.org/regional/oecd-regional-outlook-2016-9789264260245-en.htm.

OECD (2016c), *Government at a Glance: Latin America and the Caribbean 2017*, OECD Publishing, Paris, http://dx.doi.org/10.1787/9789264265554-en.

OECD (2016d), *Making the Most of Public Investment in Colombia: Working Effectively across Levels of Government*, OECD Multi-level Governance Studies, OECD Publishing, Paris, http://dx.doi.org/10.1787/9789264265288-en.

OECD (2016e), *OECD Territorial Reviews; Japan 2016,* OECD Publishing, Paris, http://dx.doi.org/10.1787/9789264250543-en.

OECD (2016f), *OECD Territorial Reviews: Córdoba, Argentina,* OECD Publishing, Paris, http://dx.doi.org/10.1787/9789264262201-en.

OECD (2016g), *OECD Regions at a Glance, 2016,* OECD Publishing, Paris, http://dx.doi.org/10.1787/reg_glance-2016-en.

OECD (2015), *The Metropolitan Century: Understanding Urbanisation and its Consequences*, OECD Publishing, Paris, http://dx.doi.org/10.1787/9789264228733-en.

OECD (2014a), *OECD Territorial Reviews: Ukraine 2013*, OECD Publishing, Paris, http://dx.doi.org/10.1787/9789264204836-en.

OECD (2014b), *OECD Regional Outlook 2014: Regions and Cities: Where Policies and People Meet,* OECD Publishing, Paris, http://dx.doi.org/10.1787/9789264201415-en.

OECD (2013a), *OECD Territorial Reviews: Brazil 2013*, OECD Publishing, Paris, http://dx.doi.org/10.1787/9789264123229-en.

OECD (2013b), *Investing Together: Working Effectively across Levels of Government*, OECD Publishing, Paris, http://dx.doi.org/10.1787/9789264197022-en.

OECD (2013c), *Poland: Developing Good Governance Indicators for Programmes Funded by the European Union*, OECD Public Governance Reviews, OECD Publishing, Paris, http://dx.doi.org/10.1787/9789264193543-en.

OECD (2012), *Promoting Growth in All Regions*, OECD Publishing, Paris, http://dx.doi.org/10.1787/9789264174634-en.

OECD (2010), *Finland: Working Together to Sustain Success*, OECD Public Governance Reviews, OECD Publishing, Paris, https://www.oecd-ilibrary.org/governance/oecd-public-governance-reviews-finland-2010_9789264086081-en.

OECD (2009a), *How Regions Grow: Trends and Analysis,* OECD Publishing, Paris, http://dx.doi.org/10.1787/9789264039469-en.

OECD (2009b), *Regions Matter: Economic Recovery, Innovation and Sustainable Growth,* OECD Publishing, Paris, http://dx.doi.org/10.1787/9789264076525-en.

Republic of Ireland, *National Spatial Strategy for Ireland 2002-2020: People, Places and Potential,* Government of Ireland, Stationary Office, Dublin, http://nss.ie/pdfs/Completea.pdf.

República de Panamá (2015), Ley No. 66, Que Reforma la Ley 37 Que Descentraliza la Administración Pública, República de Panamá, Gaceta Oficial Digital, Panama, https://www.gacetaoficial.gob.pa/pdfTemp/27901_A/GacetaNo_27901a_20151030.pdf.

República de Panamá (2009), Ley No. 37, Que Descentraliza la Administración Pública, República de Panamá, Gaceta Oficial Digital, Panama, http://www.organojudicial.gob.pa/cendoj/wp-content/blogs.dir/cendoj/ADMINISTRATIVO/ley_37_de_2009_que_descentraliza_la_administracion_publica.pdf.

República de Panamá (1973), Ley No. 106, Sobre Régimen Municipal, República de Panamá, Panama, https://panama.eregulations.org/media/ley%20106%20del%208%20de%20octubre%20de%201973%20sobre%20el%20r%C3%A9gimen%20municipal.pdf.

República de Panamá (1972), Constitución Política de la República de Panamá (amended, 2004), República de Panamá, Panama, https://panama.justia.com/federales/constitucion-politica-de-la-republica-de-panama/.

UNDP (United Nations Development Programme) (2014), *Imaginando un Futuro Común: Plan de Desarrollo Integral de los Pueblos Indígenas de Panamá*, UNDP, New York, http://www.pa.undp.org/content/panama/es/home/library/poverty/sistematizacion-plan-desarrollo-indigena.html.

Verkhovna Rada (2015), "Verkhovna Rada of Ukraine adopts law 'on fundamentals of state regional policy'", Verkhovna Rada, Kyiv, http://surdp.eu/en/news/Approval-law-on-principles-state-regional-policy.

World Bank (2018), "Banco Mundial aprueba innovador proyecto para pueblos indígenas de Panamá", World Bank Group, Washington, DC, http://www.bancomundial.org/es/news/press-release/2018/03/15/banco-mundial-aprueba-innovador-proyecto-para-pueblos-indigenas-de-panama.

World Bank (2013), *Republic of Panama: Panama Public Expenditure and Financial Accountability,* World Bank Group, Washington, DC, http://documents.worldbank.org/curated/en/499241468057554208/Panama-Public-expenditure-and-financial-accountability.

Annex A. Municipal competences in Panama versus a general schematic

The public services falling under municipal responsibility are classified into six main categories and then divided into specific tasks presented in Table A.1. Table A.2 offers a comparative, generalised look at how responsibilities are attributed across distinct levels of government in Organisation for Economic Co-operation and Development (OECD) countries.

Table A.1. Competences ascribed to Panama's municipalities

Category	Specific responsibility
Urban public services	Zoning; parks and gardens; paving and maintaining of public roads (i.e. sidewalks, avenues, lateral roads)
	Authorisation for public lighting, telephone lines and supply of potable water
	Cleaning, collection and elimination of solid waste
	Environmental protection (air, noise and aesthetics)
	Construction permits
	Granting of urban licenses in accordance with the norms established for urban development
Public transport services	Supply of vehicular license plates
	Vehicular parking
	Transport terminals
Public services for security and protection	Judicial administration[1]
	Citizen security
	Fire prevention
Public education and culture services	Education (school canteens, support for the construction of gymnasiums or areas for physical education)
	Sports fields or areas for recreation
	Public swimming pools
	Classroom construction and maintenance (support)
	Library services
	Social assistance
	Health centres
	Pre-primary schools
Public health services	Cemeteries
	Facilities for elderly care
	Orphanages
	Public hostels or dormitories
	Waste (garbage) collection
Public provisions	Public abattoirs
	Public markets
	Plazas or areas for the sale of agricultural or industrial products
	Markets for crafts, agriculture, livestock, etc.

Note: [1] This refers to local justice responsibilities (i.e. police), not to be confused with *justicia ordinaria,* which is under the responsibility of *corregidores,* a political authority within a *corregimiento*, and which will be replaced by justices of the peace as of 2018.

Source: Ministerio de Economía y Finanzas (2002), *Guía Sobre Organización Municipal y Participación Popular*, Dirección de Desarrollo Institucional del Estado, Departamento de Fortalecimiento Institucional, Ministerio de Economía y Finanzas, Gobierno de Panamá, Panama, http://www.mef.gob.pa/es/servicios/Documents/Guia%20sobre%20Organizacion%20Municipal%20y%20Participacion%20Popular.pdf.

Table A.2. Breakdown of responsibilities across subnational governments: A general scheme

Regional Level	Intermediary Level	Municipal Level
Heterogeneous and more or less extensive responsibilities, depending on country characteristics (e.g. unitary vs federal). Services of regional interest: Secondary/higher education and professional training Spatial planning Regional economic development and innovation Health (secondary care and hospitals) Social affairs (e.g. employment services, training, inclusion, support to special groups) Regional roads and public transport Culture, heritage and tourism Social housing Environmental protection Public order and safety (e.g. regional police, civil protection) Local government supervision (in federal countries)	Specialised and more limited responsibilities of supra-municipal interest. An important role in assisting small municipalities. May exercise responsibilities delegated by the regions and central government. Responsibilities determined by the functional level and geographic area: Secondary and/or specialised education Supra-municipal social and youth welfare Secondary hospitals Waste collection and treatment Secondary roads and public transport Environment	A wide range of responsibilities: General clause of competence Eventually additional allocations by law Community services: Education (nursery schools, pre-elementary and primary education) Urban planning and management Local utility networks (water, sewage, waste hygiene, etc.) Local roads and city/local public transport Social affairs (support for families, children, elderly, disabled, poverty, social benefits, etc.) Primary and preventative healthcare Recreation (sport) and culture Public order and safety (municipal police, fire brigade) Local economic development, tourism, trade fairs Environment (green areas) Social housing Administrative and permit services

Source: OECD (2016g), *Regions at a Glance, 2016*, OECD Publishing, Paris, http://dx.doi.org/10.1787/reg_glance-2016-en.

Annex B. Guidelines for effective decentralisation to support regional and local development

Through its work on regional and local development, the OECD has created a set of guidelines to support more effective decentralisation when undertaken to strengthen regional and local development. While the ideal is to have all of these dimensions in place before undergoing a decentralisation process, this is difficult to achieve in practice. Therefore, in order to maximise the possibility of success, governments should assess which areas may be weak and take steps to address these, while also reinforcing those areas that are already strong. Successful decentralisation will depend on the presence of these factors.

1. Clarify the sector responsibilities assigned to each government level: Most responsibilities are shared across levels of government, and spending responsibilities overlap in many policy areas. Therefore, it is crucial to ensure adequate clarity on the role of each level of government in the different policy areas in order to avoid duplication, waste, and loss of accountability.
2. Clarify the functions assigned to each government level: Clarity in the different functions that are assigned within specific policy areas, e.g. strategic planning, financing, regulating, implementing, or monitoring is as important or even more so than clarity in assignment of tasks.
3. Ensure coherence in the degree of decentralisation across sectors: A degree of balance in what is decentralised and to what degree should be ensured across policy sectors. In other words, decentralising one sector but not another can limit an ability to exploit cross-sectoral complementarities and integrated policy packages when implementing regional and local development policy. While decentralisation may apply differently to different sectors, there should be coherence and complementarity in the approach.
4. Align responsibilities and revenues, and enhance subnational fiscal autonomy: The allocation of resources should be matched to the assignment of responsibilities to subnational governments. Unfunded mandates or a mismatch between responsibility and financing capacity should be avoided.
5. Actively support capacity building for subnational governments with resources from the national government: Additional financial resources need to be complemented with the human resources capable of managing them. This dimension is too often underestimated, if not completely forgotten, in decentralisation reform, and is particularly important in poor or very small municipalities. At the very least, subnational governments should have the responsibility and be able to monitor employee numbers, costs, and competencies.
6. Build adequate co-ordination mechanisms across levels of government: Since most responsibilities are shared, it is crucial to establish governance mechanisms to manage these joint responsibilities. Creating a culture of co-operation and regular communication is crucial for effective multilevel governance and long-term reform success. Tools for vertical co-ordination include dialogue platforms,

fiscal councils, standing commissions and intergovernmental consultation boards and contractual arrangements.

7. Support cross-jurisdictional co-operation through specific incentives: Subnational horizontal co-ordination is essential to encourage investment in areas where there are positive spillovers, to increase efficiency through economies of scale, and to enhance synergies among policies of neighbouring jurisdictions. Intergovernmental bodies for horizontal co-ordination can be used to manage responsibilities that cut across municipal and regional borders. Determining optimal subcentral unit size is a context-specific task; it varies not only by country or region, but also by policy area – efficiency size will differ based on what is under consideration, for example waste disposal, schools, or hospitals.
8. Allow for pilot experiences and asymmetric arrangements: Allow for the possibility of asymmetric decentralisation, i.e. giving differentiated sets of responsibilities to different types of regions/cities/local governments, based on population size, rural/urban classification and fiscal capacity criteria. Ensure implementation flexibility, making room for experimenting with pilot programmes in specific places or regions and constantly adjusting through learning-by-doing.
9. Make room for complementary reforms: Effective decentralisation requires complementary reforms at the national and subnatiosnal levels in the governance of land-use, subnational public employment, regulatory frameworks, etc.
10. Improve transparency, enhance data collection and strengthen performance monitoring: Data collection should be undertaken to monitor the effectiveness of subnational public service delivery and investments. Most countries need to develop effective monitoring systems of subnational spending and outcomes.

Source: Allain-Dupré, D. (forthcoming), "Assigning Responsibilities across Levels of Government: Challenges and Guiding Principles", *OECD Regional Development Policy Working Paper*, OECD Publishing, Paris.

Annex C. Functional urban – and metropolitan – areas

Urban agglomerations are defined by their physical characteristics (such as population densities and developed land) but also by their functional relations that are expressions of the daily lives of their inhabitants. People live in one area, commute to another and go for dinner in even another. Friends might live in the same neighbourhood, but the shopping centre is located across town and business trips begin at the airport outside the city. For a single citizen, this is just a pattern of daily life. Taken together across all residents, these patterns make up the functional relations that define a city.

For several reasons, administrative borders in metropolitan areas rarely correspond to these functional relations. Often, they are based on historical settlement patterns that no longer reflect human activities. Due to population growth and improvements in transport technologies, formerly well-delimited villages have become part of the suburbs of a city or might even be fully integrated in the urban core. Often, no corresponding changes to administrative borders have occurred. Common reasons for the persistence of administrative borders are strong local identities and high costs of reforms, but also vested interests of politicians and residents.

Even if policy makers try to reorganise local governments according to functional relations within urban agglomerations, it is often difficult to identify unambiguous boundaries between functionally integrated areas. Urban agglomerations are not defined by a single functional relation, but by many overlapping ones. Generally, they are not identical in their geographical extent. For example, the functional relation defined by typical shopping patterns is different from the one defined by commuting patterns.

The mismatch between functional boundaries and administrative boundaries is well known and policy makers have long been aware of the co-ordination problems it might cause. In response, a wide range of metropolitan governance arrangements has emerged. While some countries have chosen to shift administrative boundaries to match the new urban form (e.g. via municipal mergers), others are encouraging municipalities to build partnerships – e.g. for service delivery, economic development planning – within a more or less institutionalised framework.

Source: Adapted from OECD (2015), *The Metropolitan Century: Understanding Urbanisation and its Consequences*, OECD Publishing, Paris, http://dx.doi.org/10.1787/9789264228733-en.

Chapter 4. Improving the taxation system and promoting private sector involvement to support financing for development

The preceding chapters laid out an ambitious agenda for inclusive development in Panama. To finance this development, Panama will need to significantly increase public expenditure and mobilise private investment. Current taxation levels are relatively low compared with other Latin American economies and are well below those of Organisation for Economic Co-operation and Development (OECD) economies. A better-structured taxation system, coupled with a stronger tax administration, should yield greater fiscal revenues. In addition, improvements in the regulatory and institutional framework for public-private partnerships should promote private investment for development. This chapter first summarises the revenues necessary to finance development, then presents the current fiscal framework to guarantee the solvency of the state. Third, it proposes alternative ways of increasing tax revenues that could preserve competitiveness while making the tax system more equitable. It then proposes a new framework for public-private partnerships to mobilise private investment for inclusive development and finally closes with a conclusion and policy recommendations.

Ensuring the availability of sufficient financial flows to drive Panama's continued national development and to foster social inclusion is critical to sustain the country's rapid economic expansion. Beyond funding fiscal stability, as highlighted in previous chapters, raising additional revenues is fundamental to close the gap in several policy areas. It is a priority to improve the quality and coverage of key public services, especially those that affect individuals of low socio-economic background, such as education and skills (Chapter 2; OECD, 2017a). Furthermore, financing investments that promote regional development and reduce disparities across provinces and *comarcas* is also critical for long-term sustainable growth (Chapter 3).

Current levels of investment in key socio-economic areas for development are well below those of other Latin America and the Caribbean (LAC) countries and Organisation for Economic Co-operation and Development (OECD) economies. Social expenditure in Panama is considerably below Latin America and OECD averages. Social expenditures in health, pensions, family support and other social services in 2016 were just close to 5% of Panama's gross domestic product (GDP), well below spending in LAC (around 8.6% of GDP) and in OECD countries (21.2% of GDP) (OECD, 2017a; OECD, 2017b). Investment in education also lags behind regional and OECD levels, at 3.6% of GDP in 2015, compared with close to 4.3% of GDP in LAC and 5.5% in OECD countries. Finally, investment in research and development remains well behind most Latin American countries and the gap has widened during the past decade. Panama spent only 0.07% of its GDP in 2013 in research and development, while the Latin American average was ten times higher (0.75% of GDP). The investment gap with OECD economies is even more striking, where it was 2.42% of GDP in 2013 (OECD, 2017a).

To ensure financing for development in Panama, citizens' willingness to pay taxes – known as "tax morale" – is fundamental. Trust in institutions and satisfaction with public services go hand in hand and are a key element in the "fiscal pact", understood as the agreement that citizens pay taxes to the state in exchange for certain public services and goods. It is one of the main components of the social contract. Although Panama remains slightly better than the region's average in terms of citizens' satisfaction with public services, it has shown a slight deterioration between 2010 and 2015. For instance, the share of the population that expressed being satisfied or very satisfied with public hospitals declined from 53% to 46% between 2005-15 (OECD/CAF/ECLAC, 2018). Reinforcing credibility of public policies and trust in institutions is fundamental since, similar to Latin American economies, only half of the population declares tax evasion as never justifiable. This erodes the capacity of states to raise revenues that are critical to finance good quality public goods and services, which are key to improve citizen satisfaction and respond to the greater aspirations of a larger middle class (OECD/CAF/ECLAC, 2018, OECD 2017a).

There is substantial scope to increase fiscal revenue collection in Panama. Total fiscal revenues are low compared with other countries at similar levels of development (OECD, 2017a). Tax revenues particularly are low compared with OECD and LAC averages. In 2016, tax revenues represented 16.6% of Panama's GDP, compared with 22.7% in LAC and 34.3% in OECD economies (OECD/ECLAC/CIAT/IDB, 2018). However, non-tax revenues derived from the Panama's Canal and – to a lesser extent – from other non-financial public-sector firms have accounted for 3.2% of GDP on average in the past decade; this compensates for the country's low tax efforts, but these funds tend to be earmarked or are susceptible to volatility.

Improved tax revenue collection, through a broadened tax base and strengthened tax administration, could provide a stable, long-term source of income. This is particularly evident for the value-added tax (VAT), as the tax system currently forgoes approximately 2% of GDP due to exemptions and payment evasion. Within Panama's wide array of tax exemptions, some affect the system's efficiency by potentially providing incentives to firms within sectors that do not require these benefits. Environmental taxes are also an untapped source of additional revenue that would improve the environment at the same time. Finally, curbing evasion and fraud through technology and institutional strengthening could also raise revenues.

Mobilising private sector investment, through public-private partnerships, can also help finance development. Adopting and implementing a sound regulatory and institutional public-private partnerships framework is fundamental to build effective and efficient infrastructure.

This chapter focuses on improving domestic revenue mobilisation to support inclusive and sustained growth, and on reinforcing this effort with a public-private partnership framework to promote investment in Panama. It analyses tax policies for inclusive growth that minimise the efficiency and equity trade-offs within the tax system as a whole. This is achieved through three main methods: i) reducing the efficiency costs of equitable tax policies; ii) minimising the equity costs of efficient tax policies (OECD, 2015a); and iii) implementing policies that bolster both equity and efficiency (Brys et al., 2016). In addition, this chapter presents current gaps in regulatory and institutional frameworks for public-private partnerships compared with other Latin American and OECD economies. Finally, this chapter concludes with the resulting main policy recommendations.

Fiscal stability is key to ensuring macroeconomic stability and sustained investment

While Panama's solvency has a good perception by capital markets and has contributed to reduced interest payments, capital expenditures have increased in recent years. Indeed, investment has been one of the main drivers of economic growth, with low debt cost a key factor. From 2011 to 2016, investment more than doubled from averages in the early 2000s, as public capital expenditure reached 8.8% of GDP in 2016 compared with 3.8% in 2000. Capital expenditure had an average annual expansion of 0.19 percentage points of GDP during the period 2000-16, while interest payments decreased by 0.14 percentage points during the same period. In the past, high debt levels meant high financial costs, which crowded out public productive investment. In the early 2000s, interest payments reached 4.3% of GDP. Interest costs were halved and averaged 2.0% of GDP during 2011-16 (Figure 4.1).

Reducing primary deficits through capital expenditure cuts can be costly in terms of economic growth and potential output. Capital and current expenditures have a positive and large impact on Panama's long-term GDP trajectory. For each Balboa spent by the government on a long-term horizon, the multiplier effect amounts to PAB 2.3 (Garry and Rivas Valdivia, 2017).[1] Therefore, fiscal consolidation through capital expenditure cuts is not a feasible pathway that can lead to high levels of sustainable growth despite contributing to the short-term reduction of primary fiscal deficits in the non-financial public sector (NFPS). In that context, further fiscal resources should contribute to achieving the fiscal rule and to financing capital expenditures.

Figure 4.1. Total revenue and expenditures of the non-financial public sector (NFPS)

Percentage of GDP

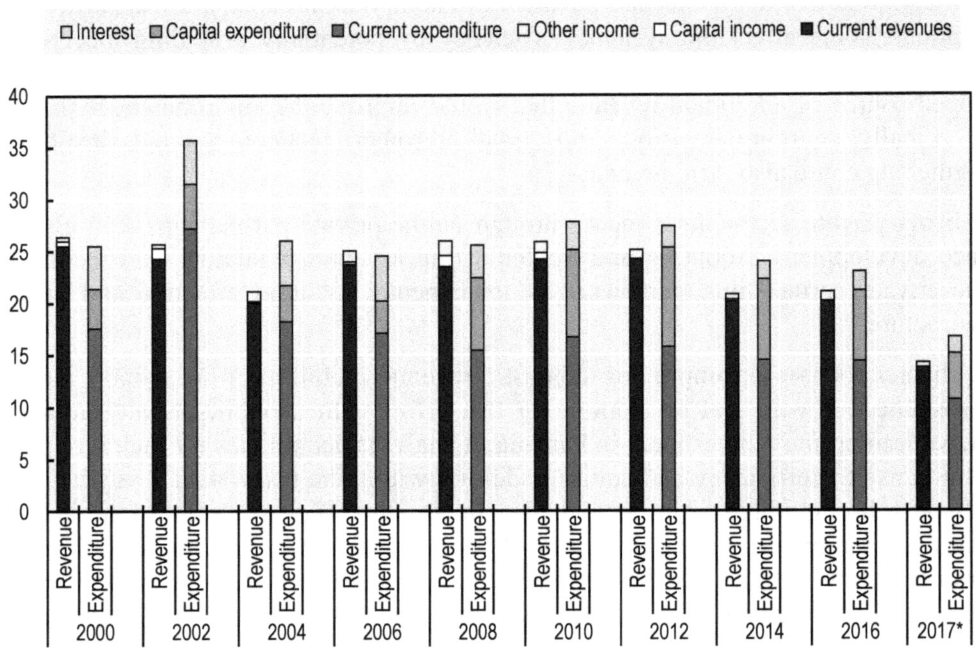

*Preliminary data up to September 2017.

Note: Other income is comprised of operational balances of public enterprises, non-consolidated agencies and donations to the NFPS.

Source: Based on IMF (2001), "Panama: Staff report for the 2000 Article IV consultation"; MEF (2017), "Fiscal balances for the years 2004-2017".

StatLink http://dx.doi.org/10.1787/888933777319

Fiscal rules are a useful tool in guaranteeing fiscal stability. Fiscal rules have been shown to improve fiscal management processes and provide a stable fiscal horizon that leads to financial certainty. These rules have usually followed three main objectives: ensuring debt sustainability; strengthening stability; and improving expenditure composition (investment) (OECD/CAF/ECLAC, 2018; Arbeloa et al., 2016).

Panama's fiscal rule promotes fiscal discipline by limiting the NFPS deficit and gross public debt. Panama's fiscal responsibility law dates back to 2002, although suspension clauses have been applied and it was subsequently refined and modified between 2008 and 2014. Essentially, the Panamanian fiscal rule imposes a double condition on public finances. First, it restricts the expansion of the NFPS's deficit as a percentage of GDP and, second, it limits the level of public debt the NFPS can acquire. The overall goal is to maintain fiscal discipline that protects public investment and provides adequate fiscal space to enact counter-cyclical policies to favour long-term fiscal sustainability.

Public debt is sustainable but rising. Economic growth and sound macroeconomic policy management have led to sustainable public debt levels. Public debt has decreased by 40 GDP percentage points from its highest peak in 1994 (82% of GDP) to the current level of 37% of GDP in 2017.[2] However, the ratio of public debt to GDP has increased in recent years, in line with primary and total fiscal deficits, and public debt is nearing the limits established by the rule (Figure 4.2, Panel A). If left unmanaged, this is likely to pose potential risks to fiscal soundness in the medium term.

Recurrent fiscal deficits are pressuring the public debt to rise. At current borrowing costs this might not seem a threat in the short term. However, a debt sustainability analysis that modelled different scenarios employing the average observed primary balance deficit, in combination with annual growth scenarios below 6%, revealed that the gross debt could surge to between 52% and 60% of GDP by 2024. Similarly, local projections have shown that scenarios in which annual growth rates are two standard deviations below the historical GDP average could potentially increase the net public debt by 15 percentage points of GDP in a five-year span (2017-22) (OECD, 2017a).

Panama's fiscal rule enforcement needs to be improved to avoid fiscal risks and ensure sustained growth. Assessing the adherence to the fiscal rule is difficult because of the numerous changes and the application of the escape clause due to economic downturns. An appraisal of the deficit clause shows that the condition was met in the years 2002 and 2008. In 2009, 2010, 2012 and 2014, the fiscal rule was met after modifications that outstretched the deficit targets (Figure 4.2, Panel B). The adjusted overall fiscal balance, which results from the difference between the unadjusted fiscal balance and the effective contribution from the Canal Authority to the *Fondo de Ahorro de Panamá* (FAP) and a constant of 3.5 GDP percentage points, has provided further leeway to increase expenditures and fiscal deficits without explicitly breaking the rule (Alonso et al., 2016).

Recent efforts to establish a fiscal council are a step in the right direction, as it will promote transparency and accountability of the fiscal framework, and will encourage informed public debate (IMF, 2017a).

Figure 4.2. Fiscal rule compliance measures

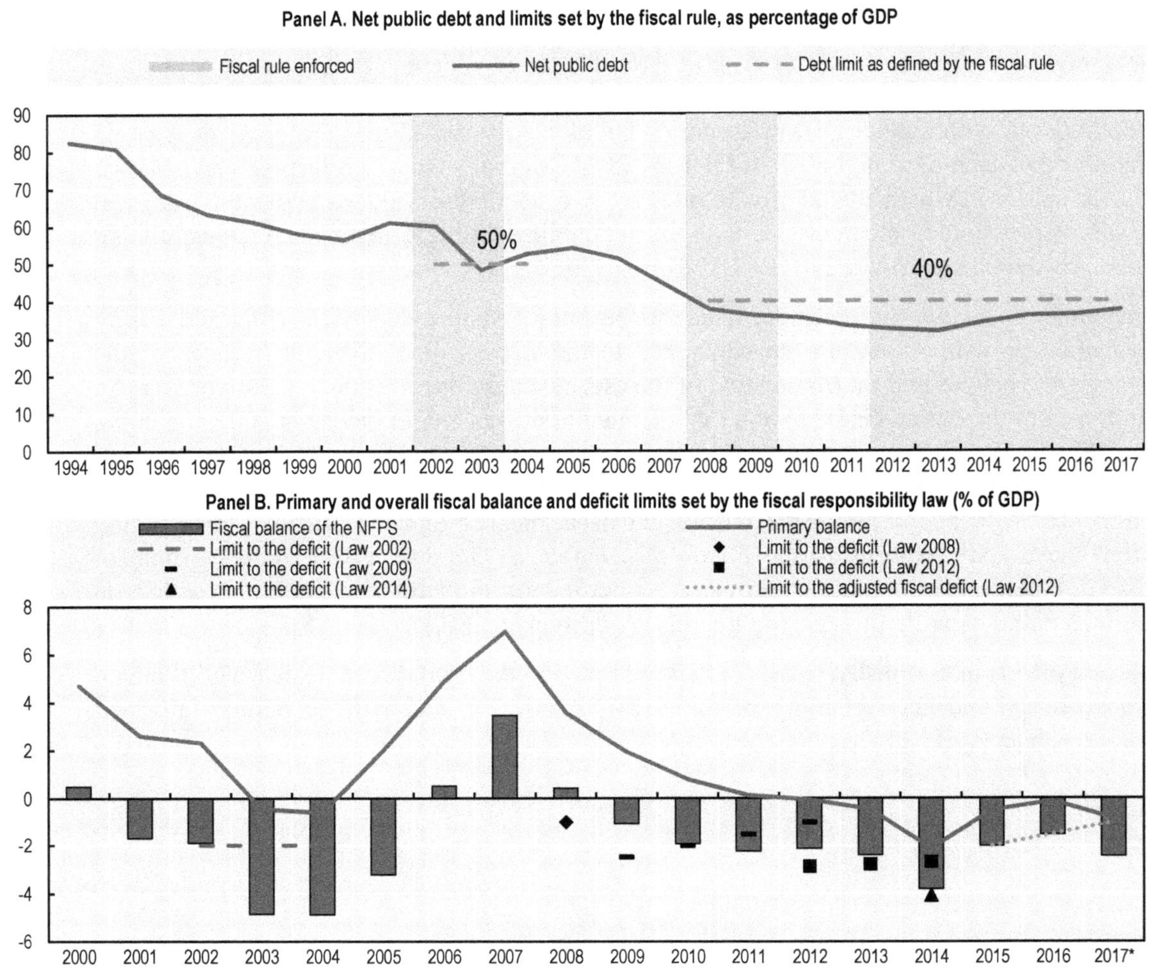

*Data for 2017 are preliminary up to September 2017.

Notes: Panel A: Fiscal balances for 2015-17 are adjusted as established by Law No. 38/2012. Panel B: Grey areas correspond to years in which the fiscal rule was in place.

Source: Barreix, Benítez and Melguizo (forthcoming), "Panama", in Fiscal Rules in Latin American Countries.

StatLink http://dx.doi.org/10.1787/888933777338

Public revenues in Panama are low

Tax revenues in Panama have remained low compared with OECD and LAC averages. In 2016, Panama's tax revenues amounted to 16.6% of GDP, compared with 22.7% in LAC and 34.3% in OECD economies (Figure 4.3). Furthermore, tax revenue collection has remained stationary during the last 27 years, averaging 16% of GDP, with a standard deviation of 1.07% of GDP throughout this period. Between 1990 and 2016, tax levels increased by 0.7 percentage points of GDP, an annual average growth of 0.03 percentage points, one of the lowest in LAC. In comparison, the LAC economies raised their tax collection by an average of 0.26 percentage points of GDP each year, a total increase of 6.8 percentage points of GDP (OECD/ECLAC/CIAT/IDB, 2018). During the same period, Panamanian GDP per capita at constant prices increased by a factor of 1.8, highlighting that Panama's high levels of growth have not translated into higher tax revenues.

Figure 4.3. Panama's tax revenue structure compared with benchmark countries

Percentage of GDP, 2016

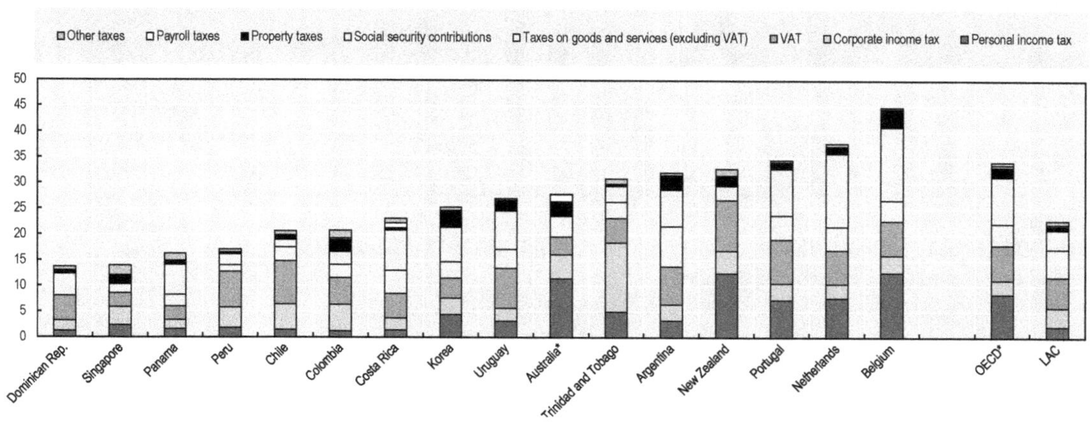

*2015 data.

Notes: As in OECD/ECLAC/CIAT/IDB (2018), taxes refer to compulsory unrequited payments to the general government. Taxes are unrequited in the sense that benefits provided by governments to taxpayers are not normally in proportion to taxes paid by them. Compulsory social security contributions paid to the general government are treated here as tax revenues. Revenues from the Canal are not included

Source: Based on OECD/ECLAC/CIAT/IDB (2018), *Revenue Statistics in Latin America and the Caribbean 2018*; OECD (2017e), Tax Administration 2017 – Comparative Information Series on OECD and Other Advanced and Emerging Economies.

StatLink http://dx.doi.org/10.1787/888933777357

Non-tax revenues from public enterprises complement the intake from tax revenues, but they tend to be more pro-cyclical and volatile than tax revenues. Non-tax revenues, including fees and dividends from the Canal, rose an average of 4% of GDP during the last five years. Countries with high levels of income from non-renewable natural resources tend to exhibit a lower tax effort (IDB, 2013). Although Panama's fees and dividends from the Canal are not a traditional non-renewable natural resource, they provide the government with a significant stream of non-tax revenue amounting to 11% of total fiscal revenues (fiscal revenue is the sum of total tax revenue and the dividends and fees of public non-financial enterprises) (Figure 4.4).

Figure 4.4. Fiscal revenue from the NFPS, 2000-16

Percentage of GDP

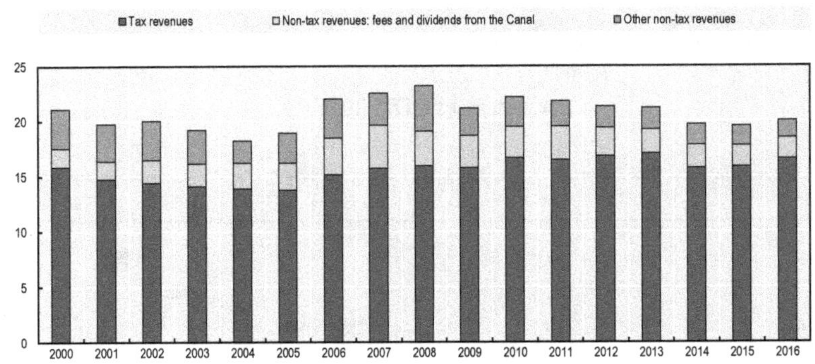

Source: OECD calculations based on OECD/ECLAC/CIAT/IDB (2018), *Revenue Statistics in Latin America and the Caribbean 2018* and MEF of Panama.

StatLink http://dx.doi.org/10.1787/888933777376

Tax structure relies heavily on social security contributions while direct and value-added taxes are relatively low

Social security contributions (SSCs) represent 37% of total tax revenues (OECD/CIAT/IDB, 2016). Taxes on goods and services accounted for 30% of Panama's total tax revenues, similar to the OECD share (32%) but significantly lower than the LAC average (51% of total tax revenues). At the same time, revenues from personal income tax (PIT) and corporate income tax (CIT) amount to 22% of total tax revenues, below the LAC average of 24% and far below the 33.7% average for OECD economies. Finally, property taxes accounted for 4% of total tax revenues, 2 percentage points higher than in LAC countries and 2 percentage points below the OECD average (Figure 4.5). 40% of total tax revenues are earmarked. SSCs are targeted to financing old-age, disability, work injury and healthcare benefits (OECD/CIAT/IDB, 2016). Taxes levied on alcohol, soft drinks and tobacco represent an additional 3.5% of total tax revenues and are also allocated to the Panamanian insurance fund (Caja de Seguro Social) (OECD/ECLAC/CIAT/IDB, 2018).

Figure 4.5. Tax revenue and composition in Panama, LAC and OECD economies, 2016

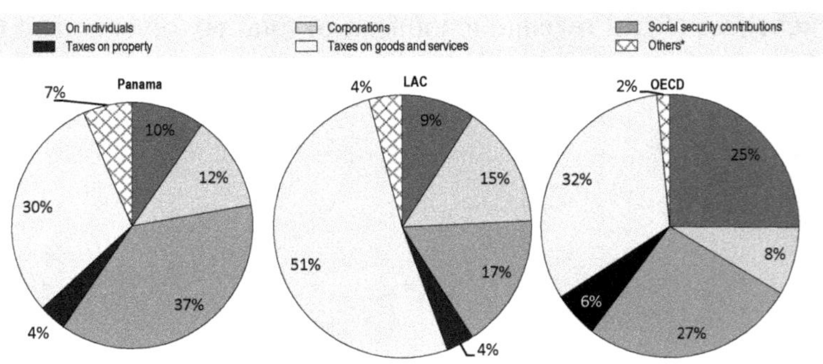

*Others: includes other unallocable taxes, including those on profits and capital gains, and payroll taxes.
Source: OECD/ECLAC/CIAT/IDB (2018), *Revenue Statistics in Latin America and the Caribbean 2018*.

StatLink http://dx.doi.org/10.1787/888933777395

Revenues from the VAT are one of the lowest in the LAC region. Panama raises 2.6% of GDP through VAT receipts. Amid LAC countries, only the Bahamas raises less (2.5% of GDP), while the averages for LAC and OECD economies are 6.3% and 6.7% of GDP, respectively.

Panama collects 62% of the VAT's potential revenue and therefore loses 38% of its potential revenue. Potential VAT revenue is estimated by levying the generalised VAT tax rate on final consumption. Although VAT's losses cannot be decomposed due to lack of information, these losses should be explained by several aspects including VAT tax expenditures, evasion, fraud and other factors that diminish the tax administration's capacity to raise revenue.[3] Estimates of the VAT revenue ratio (VRR), a measure of the amount of VAT actually collected (net of refunds) relative to the potential VAT collection show that Panama could increase tax collection by 1.6% of GDP if zero rated items, exemptions that diminish VAT collection, evasion, fraud and other forms of elusion were completely abolished. In comparison, on average, LAC countries for which data are available suggest that for each 100 monetary units of potential VAT revenue, tax administrations collect 56 units, forgive 13 units through reduced VAT rates, zero-rated items, exemptions and other benefits, and lose 31 units through other factors that cannot be explained through tax exemptions (Figure 4.6).[4] This positions Panama above the LAC average in terms of VAT collection efficiency, but highlights there is still room to increase the availability of VAT resources to finance investments without raising tax rates.

Improving the comprehensiveness of tax expenditure data will provide a more accurate depiction of foregone revenues in Panama. Tax expenditures are "provisions of tax law, regulation or practices that reduce or postpone revenue for a comparatively narrow population of taxpayers relative to a benchmark tax" (OECD, 2010). Tax expenditure estimates published by the MEF employ a different methodology based on a different benchmark, i.e. not based on the foregone-revenue approach, presumably one in which VAT exemptions are considered part of the normal tax structure rather than a tax expenditure.

Figure 4.6. The VAT revenue ratio (VRR): Decomposing the VAT's potential revenue

Share of total potential revenue, 2015

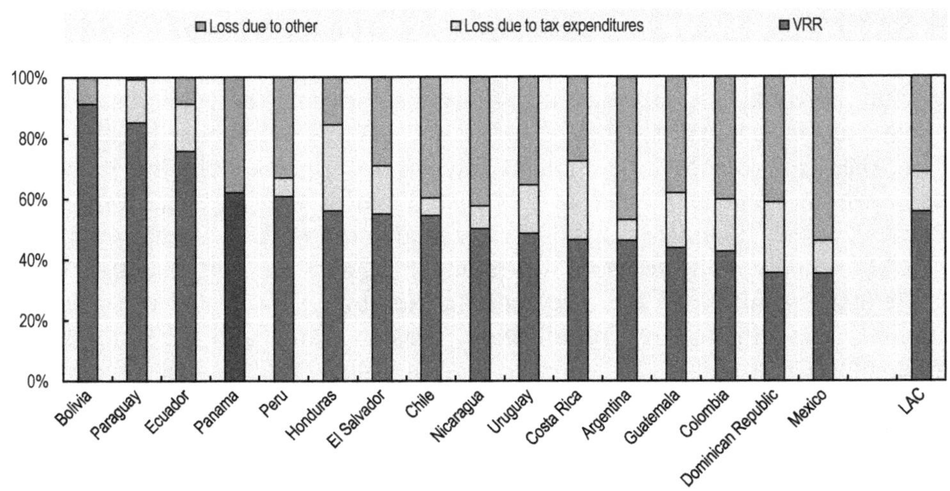

Note: The figure decomposes the potential revenue of the VAT in three categories relative to potential VAT revenue: 1) VAT revenue ratio (VRR) is the proportion of the potential VAT that is actually collected (net of VAT refunds) by the tax administration; 2) tax expenditures: are VAT tax expenditures expressed as a proportion of the potential VAT. These figures are compiled from countries' tax expenditure reports and amount to the forgone VAT revenue due to reduced rates, zero rates and other fiscal benefits or reliefs; 3) other: the rest of the potential VAT revenue base that cannot be explained through tax expenditures, i.e. it groups all of the evasion, elusion, fraud or aggressive tax planning to avoid paying the tax.
Source: OECD/ECLAC/CIAT/IDB (2018), *Revenue Statistics in Latin America and the Caribbean 2018*.

StatLink http://dx.doi.org/10.1787/888933777414

Enhancing efficiency and equity in Panama's tax system

Improvements in GDP per capita suggest a higher capacity than currently observed to mobilise tax revenue to finance development in Panama. The tax gap amounted to 9 percentage points of GDP in 2011 in Panama, implying that all else being equal, on average countries with similar characteristics collect 25% of GDP in tax revenues. This cross-country tax effort approach estimates the expected level of tax collection after considering the country's per capita income, the importance of agriculture and the industrial sector within the economy, the levels of human capital, the dependence on natural resources, the openness of the economy and its exposure to exogenous shocks (Yohou and Goujou, 2017; OECD, 2017a).

This section analyses two key items to take into consideration to enhance the taxation system in Panama: efficiency and equity. First, it presents estimates on tax expenditures to improve the tax system's efficiency. Second, it analyses the taxation system by income deciles in Panama.

Measuring tax expenditures is critical to fine-tuning the tax system's efficiency

Broadening tax bases is critical to raising additional direct revenues and maintaining current tax rates. Panama's tax bases are narrowed due to numerous tax exemptions provided to firms, individuals and special sectors through special economic zones (SEZs) to promote investment. A crucial issue lies in the quantification of the fiscal costs triggered by these benefits. According to available estimates provided by the MEF, in 2015 tax expenditures amounted to 0.8% of GDP. This does not seem high relative to the LAC average (4.6% in 2012) (Pecho, 2014); however, this figure contrasts with other estimates of tax expenditures presented for Panama, in which tax relief channelled through consumption taxes in the country amounted to 2.3% of GDP in 2012, behind only Nicaragua, Costa Rica, the Dominican Republic and Uruguay (Pelaez Longinotti, 2017; OECD, 2017c).[5] This reflects the difficulty of international comparability since differences in tax expenditure benchmarks will lead to certain tax provisions being considered as tax expenditures in one country and not in another.

Panamanian tax expenditures have declined during the last two decades according to data provided by the MEF. However these data are estimates and do not include all items related to tax benefits, such as those of VAT and SEZs. In 1995, tax benefits amounted to 2.5% of GDP. Since then, they have fallen rapidly to current levels observed in 2015 (Figure 4.7, Panel A). The downward trend can be explained mostly by a substantial decline in subsidies to energy and fuels. During 2010-15, estimated foregone revenue due to tax benefits granted through tax policy averaged 1.3% of GDP and were concentrated in fiscal documents, a kind of tax benefit provided to firms (37% of total tax expenditures), relief on imports (21%) and energy subsidies (21%) (Figure 4.7, Panel B).

Figure 4.7. Panama: Tax expenditure evolution and composition by type of benefit

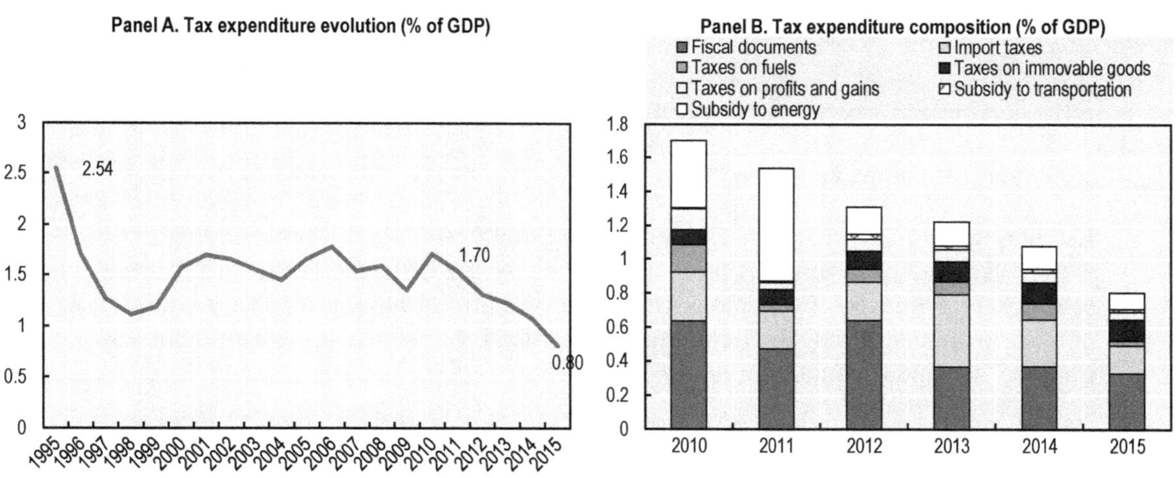

Note: Fiscal documents are issued by the government. These documents have a nominal value and can be used to pay taxes.
Source: Based on data from the MEF of Panama.

StatLink http://dx.doi.org/10.1787/888933777433

Tax expenditures are directed towards a myriad of economic goals, but it is necessary to measure their efficiency. They are aimed at social and environmental policy goals that include creating more and better jobs, boosting innovation, improving education and reducing inequality. These tax benefits are enacted and pursued through the fiscal code. Yet, it is necessary to quantify these tax expenditures to appraise their effectiveness and efficiency in achieving their intended goals (Box 4.1) (Redonda, 2016). This is particularly important since tax expenditures are automatically enforced year after year, circumventing controls and creating opportunities for tax avoidance.

Assessing efficiency draws attention to two crucial aspects of policy evaluation. First, it must be determined whether implementing a particular tax expenditure triggers effects that may impact other policy goals. For instance, there is strong consensus on the significant negative environmental impacts of tax expenditures granted to fossil fuel producers (and consumers) and, thus, on the urgent need to reduce their use. In other cases the side effects may not be as evident, but are nonetheless critical. The regressive nature of mortgage interest deductions or tax exemptions in the context of retirement schemes are examples of this (Redonda, 2016). Second, the efficiency of tax expenditures in comparison with direct spending must be determined. Under certain conditions, tax expenditures can have several advantages such as low administrative costs, low stigma for beneficiaries and/or increased political acceptability relative to direct payments from the government. In other words, tax expenditures often lead to an underestimation of their costs as well as an overestimation of their benefits (Burman and Phaup, 2012).

The design of these schemes is crucial to their effectiveness. Tax expenditures for investment are a case in point: these schemes should be well targeted so that they promote capital investment. This is not the case when a scheme has no impact at all on productive investment. For instance, whereas tax incentives targeted at export-oriented sectors and mobile capital are more likely to have the expected impact, those granted to sectors producing for domestic markets or extractive industries are significantly less effective (IMF et al., 2015). In this context, the next section analyses the equity of the tax system in Panama.

Box 4.1. Estimating and reporting of tax expenditures: International experiences

Estimating the fiscal cost of tax expenditures through sound cost-benefit analyses is a necessary step in scrutinising the effectiveness and efficiency of the different schemes implemented by the government. In addition, making those estimates publicly available through official reports is crucial to increase the government's transparency and accountability.

Various approaches can be used to measure the cost of tax expenditures. The three main methodologies are:

1. The revenue-foregone approach: estimates the amount by which taxpayers have their tax liabilities reduced as a result of a tax expenditure based on their actual current economic behaviour.
2. The revenue-gain approach: estimates the additional revenue that would be collected if a tax expenditure were removed, accounting for behavioural changes resulting from this removal.
3. The outlay-equivalent approach: estimates the government cash outlay required for an alternative direct spending programme replacing the tax expenditure that would have the same benefit for the taxpayers. As with the revenue-forgone method, it assumes no behavioural change.

Tax expenditure figures should be interpreted with caution. Not internalising behavioural changes and applying the same marginal tax rates to all tax expenditures are two of the most significant weaknesses of the revenue-foregone method. Nonetheless, and probably because of its relative simplicity, most countries base their estimates on this approach.

Whereas estimating the foregone revenue of tax expenditures for consumption taxes is based on national accounts and/or household expenditure data, and hence is relatively straightforward, the quantification of tax expenditures through direct taxes often requires the use of microsimulation techniques based on a representative sample of taxpayers. These models are static in the sense that the arithmetic simulation of taxes and benefits does not take the behavioural changes of individuals into account. Most countries have their own microsimulation model. For instance, the Institute for Fiscal Studies uses TAXBEN in the United Kingdom and the National Bureau of Economic Research works with TAXSIM in the United States.

Panama does not officially report on tax expenditures. There is significant heterogeneity in official reports across the 43 OECD and G20 countries. Whereas ten countries do not report on tax expenditures at all, ten other economies provide regular, comprehensive and detailed reports including additional information for at least some schemes – i.e. they surpass the simple revenue-foregone estimates to include, for example, cost-benefit analyses, distributive assessments, and estimates based on methods other than the revenue-foregone, such as the outlay-equivalent method (Neubig and Redonda, 2017).

Finally, whereas most countries include their tax expenditure reports within their government budgets, some have also created specific online platforms that considerably simplify accessibility to the information. Canada's official Report on Federal Tax Expenditures, for instance, provides revenue-foregone estimates of the federal income tax system (corporate and personal) as well as the goods and services tax for the current fiscal year. It also provides a forecast for the following year as well as time-series data for the previous six years. The data are classified by tax base, subject (e.g. education, business, employment), and each scheme is published with a detailed description including the beneficiaries, the type of measure, the objective, the reason the measure is not part of the benchmark tax system (and hence considered a tax expenditure), and even a legal reference. Finally, specific tax expenditure schemes are evaluated each year, moving beyond the estimation of their fiscal cost. For instance, the 2017 Report includes a paper evaluating the "relevance, effectiveness, equity and efficiency" of the Children's Fitness Tax Credit and the Children's Arts Tax Credit.

Source: Redonda (2016), "Tax Expenditures and Sustainability. An Overview", *Discussion note* 2016/3, Council on Economic Policies, Zurich, https://www.cepweb.org/tax-expenditures-and-sustainability-an-overview/.

Improving the tax system's equity

Panama should improve the potential redistributive power of the tax system to foster inclusive growth. An adequately designed tax system is a powerful instrument to achieve more equality (OECD, 2015a). Currently, exemptions, deductions and other special treatments negatively affect both the vertical and horizontal equity of the tax system. On average, individuals with higher income pay a higher share of their income in taxes, but there are several deductions and exemptions that disproportionately benefit the well-off, diminishing the average tax rate and the progressiveness of the system. The elimination of these provisions could enhance equity and revenue as well as bolster the system's redistributive power, which is currently on par with other LAC economies. Finally, informality and tax evasion diminish the system's capacity to redistribute throughout an individual's lifecycle (Brys et al., 2016).

Panama's tax system is progressive but not redistributive enough

Panama's tax system exhibits progressivity as a whole when measured by the concentration shares of tax collection.[6] The top decile pays 46.7% of total tax revenues (including SSCs), while those in the lowest three deciles of income distribution only pay a combined share of 3.4% of total tax revenues (Figure 4.8, Panel A). In terms of GDP, this translates to the former taxpayers contributing 7.7% of GDP of Panama's total revenues, while the latter group contributes 0.6% of GDP. The breakdown of the progressivity of the most important taxes shows the same pattern, although concentration magnitudes vary from tax to tax.

The Personal Income Tax (PIT) is highly progressive when viewed as a share of total revenue throughout the income distribution. The PIT is concentrated in the top two wealthiest deciles of income distribution (97% of total PIT revenue). The rest of the tax (3% of PIT) is paid by what can be considered a consolidated middle class (Easterly, 2001) (deciles 6-8)[7] (Figure 4.8, Panel B). It should be noted that the levels of concertation of the PIT are similar to other countries in Latin America (OECD/ECLAC/CIAT/IDB, 2018; Barreix, Benítez and Pecho, 2017).

Excise taxes and the VAT are concentrated at higher levels of income. The top decile pays 43.9% of total VAT collection (1.2% of GDP). At the other end of the income distribution spectrum, the poorest 5 deciles pay 15.2% of the VAT (0.4% of GDP). The tax burden on individuals, as a share of their income, is considerably lower in the lowest deciles than those who are more affluent (Figure 4.8, Panel C). This is to be expected, since wealthier individuals have greater consumption capacity and thus will pay a higher share of these taxes.

Payments to the SSCs are concentrated at the top of the income distribution. On average, the highest quintile contributes 42 times more than those in the lowest quintile (Figure 4.8, Panel D).

Figure 4.8. Concentration shares of tax payments, by deciles of market income (2016)

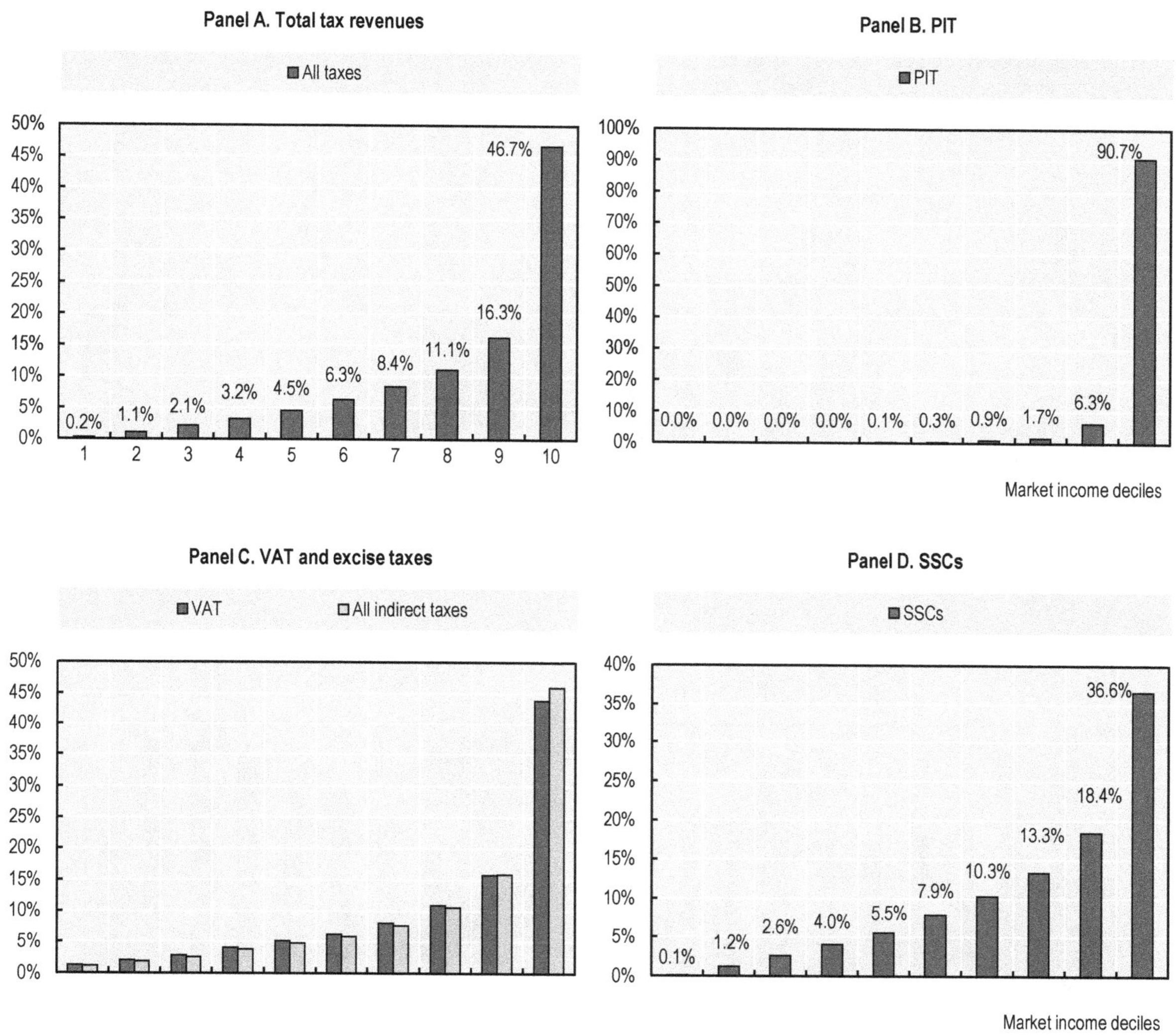

Note: The figures depict the share that each decile pays to a determined tax or the share of benefit they receive through direct transfers.

Source: OECD and the Commitment to Equity (CEQ) Institute at Tulane University, based on national household survey (INEC, 2016).

StatLink http://dx.doi.org/10.1787/888933777452

The tax system as a whole, including SSCs, remains progressive when gauged by average tax rates paid throughout the income distribution (Figure 4.9). Under this metric, individuals in the poorest decile contribute 5.5% as a share of their market income in direct and indirect taxes and SSCs. The fifth decile pays 8.4% and the richest decile pays 11.6% as a share of market gross income (Figure 4.9, Panel A). The average tax rate is the ratio between the tax paid and the total income of the decile. It is useful as it provides a better depiction of the individual's ability to pay. It can also be an approximation of the system's or the tax's fairness, as it shows the proportion of an individual's income that is used to comply with tax obligations.

The PIT is progressive although average effective tax rates remain low. The wealthiest decile is liable for only 2.7% of its market income and the second-richest decile pays only 0.3% of its income, while the rest of the deciles pay close to zero as a percentage of their market income (Figure 4.9, Panel B).

Figure 4.9. Average tax paid as a share of market income in Panama, 2016

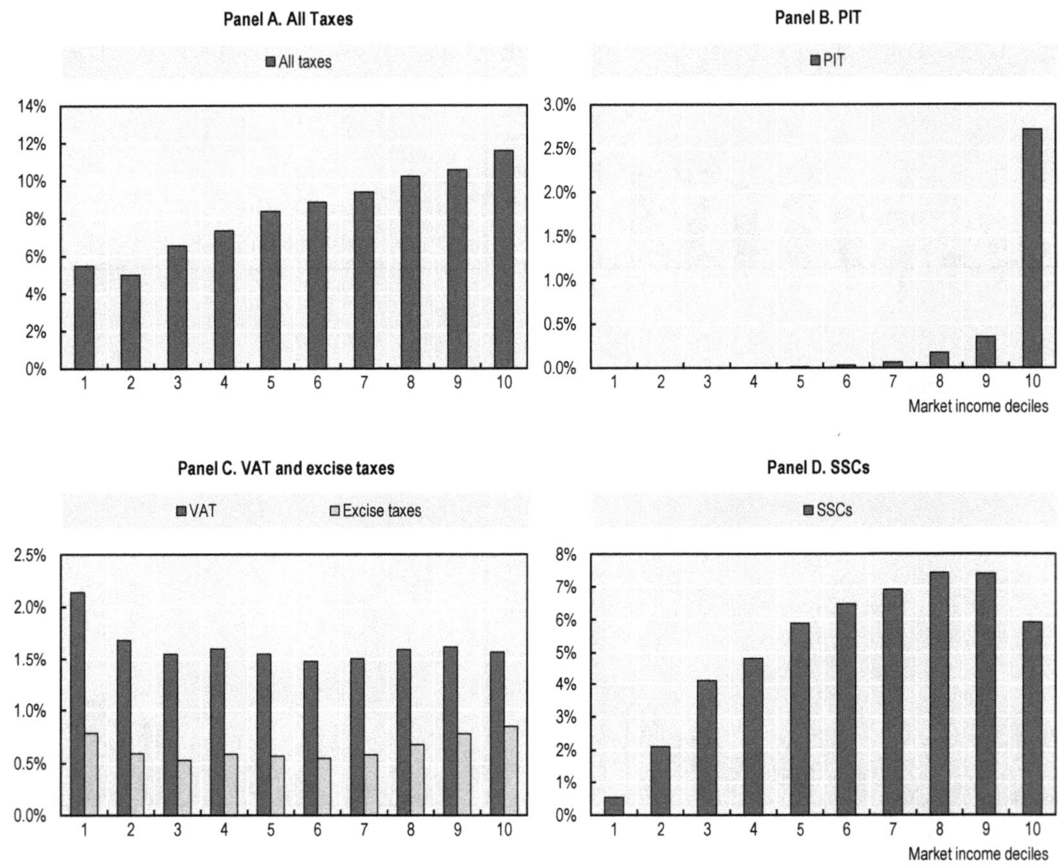

Notes: The figures depict the ratio of taxes paid to market income by decile. VAT and excise taxes are presented as a share of disposable income, which includes any direct transfer individuals might have received that affect their available income to consume.

Source: OECD and the Commitment to Equity (CEQ) Institute at Tulane University, based on national household survey (INEC, 2016).

StatLink http://dx.doi.org/10.1787/888933777471

The VAT remains regressive under this metric despite the numerous exemptions on food staples and other basic goods. On average, individuals in the lower-income deciles pay 2.1% of their disposable income on VAT, whereas high-income individuals pay 1.6% of their disposable income (Figure 4.9, Panel C). Like many other countries, Panama exempts food stuffs and other goods to benefit those at the lower end of the income scale. In this regard, evidence from Costa Rica, Mexico and Uruguay has shown that even though the poor spend a large proportion of their income on these exempted items (food), the more affluent are likely to spend more on these same items in absolute terms. Therefore, most of the foregone revenue accrues to the rich (Clements et al., 2015; Barreix, Bès and Roca, 2010; OECD, 2017c; OECD, 2007).

The middle class in Panama pays the least on excise taxes as a share of their disposable income. The average excise tax rate is slightly U-shaped (Figure 4.9, grey bars, Panel C): individuals in the wealthiest and the poorest deciles both pay 0.8% of their respective disposable incomes on 'sin' taxes. Indeed, the bulk of excise tax falls on beer, alcohol, tobacco and fuel.

The wealthiest decile's effective average SSC rate is lower than that of the fifth decile, since SSCs are levied on labour income but not on capital income. Since those in the highest deciles on the income distribution tend to derive an important proportion of their income from capital, SSCs as a share of their total income will be reduced.

The tax system does not reduce inequalities enough compared with OECD countries. Similar to Latin American economies, the tax system's redistributive power is low; it reduces the market income Gini coefficient by 0.021 Gini points (vs. 0.022 points in Latin America), while in OECD economies it decreases by 0.16 points (Figure 4.10). This does not mean that the system is not progressive, as the greater percentage change in after-tax income is in the more affluent individuals (Figure 4.9). However, average tax rates are similar among individuals across the income distribution, highlighting the available space to improve the redistributive power of the tax system.

The tax system's low redistributive power stems from low effective average tax rates which translate into few revenues to affect the disposable income distribution. Low average tax rates indicate that the income distribution is heavily skewed towards the wealthiest individuals. Tax measures that lead to a narrower distribution of disposable income include a progressive PIT design, broadening the taxable base by eliminating or reducing regressive tax expenditures and by taxing all forms of income, and reducing tax avoidance and evasion opportunities available to the wealthy through aggressive tax planning (Brys et al., 2016).

Figure 4.10. Impact of taxes and transfers on income distribution in Panama, Latin America, the European Union and selected OECD economies

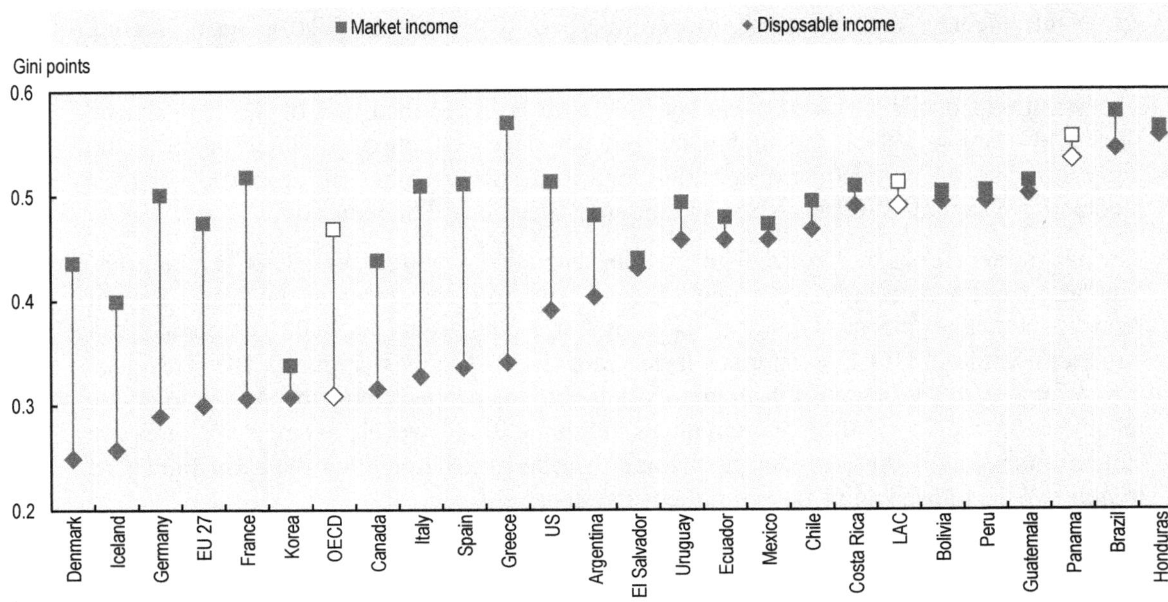

Source: OECD and the Commitment to Equity (CEQ) Institute at Tulane University, based on national household survey (INEC, 2016); OECD/CAF/ECLAC (2018), *Latin American Economic Outlook 2018: Rethinking Institutions for Development.*

StatLink http://dx.doi.org/10.1787/888933777490

Policy priorities in key tax dimensions in Panama

This section analyses and presents recommendations to improve the tax regime for several key tax dimensions in Panama. It includes the VAT, the corporate tax, the tax system for SEZs, the personal income tax and environmental taxes in Panama.

Increasing revenues from VAT

Increasing the VAT rate would yield additional resources to finance development. Panama could increase approximately 0.37% of GDP in additional revenues for each increased percentage point. A straightforward estimation of VAT shows that an additional 1 percentage point increase in the VAT rate yields USD 205 million. The analysis uses Panama's general VAT rate (7%) and assumes that behavioural responses to the higher tax rates would slightly increase evasion. An increase in the tax rate would also increase the deadweight loss on consumption. Regarding the VAT and its effect in the firms' production chain, tax paid on inputs can be credited against tax due on output at each stage of the value-added chain until the good or service reaches the final consumer. Furthermore, the VAT does not affect international competitiveness, and when it is applied on a broad-based scale it also avoids distorting consumption choices of economic agents. In fact, consumption taxes, such as the VAT, have been found to be one of the least harmful taxes to growth (Brys et al., 2016). In addition, they minimise compliance and administrative costs because economic agents can deduct the accrued VAT at intermediate stages. This increases the incentives to request receipts and hence triggers a positive effect on firm formalisation (IDB, 2013).

To increase tax revenues there is also a need to broaden the VAT's base and to increase the VAT's potential revenue. Low levels of VAT intake are a reflection on low VAT rates but also on a wide variety of tax benefits given to several products and services and high levels of evasion. Unlike other countries, Panama does not levy VAT rates that are lower than the general rate (7%). VAT rates on luxury items are levied at 10%, and on "sin" goods 15%. However, the VAT exempts several goods and services, affecting the VAT's potential revenue (Figure 4.6). Conservative estimates based on the revenue-foregone approach show that the largest exemptions are for agricultural products (0.39% of GDP), food products (0.64%) and freight and passenger transport (0.86%) (Jorrat, 2014). Yet, as these estimates were partial (they only covered the most important 14 goods and services) and are not carried out in a systematic manner, they are not comparable to other existing figures.

To compensate the poorest individuals should be a priority and this should contribute to compensate the regressive nature of the VAT for the bottom decile. Targeted programmes are more effective to reduce disparities than untargeted tax benefits. In Panama, social assistance comprises four distinct programmes: *Red de Oportunidades* (2006), a conditional cash transfer; 120 a los 65 (2014) to support the elderly; *Beca Universal* (2010), a cash transfer for households with children to encourage school attendance; and *Angel Guardian* (2012), a programme targeting poor or vulnerable people with disabilities. *Red de Oportunidades* is the only programme that has been formally evaluated and its evaluation showed that this programme increased school enrolment and was able to reduce child labour in both indigenous and rural non-indigenous areas (OECD, 2017a). In the region, other experiences are useful to show the benefits of targeted programmes compared to tax policies to reduce inequalities. In Brazil, zero-rated and exempted products of its excise tax, the *Imposto Sobre Circulação de Mercadorias e Serviços*, cost BRL 18.6 billion and improved the Gini coefficient by 0.001, whereas transfers through the *Bolsa Familia* programme cost BRL 28 and improved it by 0.017. This translates into higher rates of efficiency for the *Bolsa Familia* as each billion spent in this programme reduces the Gini coefficient by a greater proportion than those spent through exempted products, highlighting the effectiveness of targeted transfers compared to untargeted tax benefits (Bittencourt, 2017).

Taxes on corporate domestic profits can be more efficient

The CIT is the third most important tax within the Panamanian tax structure. In 2000, it represented 10.9% of total tax intake. This share increased to 18.2% in 2016. In terms of revenue, the CIT increased by 2.1% of GDP in 2016, behind only the VAT (2.7%) and SSCs (6.1%) (OECD/ECLAC/CIAT/IDB, 2018). Relative to other countries in the region, Panama's levels of CIT collection are below the averages of LAC and OECD economies, 3.4% and 2.8% respectively.

Companies' profits are subject to income tax on their Panamanian-sourced income. Panama has a territorial system of taxation. The CIT is levied at a flat 25% nominal statutory rate on the net taxable income (after exemptions and deductions are subtracted from the taxable base). This is a similar nominal rate relative to rates applied on other neighbouring or Latin American countries (26.1%) (Table 4.1). Dividends are excluded from shareholders' taxable income. Dividends and other profit distributions from companies that require an operation licence (*aviso de operación*) are subject to withholding and, in some cases, to a complementary tax. Non-resident companies are also subject to withholding taxes on dividends and interest (IBFD, 2017).

Table 4.1. Corporate taxation: selected indicators for LAC countries (2017)

Country	Statutory CIT rate	Withholding rate on dividends	Withholding rate on interest	Number of treaties
Panama	**25**	**10[g]**	**12.5[g]**	**17**
Belize	25	15	15	13
Costa Rica	10/20/30[a]	15	15	2
El Salvador	25/30[b]	5	20	1
Guatemala	25	5	10	0
Honduras	25/30[c]	10	10	0
Nicaragua	30	7.5[h]	7.5[h]	0
Argentina	35	10	35	19
Brazil	24/34[d]	0[i]	15	33
Chile	24[e]	35[e]	4/35[l]	32
Colombia	34/40[f]	0[j]	15[m]	13
Dominican Republic	27	10	10	2
Ecuador	22	0[k]	22	19
Mexico	30	10	35	56
Peru	28	6.8	30	11
Uruguay	25	7	12	18

Notes:

a. CIT rates vary by gross income; starting from CRC 105 241 000 (USD 182 128) the rate is 30%.
b. The general CIT rate is 30%; it is reduced to 25% only when taxable income does not exceed USD 150 000.
c. The general CIT rate is 25%; companies with taxable income that exceeds HNL 1 million (USD 41 975) are subject to a 5% surtax.
d. The general CIT rate is 15%; in addition, there is a social contribution tax of 9% and a 10% surtax for companies with taxable income above BRL 240 000 (USD 75 960).
e. The general CIT rate is 24%; dividends distributed to non-residents receive a tax credit for corporate income taxes paid and are subject to a 35% withholding tax.
f. The general CIT rate is 33% (for year 2018). In addition, companies with taxable income above COP 800 million (USD 282 600) face an additional surtax of 4% (for year 2018).
g. Withholding tax on dividends is 10% if the income distributed is Panamanian source, 5% if it is foreign-source income, and 20% in case of bearer shares. Withholding tax rates on interest are 25% on 50% of the gross amount.
h. Withholding tax rates on dividends and interest are 15% on 50% of the gross amount.
i. Withholding tax on dividends is zero if paid out of taxed profits and 15% otherwise.
j. Withholding tax on dividends is zero if paid out of taxed profits and 35% otherwise.
k. Withholding tax on dividends is zero if paid out of taxed profits and 22% otherwise.
l. A reduced rate of 4% withholding tax on interest is available for loans granted by foreign banks, insurance companies or financial institutions.
m. Withholding tax rates on interest are taxed at 15%; a reduced rate of 5% is levied on interest payments for loans exceeding an 8-year term for the funding of public infrastructure works under public-private partnerships.

Sources: OECD (2017c), *OECD Tax Policy Reviews: Costa Rica 2017;* DIAN (2018), "Structural tax reform".

The complementary tax and the annual licence operation tax distort investment decisions. The complementary tax is levied on companies that do not distribute profits or distribute less than 40% of the after-tax profits. The complementary tax collected an average of 0.2% of GDP during the last five years. However, a feature of this tax is that it increases the costs of not distributing profits, thus affecting investment decisions. Similarly, the annual operation licence tax also affects investment decisions. It is levied at an annual rate of 2% on the capital invested in a company and increased by an average of 0.2% of GDP. The annual licence operation tax is capped at USD 60 000 and firms with investments of less than USD 10 000 are exempted from the tax. Firms established in SEZs are subject to an annual tax at the rate of 0.5% on the capital of the enterprise, with a minimum USD 100 and a maximum USD 50 000 tax liability.

Panama should consider removing disincentives to investment. Abolishing the annual operation licence tax and the complementary tax would improve the system's neutrality and simplicity. It should be noted, however, that dividends should still be taxed. A credit can be given to the PIT for taxes paid at the CIT level to limit double taxation on corporate returns.

Differentiated tax treatments might benefit some sectors disproportionately

Differentiated tax treatment among productive sectors can lead to windfall gains in some sectors. Taxable sector profits are not proportional to the share of the CIT paid by firms. Firms that operate within the financial and insurance sectors earn 30% of all profits filed to the tax administration but only contribute 18% of the collected CIT revenue. Other sectors such as wholesale and retail face the opposite situation, as they earn 15% of total profits but contribute a quarter of total CIT revenues (Figure 4.11). The tax treatment received by firms can vary depending on the source of their income and their main activity. The tax code exempts several types of interest income (Article 708 of the Tax Code) and establishes that agricultural firms, international transportation firms, state-owned enterprises and firms that operate within SEZs are all subject to different tax rates and benefit differently from a myriad of income tax exemptions. In addition to differentiated tax treatments, firms earning more than USD 1.5 million are also required to use an alternative method to estimate CIT liability,[8] which can also affect the CIT due. Admittedly, more micro-data is required to provide a thorough explanation of the mechanisms through which these different treatments affect each sector.

Figure 4.11. Shares of sectoral distribution profits and CIT revenues

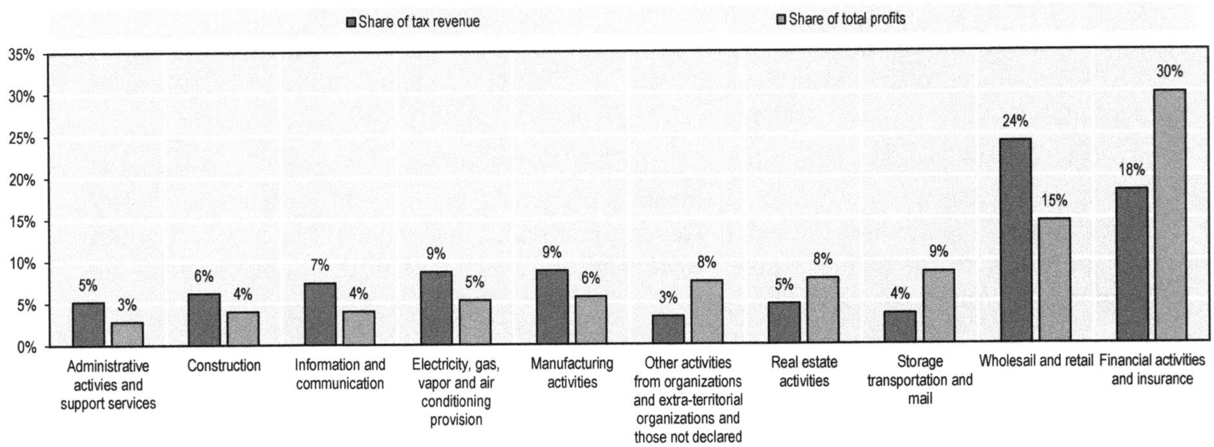

Note: Only sectors with shares of profits of 5% or higher have been considered.
Source: Based on data from the MEF (2017).

StatLink http://dx.doi.org/10.1787/888933777509

Different tax treatment for small agricultural firms and micro, small and medium-sized enterprises (SMEs) provide incentives to remain small. Small firms engaged in agricultural and farming activities are exempt from their CIT liability provided that their gross annual income is below USD 300 000 and they avoid breaking into smaller inter-related businesses for tax avoidance purposes according to the tax code (Article 708). All SMEs also face a different tax treatment. They are subject to the standard income tax schedule and rules applicable to individuals on the net taxable income (after accounting for business-related expenses and other deductions) that is attributable to a gross annual income less than PAB 100 000. On the other hand, on the part of the taxable net income attributable to a gross annual income between USD 100 001 and USD 200 000, they are subject to the CIT tax rate (25%). In addition, SMEs are exempt from the complementary tax (IBFD, 2017).

There is no conclusive evidence showing that targeted tax expenditures or tax reliefs for small firms are more cost-effective than general tax relief for businesses. Special tax treatment may prevent small businesses from growing optimally to maintain their eligibility, i.e. the so-called small-business trap (IMF et al., 2015).

Generous tax benefits and special regimes reduce corporate tax revenues

Panama has implemented a wide range of SEZs to attract foreign firms and promote innovation. The most important are the Colón Free Trade Zone, Panama Pacific *(Panamá Pacífico*) and City of Knowledge (*Ciudad del Saber*) (Table 4.2). These three SEZs host approximately 2 000 firms and employ more than 43 000 workers – 2.4% of total employment in Panama. In 2015, the Colón Free Trade Zone alone accounted for 6% of the non-financial jobs in the country (Hausmann, Obach and Santos, 2016).

Table 4.2. Main features of Panama's SEZs

	Characteristics	Tax exemptions	Incentives to immigration	Other features
Panama –Pacifico Industrial Park (2007)	251 companies (41% multinationals) 2 305 jobs	Income tax Dividend tax Import-export tax Real estate transfer tax Remittances tax Commercial license Patent & ITBMS tax	Special visa for: Investors Workers Dependents Allowed to hire more than 10% of immigrants	Labour regime: Overtime rate (25%) Days-off-rate (50%) Flexibility to operate Sundays and holidays Special custom regime One-stop shop
Cuidad del Saber Technology Park (2000)	75 SMEs 1 290 direct jobs Focus: innovation and technology	Import tax Remittances tax ITBMS tax Real estate transfer tax	Special visa for: Workers Allowed to hire more than 10% of immigrants.	
Colón Free Zone Import-Export (1948)	Oldest in the world Largest in Latin America Second-largest worldwide 2 527 companies 29 766 jobs Exports represent 4% of GDP.	Import tax Remittances tax ITBMS tax	Allowed to hire more than 10% of immigrants.	

Source: Hausmann, Santos and Obach (2017), "Special economic zones in Panama: A critical assessment".

The evolution of activity in the different SEZs is quite heterogeneous. In the Colón Free Trade Zone, the number of registered firms declined from 2 367 in 2010 to 2 058 in 2014 and total taxable income increased from USD 1 728 million to USD 2 058 million during the same period. In Panama Pacific, however, the number of registered firms significantly increased from 90 to 136 and total taxable income also went up from USD 1 778 million to USD 2 728 million during the 2010-14 period.

Labour productivity and wages are considerably higher within the SEZs. Indeed, firms within the Colón Free Trade Zone are 90% more productive than the average firm in Colón (Hausmann, Obach and Santos, 2016). Workers within SEZs earn higher wages, present lower levels of informality and a higher share of high-skilled jobs. This was observed in both the provinces of Colón and Panama. Whereas in the former wage differentials were low (USD 32 per month on average), wage gaps in Panama province were significantly higher at USD 511 (Figure 4.12).

Figure 4.12. Average monthly wages by type of job in firms within and outside of SEZs

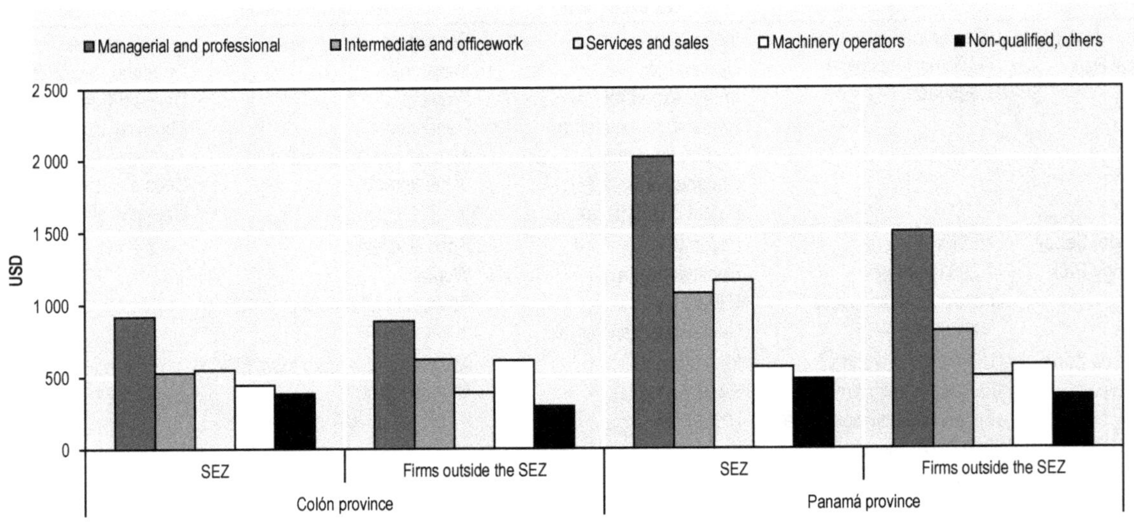

Note: Employees outside and inside of the SEZ in Colón are 76 648 and 16 356. The corresponding figures for Panama province are 744 576 and 4 889.
Source: Based on Hausmann, Obach and Santos (2016), "Special economic zones in Panama: A critical assessment".

StatLink http://dx.doi.org/10.1787/888933777528

The impact of the SEZs is less clear when it comes to foreign direct investment (FDI). Since the peak of 64% in 2007, the relative importance of SEZs in total FDI has decreased steadily while total FDI in Panama showed the opposite trend. There is no compelling evidence suggesting that without the SEZs total FDI would have been significantly lower (Hausmann, Obach and Santos, 2016). Indeed, focusing on the Colón Free Trade Zone, FDI appears to have had a minor and even negative impact on overall FDI growth in Panama during the 2011-16 period (Figure 4.13). In fact, other firms seem to have attracted FDI in higher volumes and in a more consistent manner throughout the analysed period.

For policy design and to correctly appraise the benefits or costs of tax incentives more information is needed. Striking the right balance between an attractive tax incentive for domestic and foreign investment and securing the necessary revenues for public spending is essential (IMF et al., 2015). Assessing the effective impact of SEZs on FDI is crucial as Panama is the top Latin American economy in terms of FDI inflows as percentage of GDP, a share that reached almost 10% in 2014. Unfortunately, as with tax expenditures in general, the lack of information on the tax benefits granted to firms operating in these SEZs – as well as on several target variables – prevents a sound evaluation of the effectiveness and efficiency of these schemes.

Figure 4.13. FDI growth decomposed by type of investments

Annual percentage change

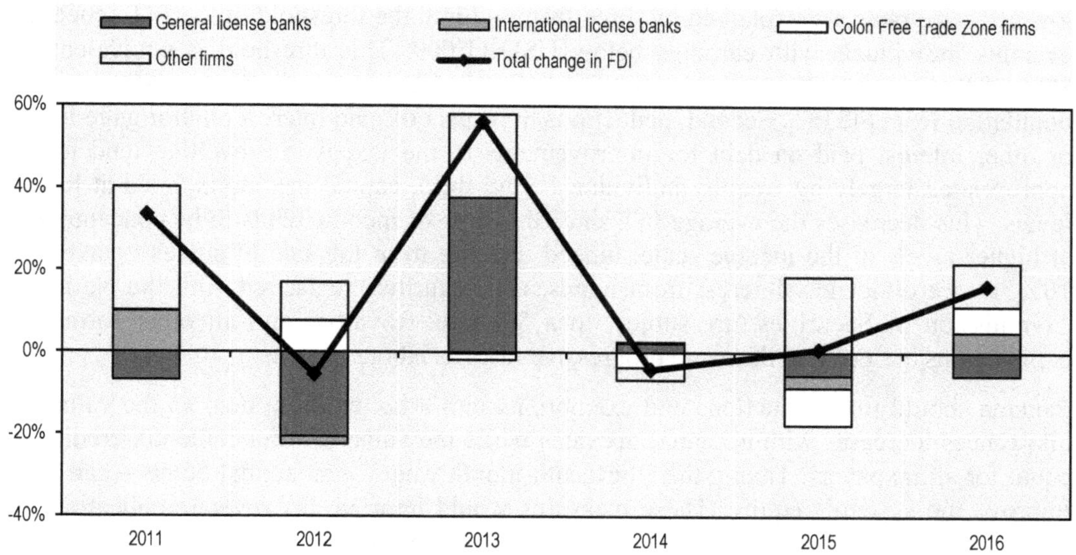

Source: Based on data from INEC, "Economic situation: Foreign direct investment", https://www.contraloria.gob.pa/inec/Publicaciones/subcategoria.aspx?ID_CATEGORIA=4&ID_SUBCATEGORIA=25&ID_IDIOMA=1.

StatLink http://dx.doi.org/10.1787/888933777547

In particular, SEZs yield direct and indirect costs that must be analysed in depth. The fiscal cost of these tax incentives arises from their direct cost as well as other indirect costs, such as making the administration of taxes more burdensome for the local authorities and creating opportunities for evasion and avoidance. These schemes are often used to reduce the tax liability from non-qualified activities – for instance by shifting taxable income to a related firm or subsidiary that resides in a tax-free economic zone (James, 2007). Indeed, the misuse of tax incentives can also result in additional leakages, further reducing public revenues. For instance, tax incentives provided to Export Free Zones were found to be redundant, created incentives to artificially readjust projects to keep receiving those benefits and favoured tax avoidance through strategic tax planning, taking advantage of subsidiaries located in eligible zones in Costa Rica, El Salvador and the Dominican Republic (Artana, 2015). Another study in the Dominican Republic showed that the greater employment created by firms within SEZs in the country came at a considerable fiscal cost, which in turn significantly hindered the government's capacity to finance other investments and social services (World Bank, 2017).

Improving the structure of the PIT

The PIT is progressive, but effective average rates (the ratio of taxes paid relative to the share of income) are very low. While the wealthiest decile is liable for a higher percentage than the second-richest decile, and well above the rest of the deciles, its proportion compared to its market income remains low (Figure 4.9, Panel B). The PIT effective average rates for the highest deciles are low compared to the nominal rates of the PIT schedule (15% and 25%) and to the theoretical average tax rates on labour income.

Low effective average rates translate into low levels of PIT revenue collection. In turn, low effective rates are explained by three factors. First, the threshold of the PIT schedule exempts individuals with earnings below USD 11 000. This threshold is equivalent to 80% of Panama's GDP per capita (USD 13 670) and exempts a large proportion of the population from the PIT. Second, deductions in respect of paid interest on mortgage loans or other interest paid on debt for improvements to the taxpayer's dwelling tend to be appropriated largely by wealthy individuals. And third, capital income is taxed at lower levels. This decreases the average PIT since this type of income tends to be concentrated at higher levels of the income scale. Indeed, income from the sale of shares is taxed at 10%, as are dividends. Interest from bonds, and securities registered with the National Commission of Securities, are subject to a 5% rate. Royalties and all other forms of capital gains are taxed at the same progressive rates as labour income.

Panama should turn deductions and exemptions into a tax credit system as the value of allowances increases with marginal tax rates while the value of refundable tax credits is equal for all taxpayers. Taxing the "thirteenth-month wage" – an annual bonus – can also improve the system's equity. These measures would improve tax revenue collection of the PIT while improving the progressivity and fairness of the taxation system.

Raising public revenues from environmentally related taxes

Environmentally related taxes in Panama remain low. On average, these taxes have collected close to 0.7% of GDP during the last five years. In 2014, LAC and OECD economies raised 0.9% and 1.6% of GDP respectively on these types of taxes (Figure 4.14).

Figure 4.14. Environmental and environmentally related taxes (2014)

Percentage of GDP

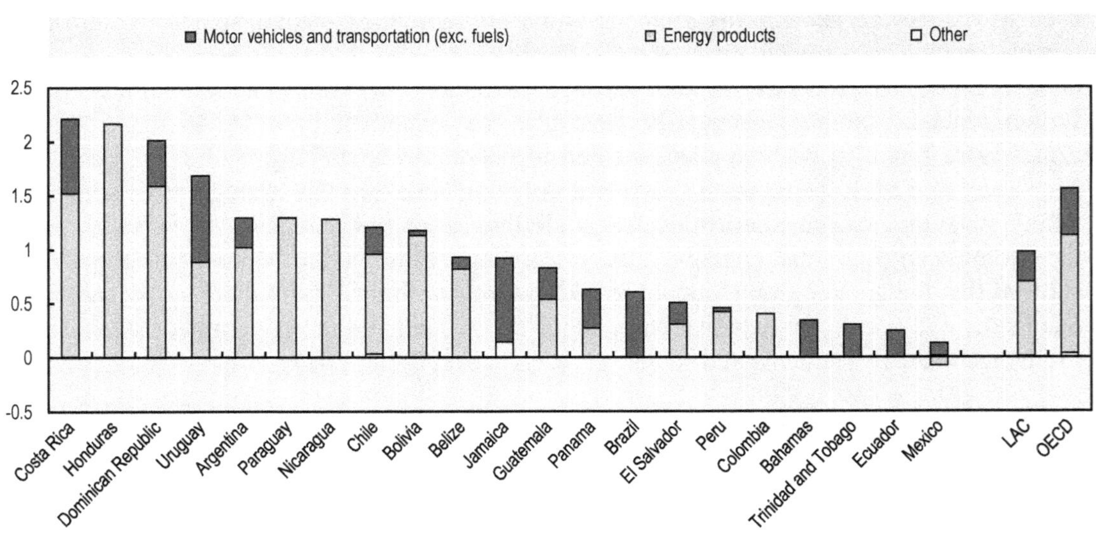

Source: OECD/CAF/ECLAC (2018), based on OECD Taxing Energy Use database.

StatLink http://dx.doi.org/10.1787/888933777566

Taxing environmental externalities can increase the government's revenue availability and help improve environmental outcomes. Green taxes are an important asset to align private and social environmental costs to encourage the efficient use of resources, to reduce waste and to advance towards a sustainable economy (OECD, 2015f).

Panama should consider designing a carbon tax and a cap-and-trade system to curb greenhouse gases and comply with the Ministry for the Environment's commitment. Panama's per capita carbon dioxide (CO_2) emissions amounted to 2.3 tonnes, below the world average of 4.97 tonnes in 2014 (World Bank, 2018). Despite its low carbon footprint, Panama is expected to increase its emissions of greenhouse gases in line with GDP growth (Bradt, 2017). Therefore, it would be useful to analyse different alternatives to taxes or enforce a cap-and-trade system among sectors such as transportation and energy. This would also reassert Panama's commitment to mitigating climate change, as expressed in Law No. 8 of 25 March promoted by the Ministry for the Environment (Bradt, 2017).

Implementing international tax rules and strengthening tax administration in Panama

This section analyses the tax administration in Panama and recent measures taken in the country to improve international tax rules. First, it summarises the progress Panama is making on addressing base erosion and profit shifting as well as strengthening the exchanges of information for tax purposes. Second, it provides recommendations to strengthen the tax administration which should deliver better revenue collection and a more equitable and efficient tax system.

Panama is making progress on addressing base erosion and profit shifting

Protecting domestic tax bases against international tax avoidance and evasion is a priority. Domestic tax base erosion and profit shifting (BEPS) arises when businesses can exploit gaps and mismatches between different countries' tax systems. BEPS negatively affects tax revenues as well as the efficiency and the ability of tax systems to provide a levelled field for all firms (OECD, 2017c). While BEPS is a worldwide concern, it is of particular importance to developing and emerging economies where tax legislation and administration are still weak and struggle with the complexities of modern business. Furthermore, anti-avoidance measures need to be strengthened in Panama, as multinational enterprises investing in the country may be able to obtain substantial tax advantages by engaging in strategies to shift profits out of the country. To prevent such tax planning and enable the collection of a fair share of tax on host-country profits from such enterprises, Panama should continue to strengthen its tax base protection rules.

Panama signed the BEPS Multilateral Convention in January 2018. This Convention updates the existing network of bilateral tax treaties and reduces opportunities for tax avoidance by multinational enterprises. It will allow Panama to integrate the results from the OECD/G20 BEPS project. To ensure a consistent global approach to the implementation of the OECD/G20 BEPS project, OECD and G20 countries have developed the Inclusive Framework on BEPS, which allows interested countries and jurisdictions to work on an equal footing with OECD and G20 members on developing standards on BEPS-related issues, and on reviewing and monitoring the implementation of the whole BEPS package.

All countries participating in the Inclusive Framework on BEPS are expected to implement the four minimum standards, and implementation will be subject to peer review. The four minimum standards relate to: harmful tax practices (Action 5) (OECD, 2015b); preventing tax treaty abuse (Action 6) (OECD, 2015c); Country-by-Country Reporting (Action 13) (OECD, 2015d); and dispute resolution mechanisms (Action 14) (OECD, 2015e). A robust process for peer review assessment of all countries' implementation of the BEPS minimum standards is being developed by its Inclusive Framework (OECD, 2017c).

Box 4.2. A comprehensive package of measures to address BEPS

The OECD/G20 BEPS project produced a 15-point Action Plan including minimum standards, common approaches, best practices and new guidance in the main policy areas.

- Minimum standards have been agreed upon in the areas of fighting harmful tax practices (Action 5), preventing treaty abuse (Action 6), Country-by-Country Reporting (Action 13) and improving dispute resolution (Action 14). All participating countries are expected to implement these minimum standards, and implementation will be subject to peer review.
- A common approach, which will facilitate the convergence of national practices by interested countries, has been outlined to limit base erosion through interest expenses (Action 4) and to neutralise hybrid mismatches (Action 2). Best practices for countries that seek to strengthen their domestic legislation are provided on the building blocks for effective controlled foreign company (CFC) rules (Action 3) and mandatory disclosure by taxpayers of aggressive or abusive transactions, arrangements or structures (Action 12).
- The permanent establishment (PE) definition in the OECD Model Tax Convention has been changed to restrict inappropriate avoidance of taxes through commissionaire arrangements or exploitation of specific exceptions (Action 7). Follow-up work undertaken in 2016 will also provide further guidance on the attribution of profits to PEs. In terms of transfer pricing, important clarifications have been made with regard to delineating the actual transaction, and the treatment of risk and intangibles. More guidance has been provided on several other issues to ensure that transfer pricing outcomes are aligned with value creation (Actions 8-10).
- The changes to the PE definition, the clarifications on transfer pricing and the guidance on CFC rules are expected to strongly address the BEPS risks exacerbated by the digital economy. Several other options, including a new nexus in the form of a significant economic presence, were considered but are not recommended at this stage given the other recommendations, plus VAT will now be levied effectively in the market country facilitating VAT collection (Action 1).
- A multilateral instrument will be implemented to facilitate the modification of bilateral tax treaties (Action 15). The modifications made to existing treaties will address the minimum standards against treaty abuse as well as the updated PE definition.

Source: OECD (2017c), *OECD Tax Policy Reviews: Costa Rica 2017*.

Implementing exchanges of information for tax purposes

Strengthening international tax rules in Panama, including the implementation of the recommendations of the BEPS project, will help create a more even playing field, which will enhance the reputation of the country. The recent move towards the Automatic Exchange of Information for Tax Purposes standard will help fight tax evasion and give greater scope to tax both domestic and foreign-source income earned by tax resident businesses and households. Panama should also strengthen its tax administration (see section below) to reduce tax evasion as part of a broader tax reform strategy that aims to increase efficiency and reduce inequality (OECD, 2017a).

In 2016, the Global Forum on Transparency and Exchange of Information for Tax Purposes rated Panama as non-compliant on the effective implementation of the international standard of exchange of information on request (EOIR). Consequently, Panama made many changes to its legal framework and practices for exchange of information to address recommendations made by the report. In 2017, Panama underwent a special fast-track review procedure by the Global Forum and was given an upgraded provisional EOIR rating of 'largely compliant'.

A comprehensive second-round EOIR review will commence in the second half of 2018. This second round of reviews by the Global Forum, launched in 2016, uses enhanced terms of reference that require jurisdictions to ensure the availability of both legal and beneficial ownership information. Beneficial ownership information is a new requirement that calls for jurisdictions to have a comprehensive legal framework and supervision practices in place to ensure such information is available and can be exchanged in practice.

In May 2016, Panama committed to implementing the international standard of Automatic Exchange of Financial Account Information (AEOI), the Common Reporting Standard (CRS) endorsed by G20 leaders and the Global Forum, with exchanges expected to begin in 2018. With this commitment, Panama joined more than 100 other jurisdictions that committed to implement the AEOI standard by 2017 or 2018. Significantly, at the end of 2016 Panama passed domestic legislation regarding the implementation of the AEOI. In addition, in January 2018 Panama signed the CRS multilateral Competent Authority Agreement to put in place an international legal framework for automatic exchanges.

At the end of October 2016, Panama signed the multilateral Convention on Mutual Administrative Assistance in Tax Matters, greatly extending its information-exchange network. This convention is the most comprehensive multilateral instrument available for all forms of tax co-operation to tackle tax evasion and avoidance, a top priority for all countries. The convention was ratified in March 2017 and went into force in July 2017.

Panama should continue to ensure that its legal framework and practices comply with the EOIR and AEOI standards and that it can effectively exchange tax information with its treaty partners; this includes delivering on its commitment to automatically exchange information with intended treaty partners by September 2018. Panama will be reviewed again later in 2018 for EOIR, including the new requirement to have beneficial ownership information available, and it is important that it achieve a satisfactory rating of either 'compliant' or 'largely compliant', as doing so will result in increased international recognition and can help mitigate efforts by institutions engaged in listing non-co-operative jurisdictions.

Strengthening tax administration should deliver better revenue collection and a more equitable and efficient tax system

Panama's tax administration is moving forward to consolidate tax transparency. Recent commitments to the BEPS multilateral convention and to the implementation of AEOI are decisive steps in this direction.

Yet, to maintain recent progress, it is necessary to further strengthen the tax administration's processes, technology platforms and human capital to ensure effective exchange of information. These institutional improvements should be a priority as they will help preserve Panama's position as a competitive and attractive destination for international financial and business services (IMF, 2017a).

Reducing evasion and fraud requires strengthening several processes throughout the tax management cycle. The registration of taxpayers, access and management of information, current tax accounts, billing systems, taxpayer services, risk management, audits, invoicing management, tax collection, and compliance initiatives can also be unified within a single platform to improve efficiency. In this area, the use of advanced technological solutions makes the difference in identifying high risks of non-compliance. Once identified, these areas should be classified and managed to prevent future occurrences. In order not to fail in the attempt, adequate planning and leadership is essential to co-ordinate within the tax administration and with other participants outside the tax administration (Arias, 2017; TADAT, 2015).

Applications of big-data analytics can combat tax evasion and promote progressivity within the system. The use and cross-reference of large datasets offer the potential to identify tax evaders by cross-referencing lifestyle patterns reflected on ownership of property and other assets on different registries with tax liabilities. This process can lead to individual audits by the tax administrations and to fine tuning risk-management models. Proper mechanisms should be enforced to safeguard individual rights to privacy, however. In addition to privacy provisions, effective tax dispute mechanisms need to be developed and enforced diligently. The Panamanian tax administration may join other government agencies to facilitate taxpayer registration or detect tax evaders. They may also work with other tax administrations in the region to identify successful strategies to broaden the tax base and reduce tax evasion.

In this respect, the Peruvian tax administration (SUNAT) carried out a project in 2015 identifying individuals who borrowed from the financial system and matched this data against taxpayers registered in the tax administration. Any individuals who had credit in the financial system and did not have a tax ID number, or for whom no payments could be identified, were flagged as potential tax evaders. The underlying assumption was that to access credit in the financial system, individuals would need to have a relatively stable income stream to pay off their credit obligations (OECD, 2017f).

Raising the likelihood of auditing can also increase tax compliance. Credible enforcement emails are a cost-effective strategy to foster compliance. A recent randomised experiment using data from Costa Rica showed that these emails doubled the income tax filing rate among previously non-filing firms (Brockmeyer et al., 2018). Similarly, messages sent to taxpayers that stated the actual fines and potential legal consequences taxpayers might face in the case of noncompliance raised enforcement perception in a municipality in Argentina. On average, tax compliance among those who received such a message increased by more than four percentage points (Castro and Scartascini, 2015).

Panama's electronic invoicing is a step in the right direction to decrease tax evasion and fraud

Electronic invoicing for the VAT will reduce the costs of compliance as well as administrative costs to the tax administration, and will contribute to scaling back the high evasion rates in Panama. The design of Panama's electronic invoice mechanism dates from late 2016. It is currently at the phase of developing adequate regulating laws and is testing a technological solution. The electronic invoice (e-bill or e-invoice) is a digital file that contains information pertaining to the sale of goods and services. The merchant transmits this e-invoice directly to the tax authority once the transaction has transpired. This enables the tax administration to exert better fiscal control in real time and at lower administrative cost.

Enforcing an e-billing programme requires a strong and modern tax administration. Ensuring a well-developed taxpayer registry and stronger departments in charge of collection, auditing and information and communications technologies will ensure that the returns to investments in e-invoicing schemes outweigh the costs to both the public and private sectors. From a public perspective, it is a process that requires investments and a modernisation strategy to deliver its benefits: increasing tax collection through reducing evasion, improving tax administration efficiency and fostering voluntary tax compliance. From the private-sector perspective, this process requires merchants to invest in training and specialised software and equipment; in exchange, merchants gain reduced filing costs for VAT payments and less unfair competition from informal firms.

Electronic invoicing encourages job and firm formality, reduces compliance costs, increases tax collection and creates positive externalities in other countries where it has been deployed. First, the e-bill increases the perception of auditing among informal firms that conduct business with formal firms. In doing so, it encourages informal firms to formalise as it becomes a requirement of their clients/suppliers to conduct business within an integrated system. For instance, in Brazil e-invoicing helped reduce informal employment from 55% to 40% in the last decade (MGI and IDV, 2014). Second, an e-billing system reduces human errors, eases access to taxing files, improves the tax administration's response times and simplifies VAT filing and reporting. The net effect is an increase in tax revenues. In Brazil, the first LAC country to implement such an e-billing scheme, tax evasion dropped from 32% to 25% (Muñoz, MacDowell and Goes, 2017), and profits reported by firms increased by 22% over four years (Naritomi, 2015). Enhanced fiscal control from these measures increased revenues. In Uruguay, e-bill application raised VAT revenues by 5.3% (Barreix and Zambrano, 2018). In Mexico, e-billing increased the amount of VAT declared to authorities by 2.2% in 2011, 3.2% in 2012 and 7.1% in 2013 (Fuentes Castro et al., 2016).

Mobilising private sector involvement in financing for development: The case of public-private partnerships

Public-private partnerships can complement improvements to the tax system and help the state finance the provision of public goods. Addressing the traditional social gaps and emerging development challenges increasingly means that public and private actors must seek greater efficiency, quality and sustainability in the delivery of public goods and services. Budget constraint is a common feature in the public sector and it can become an important barrier for the implementation of infrastructure projects. Public-private partnerships are a way of bringing together both the public and private sectors to commit to the long-term investments required. They offer private sector investment capacity and can provide efficient results. Furthermore, concessions can help to solve agency problems in traditional public provision of services and fix important failures of the state resulting from the interaction between the political cycle and the decision-making timeline.

Yet, public-private partnership arrangements are not without risks. Public-private partnership projects on transport in Latin American countries have been inefficient and have led to increases in the total cost of these projects. The performance of concessions is determined by the contract, and by regulatory and institutional designs. Flaws in the design of concession contracts have caused excessive costs in Latin America (OECD/ECLAC, 2011). For instance, in the case of Chile, Colombia and Peru for the period 1993-2010, 50 out of 61 road contracts were modified at least once, resulting in more than 540 renegotiations. All modified contracts were changed for the first time less than three years after the initial signing of the concession (Bitran, Nieto-Parra and Robledo, 2013). Furthermore, based on more than 30 interviews conducted with different agents involved in 200 conflict-affected infrastructure projects across six infrastructure sectors in the past 40 years in Latin American economies, deficient planning, reduced access to resources, lack of community benefits and lack of adequate consultation were the most prominent conflict drivers (Watkins et al., 2017).

Taking public-private partnerships as a possible means of increasing fiscal space can end up being costly for future governments. Whether to opt for a public-private partnership or another modality to finance infrastructure projects depends on several criteria, including the expertise of risk management between the private and public sectors on the specific steps of a infrastructure project. Concessions should be chosen based on an evaluation of value for money. Cost-benefit analyses essentially aim to work out which infrastructure projects offer the best value for money (OECD, 2011), helping determine which mode of financing is most appropriate. Following a social feasibility analysis, policy makers can use value-for-money evaluations to assess whether or not a concession model is preferable to direct public-sector provision. In contrast, some countries in Latin America have used public-private partnerships to create fiscal space without undertaking a detailed value-for money-analysis, which in the end has been costly for future governments (Engel, Fischer and Galetovic, 2009).

Panama still lacks sound regulations and an institutional framework for public-private partnerships. The country awarded a total of 36 public-private partnerships in infrastructure projects worth approximately USD 10.1 billion during 1990-2016 (EIU and IDB, 2017). In addition, total investment committed to public-private partnerships since 1990 has been higher than in other Central American countries such as Costa Rica, El Salvador, Guatemala, Honduras and Nicaragua. However, the potential of effective and well-implemented public-private partnerships is limited by outdated legislation and the need to establish new norms. The law regulating concession projects, including roads and airports, is from 1988 (Law No. 5 of 1988). In 2011, a law proposal was withdrawn from Congress due mainly to a misunderstanding on the part of public-sector workers who felt that their job security was threatened by greater private-sector participation. That law proposal included some useful elements for improving the regulatory and institutional frameworks for public-private partnerships in Panama, such as the analysis of value for money, transparency and competition in the auction process, fiscal responsibility and the creation of a public-private partnerships unit.

Panama performs below the LAC average. The Infrascope index evaluates the capacity of countries to implement sustainable and efficient public-private partnerships in infrastructure (EIU and IDB, 2017). Within its different components – regulations, institutions, maturity, investment and business climate, and financing – Panama performs below the LAC average in the first two. Panama is among the few LAC countries that lack an agency dedicated to public-private partnerships. This contributes to the lack of reports on public-private partnership projects and the absence of publication of assessment, monitoring and evaluation documents that affect transparency and accountability.

Regarding the regulatory framework, Panama should improve in key areas to make public-private partnership procedures more effective and efficient. A sound regulatory framework is crucial for mobilising private investment through public-private partnerships. This means having clear and systematised procedures for selection criteria, bidding, contract changes and renegotiations, as well as having a clear national policy and co-ordination among the institutions concerned. Panama lacks specific features in this regard, placing the country among the lowest ranked of Latin American countries (Figure 4.15, Panel A). For instance, the country lacks online manuals and policies for public-private partnership procurement that would allow for more transparent procurement processes. The legislation does not yet require sound economic assessments for project selection such as cost-benefit analysis or value-for-money assessment. Policies and procedures are not yet established for unsolicited biddings, and despite having a National Infrastructure Plan, explicit prioritisation of public-private partnerships is still unclear. Finally, effective and efficient participation of citizens in the grant process for environmental and social licenses and the execution of land permits should be implemented for concessions.

Additionally, Panama must improve its institutional framework for implementing public-private partnerships. In contrast to other countries in the region, Panama lacks an agency dedicated to public-private partnerships, and as a result the country has one of the poorest institutional frameworks for public-private partnerships (Figure 4.15, Panel B). This institutional arrangement is crucial for developing stable concession processes, and for having sound guidelines and project preparation facilities. Lacking such institutions affects transparency and accountability procedures that make it more difficult for the country to mobilise private investment.

Figure 4.15. Regulatory and institutional frameworks in Panama vs. Latin American economies (2017)

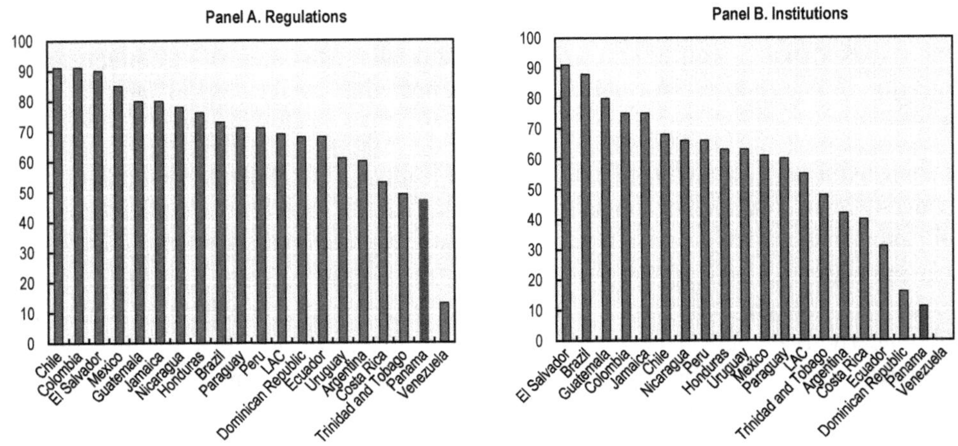

Notes: The Infrascope index evaluates the capacity of countries to implement sustainable and efficient public-private partnerships in infrastructure. This index is composed of five categories: Regulations, Institutions, Maturity, Investment and Business Climate, and Financing. The index assesses the capacity of countries in Latin America to carry out sustainable public-private partnerships in infrastructure. It ranges from 0 to 100, with countries ranked 0-29 classified as nascent, 30-59 as emerging, 60-79 as developed and 80-100 as mature.
Source: EIU and IDB (2017) "Evaluating the environment for public-private partnerships in Latin America and the Caribbean: The 2017 Infrascope".

StatLink http://dx.doi.org/10.1787/888933777585

In contrast, some countries in the region have improved their regulatory and institutional frameworks in the past five years, thereby achieving more effective private participation in infrastructure. Since 2012, for instance, the contract term and resources committed to it in Colombia cannot be increased by more than 20%. The new framework also requires value-for-money analysis to justify executing projects through a public-private partnership instead of through regular public procurement. Further, a new National Infrastructure Agency was created with greater administrative capacity and technical expertise in designing, structuring, tendering and monitoring contracts (OECD, 2015g). In Honduras, a new independent Fiscal Contingency Unit within the Ministry of Finance has the explicit purpose of approving public-private partnership projects and conducting oversight. Quantifiable firm and contingent commitments by the non-financial public sector in public-private partnership contracts, calculated at present value, may not exceed a limit equivalent to 5% of GDP (Reyes-Tagle and Tejada, 2015). In Peru, recent efforts to increase efficiencies in environmental and land licensing should improve the timing and certainty of concession contracts (OECD/ECLAC/CAF, 2018).[9]

Following the experiences of some countries in the region, technical analyses can help increase the effectiveness of public-private partnerships. LACs are beginning to require deeper economic analyses, both ex-ante and ex-post the implementation of public-private partnership projects. Before proceeding with public-private partnerships, public institutions are requiring cost-benefit analyses that result in more informed decision making. Analysing the economic returns to users can inform good practices and the effects of public-private partnerships in infrastructure. Only Panama and Venezuela do not have these assessments properly codified in their public-private partnership legislation (EIU and IDB, 2017). In the case of Panama, while the National System of Public Investment (*Sistema Nacional de Inversión Pública*) was developed to evaluate and oversee public investment decisions, it has not yet been fully implemented.

Exploiting the benefits of concessions requires strong regulatory capacity in terms of evaluating, tendering and managing the concession contracts. Following a social-feasibility analysis, value-for-money assessments can be used to decide whether a concession contract would be more appropriate than publicly funded work. Most OECD economies do a cost-benefit analysis or use a public-sector comparator (OECD, 2008). Additionally, mechanisms must be put in place to limit the possibility of projects running over schedule or above budget.

A change in fiscal-accounting procedures could improve how contractors are selected by preventing the use of public-private partnerships purely because of tax incentives. Given that the state controls the economic results of the concession through regulations and is also the recipient of the work at the end of the contract, considering concessions as public projects can provide transparency to public accounts. Thus, if investment in concessions is accounted for within a comprehensive framework for public infrastructure expenditure, concessions would be chosen based on a value-for-money analysis.

In sum, Panama needs to adopt and implement a public-private partnership law that includes the regulation and institutional frameworks that improve private sector involvement in investment in infrastructure, and therefore contribute to financing development. Regarding the institutional framework, Panama needs to create a public-private partnership unit and thus improve the quality of institutional design, the design of public-private partnership contracts, and the management of hold-up and expropriation risks. In terms of regulation, better procedures are needed. These include value-for-money or cost-benefit analyses, transparency and competition in the auction process and public-private partnership fiscal accounting. As well, Panama needs to effectively and efficiently implement the participation of citizens in the grant process for environmental and social licences and the execution of land permits. Finally, due to the unsuccessful experience of the 2011 proposal law, it is crucial that a communication strategy with citizens be adopted, which highlights the socio-economic benefits of sound regulatory and institutional frameworks for public-private partnerships in Panama.

Conclusions and policy recommendations

Improving Panama's tax collection should provide further financial resources for development, which are crucial to respond to socio-economic challenges and to sustain recent macroeconomic performance. Panama's economy has performed relatively well compared with other Latin American economies. Sustaining this position demands continued growth through efforts to fund public investments in physical and digital infrastructure and social expenditure in human capital development at both national and regional levels (Chapters 2 and 3). In turn, ensuring higher fiscal revenues is critical to maintain macroeconomic stability, ensure compliance with the Fiscal Responsibility Law and fund the necessary investments to achieve development goals. In recent years, repeated primary deficits have begun to pressure the public debt and risk constraining capital expenditures to prevent the debt from rising.

Panama's total tax revenues have remained stable during the past two decades. Total taxes and social security contributions in Panama (at 16.6% of GDP) remain well below those in OECD economies (34.3% of GDP) and in LAC countries (22.7% of GDP).

However, revenues from the Canal and other public enterprises – on average 3.2% of GDP in the past decade – have in part compensated for low fiscal revenue intake.

Improved tax revenue collection, by broadening the tax base and strengthening the tax administration, could provide a stable, long-term source of income to finance inclusive growth through sustained investments without harming Panama's international competitiveness or hampering growth. Revenues can potentially be increased by improving tax collection. For instance, the VAT forgoes approximately 2% of GDP due to currently excluded items, fraud and evasion (Jorrat, 2014). Furthermore, Panama provides a wide array of tax benefits: some of these affect the system's efficiency by potentially providing incentives to firms within sectors that do not require these benefits. Rationalising these incentives and eliminating distortions to the allocation of investments can enhance both revenue and efficiency. Moreover, exemptions, deductions and other special treatments affect both the vertical and horizontal equity of the tax system, thus requiring further in-depth analysis. All of these exemptions diminish average tax rates, which in turn decreases the system's redistributive power. Environmental taxes are also an untapped source of potential revenue that could provide additional revenue while improving environmental outcomes. Finally, curbing evasion and fraud through the use of technology and institutional strengthening can also provide additional revenues.

Private-sector involvement, through public-private partnerships, should help increase resources for development. However, Panama needs to adopt and implement a public-private partnerships framework to deliver effective and efficient infrastructures.

Box 4.3 summarises the main policy recommendations and requirements for each area covered in this chapter.

Box 4.3. Main policy recommendations to finance development through improved tax collection

1. Ensure macroeconomic stability and bolster international creditworthiness

1.1 Improve compliance of the fiscal rule and its transparency

- Establish an independent fiscal council to promote transparency and accountability of the fiscal framework.
- Revise the adjusted overall fiscal balance target to curb unnecessary current spending and increase contributions to the Panamanian Savings Fund.
- Substitute annual budget targets for a multi-annual approach that aims to generate a cumulative adjustment of the primary and overall budget results that is enough to ensure the targeted public debt trajectory.

1.2 Increase fiscal revenues to achieve surplus in the primary fiscal balances and guarantee the solvency of the state in the future

2 Improve the efficiency, equity and revenue-raising capacity of the tax system

2.1 Enhance the tax system's efficiency

- Adopt a methodology to measure and report tax expenditures on an annual basis.

- Review tax expenditures and incentives periodically to ensure they are achieving their intended goals and reaching their intended targets.
- Revise benefits provided to economic sectors, as the tax system might be subsidising otherwise unprofitable businesses or firms within these sectors.
- Broaden the tax base by scaling back tax benefits provided to well-established and consolidated industries within Special Economic Zones.
- Abolish the annual operation licence tax and the complementary tax to improve the system's neutrality and simplicity.
- Adopt strong mechanisms to prevent firms abusing granted tax benefits and shifting profits.
- Adopt environmental taxes that align private and social costs with the environment.

2.2 Increase the redistributive power of the tax system

- Expand the VAT's base to include currently exempted services while maintaining current exclusion of basic food staples and goods and compensating poorer households through direct transfers.
- Turn PIT allowances into tax credits as the value of allowances increases with marginal tax rates while the value tax credits is equal for all taxpayers. Make the tax credits refundable.
- Expand the PIT base to include the currently exempted 'thirteenth-month wage' since those that earn more benefit the most.

3 Modernise the tax administration.

- Integrate critical processes (registration of taxpayers, access and management of information, current tax accounts, billing systems, taxpayer service, risk management, auditing, invoicing management, tax collection, and compliance) of the tax administration to improve efficiency and reduce administrative costs.
- Raise the likelihood of auditing to increase voluntary tax compliance.
- Employ big-data analytics to identify evasion and fine tune risk-management models
- Continue the development of electronic invoicing to fight fraud and evasion, and to encourage compliance.

4 Adopt and implement sound regulatory and institutional frameworks for public-private partnerships

- Create a public-private partnerships unit to improve the quality of institutional design, the design of public-private partnerships contracts, and the management of hold-up and expropriation risks.
- Adopt regulatory procedures, such as value-for-money or cost-benefit

analyses, transparency and competition in the auction process and public-private partnership fiscal accounting.

- Implement the effective and efficient participation of citizens in the grant process for environmental and social licences.
- Achieve a communication strategy with citizens, highlighting the benefits of having sound regulatory and institutional frameworks for public-private partnerships in Panama.

Notes

[1] The official currency in Panama is the Panamanian Balboa (PAB). This currency has been tied to the United States Dollar since 1904; 1 PAB equals 1 USD (US dollar).

[2] Preliminary data. Updated by the Ministry of Finance up to September 2017.

[3] Other factors that affect the VRR estimates are measurement errors of the GDP and final household consumption (Keen, 2013 and Diaz de Sarralde, 2017).

[4] Exemption breaks the VAT chain. Whether this increases or decreases the net revenue raised by the VAT depends where the break occurs in the chain of supply. If the exemption occurs immediately prior to final sale, the consequence is a loss of revenue since value added at the final stage escapes tax. If the exemption occurs at some intermediate stage, however, the consequence is actually an increase in net revenues: the cascading of tax on inputs means that, as the price charged by downstream firms using the exempt item rises in order to cover their increased costs, so the tax on output downstream increases. Thus, value added prior to the exempt stage is effectively taxed more than once (Ebrill et al., 2001).

[5] It should be noted that caution is warranted as countries employ different methods to estimate their tax expenditures and comparisons might be misleading.

[6] The results and shares have been estimated by analysing information on the national household survey from 2016.

[7] Refer to Easterly, W. (2001) for a detailed discussion on the classification of the middle class.

[8] Companies whose annual taxable income surpasses USD 1.5 million must undergo additional procedures, as they must also determine their CIT through an alternative calculation (cálculo *alterno del impuesto sobre la renta*, CAIR). The resulting tax will be the highest amount resulting from the application of the traditional method (the net taxable income multiplied by the general rate) or applying the 4.67% rate to the total taxable income.

[9] Furthermore, new legislation is being implemented in Argentina, El Salvador and Nicaragua, while other countries with more public-private partnerships experience, such as Chile, Brazil and Mexico, have opened up the public-private partnerships scheme to new areas beyond traditional infrastructure, to include sports arenas, parks, and educational and prison facilities (EIU, 2017).

References

Alberola, E. et al. (2017), “Fiscal policy and the cycle in Latin America: The role of financing conditions and fiscal rules”, *Bank for International Settlements Working Papers*, No. 543, Bank for International Settlements.

Alonso, V. et al. (2016), *Panamá. Fortalecimiento del marco de responsabilidad fiscal*, Fondo Monetario Internacional/International Monetary Fund, Washington, DC.

Arias, G. (2017), “Los retos de las administraciones tributarias” [“The challenges of tax administrations in Latin America”], CIATblog, Inter-American Center for Tax Administrations (CIAT), Panama City, https://www.ciat.org/the-challenges-of-tax-administrations-in-latin-america/?lang=en.

Artana, D. (2015), “The effectiveness of fiscal incentives: The case of the export free zone of Costa Rica, El Salvador and Dominican Republic”, in O. Manzano, M. Cuevas and S. Auguste (eds.), *Partners or Creditors? Attracting Foreign Investment and Productive Development to Central America and Dominican Republic*, Inter-American Development Bank (IDB), Washington, DC.

Barreix, A., J.C. Benítez and A. Melguizo (forthcoming), “Panama”, in Fiscal Rules in Latin American Countries.

Barreix, A., J.C. Benítez and M. Pecho (2017), “Revisiting personal income tax in Latin America: Evolution and impact”, *OECD Development Centre Working Papers*, No. 338, OECD Publishing, Paris, http://dx.doi.org/10.1787/16d42b4a-en.

Barreix, A., M. Bès and J. Roca (2010), “El IVA personalizado. Aumentado la recaudación y compensando a los más pobres,” https://www.cepal.org/ilpes/noticias/paginas/1/41751/alberto_barreix_El_IVA_Personalizado_BID_Eurosocial_IEF_2010_doc.pdf.

Barreix, A. and R. Zambrano (2018), *Electronic Invoicing in Latin America*, IDB, Washington, DC, and CIAT, Panama City.

Benitez, J.C. and F. Velayos (2018), “Impuestos a la Riqueza o al Patrimonio de las Personas Físicas con especial mención a América Latina y el Caribe”, CIAT, Panama City, ISSN 2219-780X.

Bitran, E., S. Nieto-Parra and J.S. Robledo (2013), “Opening the black box of contract renegotiations: An analysis of road concessions in Chile, Colombia and Peru”, *OECD Development Centre Working Papers*, No. 317, OECD Publishing, Paris, http://dx.doi.org/10.1787/5k46n3wwxxq3-en.

Bittencourt, J.L. (2017), “Eficiencia e Ineficiencia de los gastos fiscales: Una perspectiva Brasilera”, paper presented at the 7th LAC Fiscal Policy Forum, Asuncion, Paraguay, 17 November 2017.

Bloomberg (2018), “A new contender has emerged for the best credit in Latin America”, https://www.bloomberg.com/news/articles/2018-01-09/there-s-a-new-contender-for-the-best-credit-in-latin-america.

Bradt, A. (2017) “Estudio de las opciones y las repercusiones de la aplicación de un sistema de permisos comercializables de reducción de emisiones de carbono en Panamá”, Comisión Económica para América Latina y el Caribe, Santiago, Chile.

Brockmeyer, A.M. Hernandez, S. Kettle, and S. Smith. (2018), “Casting the tax net wider: Experimental evidence from Costa Rica”, http://documents.worldbank.org/curated/en/660661475679714942/Casting-the-tax-net-wider-experimental-evidence-from-Costa-Rica.

Brys, B.P. O'Reilly, S. Perret and A. Thomas (2016), "Tax design for inclusive economic growth", *OECD Taxation Working Papers*, No. 26, OECD Publishing, Paris, http://dx.doi.org/10.1787/5jlv74ggk0g7-en.

Burman, L. and M. Phaup (2012), "Tax expenditures, the size and efficiency of government, and implications for budget reform", *Tax Policy and the Economy*, Vol. 26, University of Chicago Press, Chicago, pp. 93-124.

Castro, L. and C. Scartascini (2015), "Tax compliance and enforcement in the Pampas. Evidence from a field experiment", *Journal of Economic Behavior and Organization*, Vol. 116, pp. 65-82.

Clements, B.R. de Mooji, S. Gupta and M. Keen.(eds.) (2015), *Inequality and Fiscal Policy*, International Monetary Fund, Washington, DC.

DIAN (2018), "Structural tax reform", https://www.dian.gov.co/impuestos/Paginas/RefTribuEstructu.aspx.

Diaz de Sarralde, S. (2017), "Value added tax: Revenue, efficiency, tax expenditure and inefficiencies in Latin America", *Working Paper* WP-05-2017, CIAT, Panama City, https://biblioteca.ciat.org/opac/?v=5556.

Easterly, W. (2001), "The middle class consensus and economic development", *Journal of Economic Growth*, Vol. 6/4, pp. 317-335.

Ebrill, L. et al. (2001), The Modern VAT, IMF, Washington, DC.

ECLAC (2016), *Economic Survey of Latin America and the Caribbean 2016: The 2030 Agenda for Sustainable Development and the Challenges of Financing for Development*, UN Economic Commission for Latin America and the Caribbean, Santiago.

EIU and IDB (2017), "Evaluating the environment for public-private partnerships in Latin America and the Caribbean: The 2017 Infrascope", Economist Intelligence Unit and Inter-American Development Bank, Washington, DC, https://infrascope.eiu.com/wp-content/uploads/2017/02/EIU_IDB_INFRASCOPE_2017-FINAL-1.pdf.

Engel, E., R. Fischer and A. Galetovic (2009), "Public-private partnerships: When and how", *Centre for Applied EconomicsWorking Papers*, No. 257, University of Chile.

Fuentes Castro, H.J. et al. (2016), "Impacto en la evasión por la introducción de la factura electronica", *Working Papers*, No. IA-006E00002-E37-2016, Instituto Tecnológico de Estudios Superiores de Monterrey, Mexico City.

Garry, S. and J.C. Rivas Valdivia (2017), "An analysis of the contribution of public expenditures to economic growth and fiscal multipliers in Mexico, Central America and Dominican Republic, 1990-2015", UN, Mexico City, https://repositorio.cepal.org/bitstream/handle/11362/42062/1/S1700766_en.pdf.

Gebauer, A. et al. (2010), "Tax expenditures in Nordic countries", paper presented at the Nordic Tax Economist Meeting, Oslo, June 2009.

Hausmann, R., M.A. Santos and J. Obach (2017), "Appraising the economic potential of Panama: Policy recommendations for sustainable and inclusive growth", Center for International Development Working Papers, No. 334, Harvard University, Cambridge, MA, https://growthlab.cid.harvard.edu/publications/panama-policy-recommendations.

Hausmann, R., J. Obach and M.A. Santos (2016), "Special economic zones in Panama: A critical assessment", *Harvard Kennedy School Working Papers*, No. RWP16-044, Harvard University, Cambridge, MA, https://papers.ssrn.com/sol3/papers.cfm?abstract_id=2880636.

IBFD (2017), Panama Corporate Taxation, IBDF Office for Americas, International Bureau of Fiscal Documentation.

IDB (2013), *More than Revenue: Taxation as a Development Tool*, Inter-American Development Bank, Palgrave Macmillan, Washington, DC, https://www.slideshare.net/svend3ew/download-pdf-more-than-revenue-taxation-as-a-development-tool-development-in-the-americas-paperback.

IMF (International Monetary Fund) Western Hemisphere Department (2017), "Article IV consultation – Press release and staff report for Panama", *IMF Country Reports*, No. 17/105, IMF, Washington, DC, http://www.imf.org/en/Publications/CR/Issues/2017/05/04/Panama-2017-Article-IV-Consultation-Press-Release-and-Staff-Report-for-Panama-44875.

IMF Western Hemisphere Department (2016), "El Salvador: Selected issues", *IMF Country Reports*, No. 16/209, Washington, DC, http://www.imf.org/en/Publications/Search?series=IMF%20Staff%20Country%20Reports&when=During&year=2016.

IMF (2001), "Panama: Staff report for the 2000 Article IV consultation", *IMF Country Reports*, No. 01/39, Washington, DC, http://www.imf.org/en/Publications/Search?series=IMF+Staff+Country+Reports&when=During&year=2001&title=Panama%3A+Article+IV+Consultation.

IMF, OECD, UN and WB (2015), "Options for low income countries' effective and efficient use of tax incentives for investment", a report to the G-20 Development Working Group, IMF, Washington, DC, https://www.imf.org/external/np/g20/pdf/101515.pdf.

INEC (National Institute of Statistics and Census of Panama) (2016), "Encuesta continua de hogares" ["National household survey"], INEC, https://www.contraloria.gob.pa/inec/.

Jacobsen, M. et al. (2010), "Tax expenditures in the Nordic countries", paper presented at the Nordic Tax Economist Meeting, Oslo, June 2009, http://www.skm.dk/media/110391/tax_expenditures_in_the_nordic_countries.pdf.

James, S. (2007), "The effect of tax rates on declared income: An analysis of Indian taxpayer response to changes in income tax rates", PhD Thesis, Harvard University, Cambridge, MA.

Jorratt, M. (2014), "Estimación del gasto tributario en Panamá, mediante el señalamiento de pautas y criterios para el establecimiento de una metodología de medición", Informe Técnico.

Keen, M. (2013), "The anatomy of the VAT", *IMF Working Papers*, No. 13/111, IMF, Washington, DC, https://www.imf.org/external/pubs/ft/wp/2013/wp13111.pdf.

McDonald, M. (2018), "A new contender has emerged for the best credit in Latin America", https://www.bloomberg.com/news/articles/2018-01-09/there-s-a-new-contender-for-the-best-credit-in-latin-america.

MEF (Ministerio de Economía y Finanzas/Ministry of Economy and Finance) (2017), "Balances fiscales para los años 2004-2017" ["Fiscal balances for the years 2004-2017"], Ministerio de Economía y Finanzas de Panamá, http://www.mef.gob.pa/es/informes/Paginas/informes.aspx.

MGI and IDV (2014), *Eliminating Barriers to Economic Growth: An Update Focused on Retail*, MGI, London, and IDV, Sao Paulo.

Muñoz, A., M.C. MacDowell and P. Goes (27 March 2017), "La factura electrónica: una herramienta eficaz contra la evasión de impuestos", IDB Recaudando Bienestar blog, https://blogs.iadb.org/recaudandobienestar/es/2017/03/27/factura-electronica-herramienta-contra-la-evasion-de-impuestos/.

Naritomi, J. (2015), "Consumers as tax auditors", London School of Economics, London, http://www.iipf.org/papers/Naritomi-Consumers_as_tax_auditors-151.pdf.

Neubig, T. and A. Redonda (2017), "Shedding light on hidden government spending: Tax expenditures", IMF Public Financial Management blog, http://blog-pfm.imf.org/pfmblog/2017/12/shedding-light-on-hidden-government-spending-tax-expenditures.html.

OECD (2018), *Taxing Energy Use 2018: Companion to the Taxing Energy Use Database*, OECD Publishing, Paris, http://dx.doi.org/10.1787/9789264289635-en.

OECD (2017a), *Multi-dimensional Review of Panama: Volume 1: Initial Assessment*, OECD Development Pathways, OECD Publishing, Paris, http://dx.doi.org/10.1787/9789264278547-en.

OECD (2017b), *Enhancing Social Inclusion in Latin America: Key Issues and the Role of Social Protection Systems*, OECD Publishing, Paris, http://www.oecd.org/latin-america/regionalprogramme/Enhancing-Social-Inclusion-LAC.pdf.

OECD (2017c), *OECD Tax Policy Reviews: Costa Rica 2017*, OECD Publishing, Paris, http://dx.doi.org/10.1787/9789264277724-en.

OECD (2017d), *OECD Economic Surveys: Mexico 2017*, OECD Publishing, Paris, http://dx.doi.org/10.1787/eco_surveys-mex-2017-en.

OECD (2017e), *Revenue Statistics: 1965-2016*, OECD Publishing, Paris, http://dx.doi.org/10.1787/9789264283183-en.

OECD (2017f), *Tax Administration 2017 – Comparative Information Series on OECD and Other Advanced and Emerging Economies*, OECD Publishing, Paris, http://www.oecd.org/ctp/administration/tax-administration-23077727.htm.

OECD (2015a), *In It Together: Why Less Inequality Benefits All*, OECD Publishing, Paris, http://dx.doi.org/10.1787/9789264235120-en.

OECD (2015b), *Countering Harmful Tax Practices More Effectively, Taking into Account Transparency and Substance, Action 5 – 2015 Final Report*, OECD/G20 Base Erosion and Profit Shifting Project, OECD Publishing, Paris, http://dx.doi.org/10.1787/9789264241190-en.

OECD (2015c), *Preventing the Granting of Treaty Benefits in Inappropriate Circumstances, Action 6 – 2015 Final Report*, OECD/G20 Base Erosion and Profit Shifting Project, OECD Publishing, Paris, http://dx.doi.org/10.1787/9789264241695-en.

OECD (2015d), *Transfer Pricing Documentation and Country-by-Country Reporting, Action 13 – 2015 Final Report*, OECD/G20 Base Erosion and Profit Shifting Project, OECD Publishing, Paris, http://dx.doi.org/10.1787/9789264241480-en.

OECD (2015e), *Making Dispute Resolution Mechanisms More Effective, Action 14 – 2015 Final Report*, OECD/G20 Base Erosion and Profit Shifting Project, OECD Publishing, Paris, http://dx.doi.org/10.1787/9789264241633-en.

OCDE (2015f), *Towards Green Growth? Tracking Progress*, OCDE Publishing, Paris, http://dx.doi.org/10.1787/9789264234437-en.

OECD (2015g), *Colombia: Policy Priorities for Inclusive Development*, Better Policies Series, OECD Publishing, Paris, https://www.oecd.org/about/publishing/colombia-policy-priorities-for-inclusive-development.pdf.

OECD (2011), *Improving the Practice of Transport Project Appraisal*, ITF Round Tables, No. 149, OECD Publishing, Paris, http://dx.doi.org/10.1787/9789282103081-en.

OECD (2010), *Tax Expenditures in OECD Countries*, OECD Publishing, Paris.

OECD (2008), *Public-Private Partnerships: In Pursuit of Risk Sharing and Value for Money*, OECD Publishing, Paris, http://www.oecd.org/gov/budgeting/public-privatepartnershipsinpursuitofrisksharingandvalueformoney.htm.

OECD (2007), *OECD Economic Surveys: Mexico 2007*, OECD Publishing, Paris, http://dx.doi.org/10.1787/eco_surveys-mex-2007-en.

OECD/CAF (Development Bank of Latin America)/ECLAC (2018), *Latin American Economic Outlook 2018: Rethinking Institutions for Development*, OECD Publishing, Paris, http://dx.doi.org/10.1787/leo-2018-en.

OECD/ECLAC (2011), *Latin American Economic Outlook 2012: Transforming the State for Development*, OECD Publishing, Paris, http://dx.doi.org/10.1787/leo-2012-en.

OECD/IDB/CIAT (2016), *Taxing Wages in Latin America and the Caribbean 2016*, OECD Publishing, Paris, http://dx.doi.org/10.1787/9789264262607-en.

OECD/CAF/ECLAC (2018), *Latin American Economic Outlook 2018: Rethinking Institutions for Development*, OECD Publishing, Paris, http://dx.doi.org/10.1787/leo-2018-en.

OECD/ECLAC/CIAT/IDB (2018), *Revenue Statistics in Latin America and the Caribbean 2018*, OECD Publishing, Paris, http://dx.doi.org/10.1787/rev_lat_car-2018-en-fr.

Pecho, M. (2014), "Tax expenditures in Latin America: 2008-2012", *Tax Studies and Research Directorate Working Papers*, No. 2-2014, CIAT, Panama City.

Pelaez Longinotti, F. (2017), "Overview of tax expenditures in Latin America, main statistics of the CIAT database", *Working Papers*, No. 06-2017, CIAT, Panama City.

Redonda, A. (2016), "Tax Expenditures and Sustainability. An Overview", *Discussion Note* 2016/3, Council on Economic Policies, Zurich, https://www.cepweb.org/tax-expenditures-and-sustainability-an-overview/.

Reyes-Tagle, G. and M. Tejada (2015), "The Fiscal Implications of Public-Private Partnerships in Honduras: Current Developments and the Road Ahead", *Discussion Paper* No. IDB-DP- 391, IDB, Washington, DC, https://publications.iadb.org/handle/11319/6991#sthash.dFBKhJce.dpuf.

TADAT (2015), *Tax Administration Diagnostic Assessment Tool: Field Guide*, Tax Administration Diagnostic Assessment Tool http://www.tadat.org/Field_Guide/FieldGuide.html.

Watkins, G.G. et al. (2017), *Lessons from Four Decades of Infrastructure Project-Related Conflicts in Latin America and the Caribbean*, IDB, Washington, DC, http://dx.doi.org/10.18235/0000803.

World Bank (2018), "World Development Indicators dataset. CO2 emissions (metric tons per capita) indicator", World Bank, https://data.worldbank.org/indicator/EN.ATM.CO2E.PC.

World Bank (2017), Hacia un sistema tributario más eficiente. Evaluación de la eficiencia fiscal, análisis de costos y beneficios de los gastos fiscales y estudio sobre el empleo informal y sus repercusiones en el sistema tributario, World Bank, http://dgii.gov.do/informacionTributaria/publicaciones/estudios/Documents/HaciaUnSistemaTributarioM%C3%A1sEficiente-BancoMundial.pdf.

Yohou, H. and M. Goujou (2017), "Reassessing tax effort in developing countries: A proposal of vulnerability-adjusted tax effort index (VATEI)," FERDI Working Papers, No. 186, Fondation pour les études et recherches sur le développement international, Clermont-Ferrand, France, http://www.ferdi.fr/sites/www.ferdi.fr/files/publication/fichiers/p186-ferdi_hyohou-mgoujon_0.pdf.

ORGANISATION FOR ECONOMIC CO-OPERATION AND DEVELOPMENT

The OECD is a unique forum where governments work together to address the economic, social and environmental challenges of globalisation. The OECD is also at the forefront of efforts to understand and to help governments respond to new developments and concerns, such as corporate governance, the information economy and the challenges of an ageing population. The Organisation provides a setting where governments can compare policy experiences, seek answers to common problems, identify good practice and work to co-ordinate domestic and international policies.

The OECD member countries are: Australia, Austria, Belgium, Canada, Chile, Colombia, the Czech Republic, Denmark, Estonia, Finland, France, Germany, Greece, Hungary, Iceland, Ireland, Israel, Italy, Japan, Korea, Latvia, Lithuania, Luxembourg, Mexico, the Netherlands, New Zealand, Norway, Poland, Portugal, the Slovak Republic, Slovenia, Spain, Sweden, Switzerland, Turkey, the United Kingdom and the United States. The European Union takes part in the work of the OECD.

OECD Publishing disseminates widely the results of the Organisation's statistics gathering and research on economic, social and environmental issues, as well as the conventions, guidelines and standards agreed by its members.

OECD DEVELOPMENT CENTRE

The OECD Development Centre was established in 1962 as an independent platform for knowledge sharing and policy dialogue between OECD member countries and developing economies, allowing these countries to interact on an equal footing. Today, 27 OECD countries and 25 non-OECD countries are members of the Centre. The Centre draws attention to emerging systemic issues likely to have an impact on global development and more specific development challenges faced by today's developing and emerging economies. It uses evidence-based analysis and strategic partnerships to help countries formulate innovative policy solutions to the global challenges of development.

For more information on the Centre and its members, please see *www.oecd.org/dev*.

OECD PUBLISHING, 2, rue André-Pascal, 75775 PARIS CEDEX 16
(41 2018 23 1 P) ISBN 978-92-64-30253-2 – 2018

www.ingramcontent.com/pod-product-compliance
Lightning Source LLC
Chambersburg PA
CBHW061213240926
51846CB00006B/1214
* 9 7 8 9 2 6 4 3 0 2 5 3 2 *